Beautifully written, with an attentio
to wince, at times causes you to sig
remarkable story will offer hope to all who are fighting a hard battle.

—**Ed Piorek,** author of The Father's Love and The Central Event

At first glance, *Dry Bones Dance Again* provides an essential commentary for our society on the challenges and victories associated with life in a wheelchair. Yet author, Lynn Miller's compelling vulnerability launches the reader much deeper into the more universal issues of loneliness, identity, love, relationships, suffering, hope and faith.
My own emotional response while reading Lynn's book reminded me that a well-crafted story possesses the power not to only communicate the author's journey, but also, through the communion of tears, to reveal the secrets of who you are, where you have been, and where you are going. The book capture's Lynn's unique ability to light up any room with hope and love, and I feel enlarged by reading it.

—**Dan McCollam**, The Mission, Vacaville, California International
Director of Sounds of the Nations and the Prophetic Company;
author of *God Vibrations, The Good Fight*, and *Finding Your Song*

Have you ever read the story of someone with a life-altering disability? It's time. In this well-written book, Lynn candidly opens the curtains. We're given a window into a world that's so personal and tender we wonder if we should be allowed this seat. We come away enriched with understanding, gratefulness, compassion, wisdom, and a deeper love for God. Thank you, Lynn, for gathering your courage and giving us a narrative that will imprint and enlarge our souls.

—**Bob Sorge**, author of Secrets of the Secret Place and Fire of God's
Love

A tale of triumph over suffering marked by tenderness, humor and grace, that will resonate with all who read it.

—**Lindsay Linegar**, author of You Need Africa More Than Africa
Needs You

Lynn Miller's *Dry Bones Dance Again* is an exceptional book. Though it covers the author's lifetime struggle with an unforgiving malady, it overflows with good spirits, humor, and exceptional courage. And it's beautifully written. None of this surprises me. For several semesters Lynn was a student in my writing class, where she left behind an indelible image of happiness, and, yes, love—in the face of what we recognized as a brutal handicap. Yet none of us felt obligated to help her, because Lynn was so clearly in charge of her own daily destiny. Rereading her pages reminds me of the bountiful spirit she's attained through remarkable insights and through her ongoing relationship with her own students, her friends, and her God.

—**Maralys Wills**, author of *Higher Than Eagles*

Dry Bones Dance Again is funny, it's real, it's heart wrenching, it's hope inspiring, and it clarifies and glorifies God. Lynn is a masterful storyteller. I didn't want to stop reading!

—**Pat Novak**, educator, retired principal Orange County Department of Education

For starters, *Dry Bones Dance Again* is a wonderfully written work about real life, real challenge, and real victory, one that will touch all emotions at a meaningful level. Beyond that, it enlightens, clarifies, and enhances our view of the life we've been given and provides perspectives that will bring hope, growth, and empowerment to anyone who reads it.

—**Dean del Sesto**, author of *Shift Your Thinking* and *Shift Points*, speaker, entrepreneur

LYNN MILLER

dry bones dance again

A Journey from Suffering
to Comfort, Purpose, and Joy

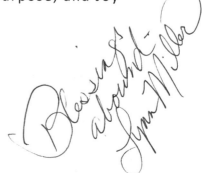

Blessings
abound -
Lynn Miller

Lynn Miller
www.drybonesdanceagain.com
drybonesdanceagain@gmail.com

Cover Design by Sarah Smith @ Reedsy

Ordering Information:
Discounts are available on quantity purchases by corporations, associations, churches, large groups and others. For details, contact drybonesdanceagain.com.

Names, identifying characteristics, and some details have been changed to protect the privacy of certain individuals. Some events depicted are not told in chronological order. However, they are true to the best of the author's memory.

Dry Bones Dance Again/ Lynn Miller.—1st ed.
ISBN-13: 978-0-692-15330-7

To Mom and Dad who taught us kids to play cards.
Thanks for the lessons on winning with
the hand I was dealt.

Then He said to me,
"Prophesy to the breath; prophesy, son of man, and say to it,
'This is what the Sovereign Lord says: Come, breath, from the
four winds and breathe into these slain, that they may live.'"
Ezekiel 37:9

THE HOLY BIBLE (NIV)

Table of Contents

Foreword

WHAT DO YOU DO when your hopes and dreams are repeatedly dashed? How can you take your vulnerability and turn it into the key to a life of joy and service? These are questions we all face at one time or another in our lives.

Dry Bones Dance Again tells how Lynn Miller answers these questions. The title of her book gives you a hint about her philosophy of life. We have had the opportunity to see her put her answers into practice.

We met Lynn almost twenty years ago and were immediately captivated by her radiant spirit. Our children were seven and five at the time and we were having trouble finding a church that was prepared to welcome our son Ben. His dual diagnosis of Down Syndrome and autism meant that he did not fit into traditional church structures. Lynn welcomed Ben and our energetic daughter Brianne to the church where she serves as children's minister. She became a true friend for life.

We have seen Lynn's life across many years as she has navigated challenges and celebrated milestones with grace, hope, and joy. She has a deep reliance on God's love and an identity rooted in the moment-by-moment presence of Jesus in her life. Lynn is an overcomer.

As parents of a child with special needs and as life-long educators, we are aware of the challenges that Lynn has faced and continues to face every day. Rather than holding her back from pursuing her mission in life, Lynn has turned these challenges into assets that have shaped her into a person who readily accepts the differences in others, who exercises a growth mindset in every situation, and who cultivates a community where every child feels loved and accepted.

Dry Bones Dance Again is a story of courage in the face of hardship. Lynn shows what it looks like to have an intimate relationship with God. Her faith is inclusive, inspiring, and embracing. Knowing Lynn as we do, we are delighted that you will get to know her as you read this book. As you do, you might just see bright new possibilities for your own life.

-- Jeff Hittenberger, Ph.D., and Christine Corbin Hittenberger

Preface

I LEARNED MY FIRST survival skills from Dad.

He loves movies, especially war films like *Kelly's Heroes* and *The Green Berets* with John Wayne. On a warm Friday night in summer, we'd often hear a shout from Mom, "We're going to the movies, everybody!" My brothers, sister, and I would squeal with delight, and each of us shifted into gear. We donned our pj's and grabbed a favorite pillow, while Mom cooked popcorn. Dad got Windex and bug repellent. We lived in Florida, the home of swampland, alligators, and vulture-sized mosquitoes. Off, we'd go to the drive-in theater.

Inevitably in those old war flicks, there would come a scene with troops walking in a beautiful European countryside, and suddenly a soldier would step on a landmine. Unwittingly, the company had entered into dangerous territory. Then the troops would often crawl over the ground, dig carefully with a knife, and place a stick next to the just-discovered explosives to warn those following behind. In doing so, they created a safe path through to the other side.

Suffering and chronic sickness are like stumbling through a minefield. We never willingly walk into one, but once there, we are not sure if we will make it out alive, or with all our limbs attached. My life

has been about getting to the other side. In this memoir I offer words—
stories—as sticks in the ground to identify places of potential harm and
provide a safe path for those who know similar misfortune.

Introduction

Loneliness is the most terrible poverty.

—Mother Teresa

OVER FORTY MILLION NONINSTITUTIONALIZED Americans are disabled. These survivors of diseases, genetic disorders, accidents, war, and violence will face challenges in almost every aspect of life. They are more likely to be poor and less likely to be employed. They are also less likely to graduate from high school or college. And for those fortunate enough to work full-time, many will earn a significantly lower wage (Erickson, Lee, and von Schrader 2018). As sobering as these statistics are, for children with disabilities, their plight is even more alarming.

As Mother Teresa describes, there is a poverty that strikes much deeper to the heart. For children with disabilities, having friends doesn't come easy. Some children have a difficult time forming meaningful peer relationships because of social communication deficits due to developmental delays or autism. Others may be friendless because of physical differences. In one research study interviewing 166 families, Dr. Anne Snowden, a professor and leader in health research, found that outside of the classroom, 53 percent of disabled children had no friends (Picard 2012, updated 2018). For the majority of these children, the benefits of socialization with peers is a missing ingredient in the child's preparation for adulthood, though they are more likely to face discrimination both in the marketplace and in personal relationships. Most heartbreaking of all, disabled children are more likely to suffer bullying, sexual abuse, and physical violence (Dawkins 1996).

I am one of the forty million people living with a disability. As a young adult, I looked for books that would help me navigate my world, early on realizing the unique obstacles I faced. Nothing I read addressed my struggles or gave me a clue on how to tackle them. Despite this, when friends and even a few strangers told me to write a book, I resisted the idea. The first time, when I was twenty-one, a man who spoke like a prophet said, "You will one day write a book about your life." I thought he was nuts.

So for twenty years, I ignored the suggestion, but in time, I realized I had something to offer you—something that might help. For those with a disability like me, especially people who began that journey in childhood, for other sufferers, and for their families and caregivers, I came to believe that I could offer the gift of an account of my life. It would take another twelve years to write my story.

As you read, you might find how well you can relate, and most likely you will laugh. Perhaps you will be inspired, and that is my prayer. So maybe you will see better the face of God as I tell you the stories of my childhood, of coming to grief time and again as I tried to accept my disability, of getting around in a wheelchair, and of my growing hunger to know God. For mostly, this memoir is a story of God meeting me in my suffering, and the joy I found in his presence. Of how his truth freed me to reach for more in life, instead of settling for restrictions defined by my disability and my culture.

When God visited the prophet, Ezekiel, he carried him away to a valley in the desert, a graveyard of skeletons. God told him to prophesy life into the dry bones (Ezekiel 37). As the doubting prophet spoke in faith over the rubble, the bones took on flesh and sinew and joined together, becoming an army. My story is about a similar transformation. Having a chronic bone disease at first seemed to sentence me to a painful and unhappy existence. Instead my life has become not a dirge, but a dance. For this reason, I'll tell you the story of how it came to pass that "dry bones dance again."

CHAPTER 1

The Discovery

"FASTER! FASTER!" I CRIED, begging for more.

"Okay. Hang on!" My sister, Beth, took a deep breath and pushed with all the strength of her six-year-old body.

The wind tousled my hair as I straddled the pretend motorcycle, relishing the unexpected bumps that flung me into the air like Evel Knievel. As a four-year-old, this tricycle ride around my grandparent's backyard was a daredevil adventure equal to my love for soaring into the clouds on my swing. Clenching the handlebars tighter in anticipation, I added special effects, "Vaaa...roooom...varoom!"

I have heard it said, "Little things make big things happen." Such was the case with me. An unexpected clump of grass stopped my front tricycle tire, and I keeled over. My screams declared this no ordinary fall, and Beth ran for help.

Daddy came running.

I always thought him the most handsome man in the world. He had a perpetual tan, either because he was half-Italian or because he was an athlete his whole life, I do not know which. In 1965, at only twenty-three, he had already fathered four kids. When I hit my teens, I thought him hip because he could dance better than my friends.

As I lay in the grass, piercing the air with my shrill cries, I saw him coming, my knight, and could only think, *It's going to be okay. Daddy's here.*

He swooped me up in his arms, but instead of safety, I plummeted into new depths of pain in both my legs. Holding me to his chest, he rushed me to the car.

Mommy came running, too, eyes wide and darkened with fear, an image I'd never seen before. She clutched my blue blanket, the one with the stars and a cow jumping over the moon.

Daddy said, "Betty, get in. I'll put her in your arms."

She held me like a piece of china—careful but tight—and wrapped the blanket around me. My anguish continued, but her comfort muffled its voice.

MY FALL HAD FRACTURED my right femur and left hip, so the doctor at Morton Plant Hospital put me in traction, both legs sticking straight up in the air. Long hours drifted into dreary days, my broken legs throbbing like the beat of a drum. But how I loved my toy carousel playing, "Hey diddle, diddle, the cat and the fiddle, the cow jumped over the moon." I sang and sang, watching the white starched, uniformed nurses pass by in the hallway.

After several weeks in traction, the nurse gave me a shot that put me to sleep. When I awoke, a cast covered me from armpits to toes. My immobilized legs ached, so I begged, "Mom, would you rub my toes?" longing for her soothing touch on the only part of my lower extremities not covered in plaster. Though I saw her tiredness and reluctance, she would reach out and squeeze my toes, release, squeeze my toes, till her hand hurt.

Gifts from family friends began to pour in, decorating my half of the hospital room and bringing some small measure of relief to my incarceration. Picking up the Etch A Sketch, I made a house like the Leaning Tower of Pisa, and then a face—the kind Picasso would draw. Drawn to the tiny toy much easier to master—a monkey dangling from a trapeze, I pushed my thumb under the plastic base, flipping the ape one way, then the other. Sometimes, he would even flip twice.

I would put a toy down and look toward the door, longing for Mommy or Daddy to come, though they usually visited later in the day. No one. After six weeks in the hospital, the doctor sent me home to finish out another six months in my stiff body suit.

The following fall I started kindergarten. Except for a slight limp, I seemed recovered. One day during outdoor recess, our teacher lined us up about thirty yards away from the school. She said, "Run as fast as you can to the wall. Let's see who wins."

Fixing my eyes on the finish line, I held my right arm outstretched in front of me and crouched ever so slightly, waiting for the signal.

"On your mark. Get set. Go!"

Like an Olympian going for the gold, I flew across that sun-glazed patch of grass. With limited grace but utter abandon, I strained toward the wall. Muscles screeched in rebellion, but my soul soared free in a rush of wind and pounding feet. Aching for air in short gasps, I pressed on to catch the others landing at the wall, heaving and chuckling. I had come in last.

This kindergarten moment is my only memory of running.

For the next few years, it became evident that I never fully recovered from my fall, walking always felt labored, and I limped. Then at seven years old, the morning after my first Holy Communion, I tried out my new bathing suit while my brother, Don, chased me with a hose. As I darted frantically from the cold spray, I slipped on grease in the driveway and fractured my right hip. My physician wrapped me in another body cast.

Soon after, the doctor sent me up to Gainesville Medical Center in northern Florida to see why my bones were so fragile. Mom and Dad packed the station wagon with pillows and a bedpan for the four-hour drive and laid me in the back like luggage.

"Now, we are not going to be able to stay or come see you because you will be far from home," Mom consoled. "But you can call us anytime you want."

My heart ached at the thought of not seeing them.

After check-in, my parents pushed me on a stretcher to my

home away from home—a white, sterile room with four beds, one in each corner. Mom unpacked my yellow-flowered suitcase at the bed near the far window, laying my brush within reach. Then Dad said, "Let's take a tour of this place."

Mom and Dad rolled me to a dingy playroom, painted orange. I hated orange. Dad said, "Look here at this abacus, Lynn. Do you know what it is?"

I did not. I noticed rows of colorful beads. As Dad explained the mathematics of the colorful abacus, I slid the beads along the wire and decided, *I am going to be brave about Mom and Dad leaving.*

Although quite young, it dawned on me that my parents struggled with leaving me. I understood their dilemma. Mom had three other young kids at home, and Dad worked a demanding job running his own men's clothing store, vital to paying the bills.

Gainesville Medical Center became my playground with exploratory trips and push-the-limit exploits, which earned a few tongue-in-cheek smiles from nurses. With limited mobility and the context of a hospital as inspiration, my imaginative play turned somewhat morbid and confined to activities on one of the floor gurneys. Already boy crazy, I adored my handsome doctors. The girl in the bed next to mine would park me in the hallway or deposit me at a busy location on the floor next to the nurses' station, where I covered my head with a sheet and pretended to be dead. From this stealthy hideout, I spied on all the happenings on the floor and got a glimpse of my cute doctors. Pretending to be a forgotten corpse felt delightfully wicked and fun.

Three other children stayed in my hospital room. I felt an uncomfortable heaviness whenever their families came to visit. Whispered words seemed full of fear and dread. My friend, Charlotte, also seven, had steadily lost weight, and they didn't know why. Wiry brown hair smothered her tiny pointed face dotted with playful freckles. She pushed me everywhere, racing up and down the halls giggling. Another child had broken all the bones in her face from a car accident. Eventually, she went home, replaced by a little girl having corrective surgeries, born with a claw for a hand and no rectum. In the bed across from me, a Korean child about my age kept to herself. Darkness shrouded her corner of the room. Charlotte told me she was going blind.

Their peculiar medical conditions frightened me.

One morning I awoke to the sound of my doctors standing around my bed. I pretended to still be asleep so that I could continue my spying, but then I heard, "Lynn is seven years old, and is a such pretty child."

"Oh yes, she is a lovely girl" another doctor chimed in.

My fluttering lashes and sublime smile were a giveaway, I am sure, because the doctors took a suspicious amount of time commenting on my beauty before they got down to business. "Lynn has eyes with blue sclera," said the head physician. I thought it an odd comment since I have hazel eyes. (Later, I found out sclera was the white part of my eyes. They had detected a slightly bluish tinge.) He continued, "This is indicative of a bone disease called osteogenesis imperfecta tarda."

Although it would be a few years before I could pronounce it, the news would forever shape my life. My bones didn't break because of freak accidents. I had a genetic abnormality that would never change—a disease without a cure. My body couldn't absorb calcium, so my bones were not strong, but soft and porous. In time, this would cause my bones to bow and create the curvature of my spine, dwarfism, and other deformities. Every aspect of my future would be affected by this reality.

Mercifully, I could not grasp the weight of his announcement.

THE YEARS FOLLOWING SAW a series of broken bones. I never became used to these sudden life interruptions that thrust me into pain, isolation, and body casts for months at a time. My siblings have memories of neighborhood friends and a tree house in the woods, things of which I have no experience or recollection. Hospitals became my home turf.

The smells and sounds of a hospital, are as distinctive as those of the beach. The familiarity of the hospital's unique milieu left its imprint on my childhood, as surely as the segregated south forged heavyweight champion Muhammad Ali. Gray and aseptic, hospitals have a precise order and culture revolving around the godlike doctors. Other citizens made up this little world: the staff who delivered food; the crotchety old nurse on night duty; the kind nurse who worked weekends;

and the bubbly teen dressed in red-and-white stripes, offering magazines. The African American cleaning woman became my dearest angel. One night she brought in green knitting needles and thick, hot-pink yarn. She leaned over the bed rails with her big bosomy body to guide my hands as she taught me how to hold the needles and wrap the yarn around, pulling it through until a loose knot formed. My angel came each night, cleaned the floor, and taught me how to knit.

In third grade, I spent lots of time at Morton Plant Hospital. While on the monkey bars, I grabbed the metal rung with my right hand to pull myself higher, but my collarbone gave way and broke. A few months later, while playing at home, I broke my left arm. Then, toward the end of the school year during recess, I slipped at the drinking fountain and broke my left hip.

In fourth grade, my parents took me to see Dr. Linebach, a kind man, famous for being the first doctor in America to do hip replacement surgery. He decided I needed corrective surgery to insert a pin in my right femur to strengthen the weak bone. At St. Petersburg General Hospital, they dedicated an entire floor to Dr. Linebach's specialty, and I was the only child there. On my first day, I raced the elderly patients in wheelchairs and visited the ones stuck in bed. By the next day, everyone knew Lynn.

My roommate, Ruth, probably got shocked when I climbed into bed with her so we could sing the novena together. The novena is a service in the Catholic Church dedicated to Mary. Every Monday night I would go with my grandma Daughberger (Mom's mum) because she had it in her heart to pray for me regularly. Since it was Monday night, Ruth and I prayed together.

The next day I visited another one of the elderly patients in her hospital room. I climbed into her bed and snuggled next to her under the crisp white sheets. We played with the electric controls raising our feet, lowering our head, raising our head, and then lowering our feet. Within a few minutes of my visit, we stuck together like a folded peanut butter sandwich—head up and feet up, too. The nurses called the maintenance man and my new gray-haired friend and I giggled as we waited.

After my surgery, once again, I spent the next four months in a body cast—my legs and torso covered in plaster.

9

CHAPTER 2

Life as a Mummy

"MOM! DAD! MOOOOM!" MY hollers shattered the stillness. It was 2:00 a.m. and the third night in a row my agony set the house in motion. Though tired and sleepless, Mom and Dad came quickly.

"What's wrong, honey?"

Between sobs, I said, "I c-c-can't sleep. My cast is itchy."

"Betty, get me the blow dryer."

"Bob, I'll take care of it. You go to bed." But they both continued to hover as the soothing air penetrated the tight areas where my flaking skin ached for relief.

Hot summer nights further aggravated the discomfort of my plaster bodysuit. Dad turned the air conditioner down to arctic temperatures, and the family bundled in blankets, but the tickling of dried skin and moist heat brought me to a frenzy of nerves and itchiness. We lived in hot, humid Florida, where flying cockroaches are hailed as the state bird. In my childish thinking, I had a hundred of those nasty, six-legged insects crawling around inside my cast, causing my itchiness.

Probably one of my teasing brothers planted the idea.

For many children kicking a soccer ball with pinpoint accuracy or performing a plié while maintaining balance are the skills developed in childhood. Confined ten times to body casts during my first twenty-one years, meant that I instead spent much of my childhood mastering the maneuverings of life as a mummy. Altogether, I spent four and a half of those years in body plaster.

I used crutches, a walker, and a metal leg brace with two prongs that hooked into clunky, ugly saddle shoes. These were awkward and uncomfortable, the body cast—a prison—a coffin. Words fail me. At the time, I did not know that I learned best through movement, and like an athlete or a dancer, I ranked bodily intelligent. Though unable to assess the effects of this straightjacket and the inactivity upon my young psyche, the poundage of my plaster-encased body weighted my spirit like a chained bird's.

Being covered in stiff plaster made it vital for me to explore the outer limits of mobility. Sitting up was unattainable, and I could not bend my knees, stretch my ankles, or twist around; so ambulation seemed impossible. The whole idea of a body cast is to prevent movement of the limbs and torso, but I am convinced that the spirit longs to be free and will therefore put to use whatever little mobility remains. Just as a blind man refines his sense of hearing, I learned to be active in my casts.

Restrained by my first body cast at age four, I mastered the art of pulling on the rail of the hospital bed so I could roll onto my side. Then, by shifting my shoulders and using the smoothness of the sheets to help me slide to the center of the bed, I flipped onto my tummy. An amazing accomplishment! With a slight push-up, I shoved a pillow under my knee on each side so that my toes would not get squished while I lay face down. This may seem like no big deal, but when lying on my back all day, every day, a change of position meant a whole new world.

Some casts reached down to my toes on one leg but only down to my knee on the other. I became good at picking up things with my foot and even developed a prehensile toe over the years, kind of like a chimpanzee. Even as an adult, without thinking, I will quickly slip off a shoe and pick up items left on the floor. I have impressed many a child this way.

By the time my fourth body cast came along at age nine, Dad had hit on an ingenious idea. Dad sounded crazy to my doctor, but he obediently sawed a small window in my cast at the knee. Though only a two-inch by two-inch opening, it allowed air to enter into the dark, tight areas of the plaster. The much-needed ventilation lessened the itching and also gave me access to hard-to-reach areas with a long skinny, knitting needle. How I came to love this soothing, makeshift scratcher.

This victory proved a valuable life lesson Dad passed on to me: hardships created by my disability must be challenged. Learning to defy my limits became a passion for independence, a kind of game to overcome the odds. Through his creativity, Dad empowered this attitude. In the minefield I had stumbled into, I shoved my first stake in the ground.

One time, I came home in a new body cast, expecting the hospital bed as usual. Instead, Dad had put my mattress on the ground,  like a futon, and created a cart with casters. I could now roll out of my bed on my own, slide onto the vinyl-covered cart, and push myself all over the house—like riding a long skateboard. Living on this cart, six inches above the ground, I navigated through tight corners and narrow hallways and bulldozed through discarded clothes and shoes with the skill of a hockey player scoring a goal. From my cart, I played Ping-Pong against the wall and accessed potato chips for a late-night snack. Mom strategically placed my favorite foods down low in the pantry so I could pour a bowl of Cheerios for breakfast or bake homemade chocolate-chip cookies for the family.

Impressed by my mobility, the doctors took pictures and shared it with other orthopedists. In this small way, I felt the accomplishment of a noble exploit, kind of like my friends outside winning soccer trophies. Dad's innovative problem solving not only relieved my discomfort but also allowed me to enjoy independence and a feeling of normalcy. This approach to life's roadblocks would become invaluable in the years ahead.

CHAPTER 3

The Miller Family

I WAS NOT SUPPOSED to be born.

The doctor said, "Betty, you are risking your life if you have another child."

After dating for four years, in 1957, my dad, Bob Miller—at nineteen, married my mom, Betty Daughberger—at only eighteen. Don arrived on the scene within the first year, followed by Beth less than a year later. Obeying the doctor's advice would not be a tragedy after Don and Beth's births. But Mom and Dad found out soon enough that, for a good Catholic, the only acceptable form of birth control in the 1960s—the rhythm method—did not work so well. David came fourteen months later.

With Mother already caring for three small children, her physician cautioned her yet again about the dangers of having another child. But despite the warnings to thwart my conception, I was born a year after David in Orlando, Florida, on October 10, 1961, sandwiched between the Bay of Pigs and the Cuban Missile Crisis.

Having survived attempts to prevent my existence by doctors, and nuclear annihilation by Castro, after I arrived on the scene, Mom and Dad decided it best to stop having kids. They sought out permission from a young Catholic priest at their local parish. A modern thinker, he said, "Betty, you have done your duty by having four beautiful children. I think you should stay alive and care for them."

Being the caboose of the family came with certain perks. Worn down by older siblings pushing the limits, Mom and Dad often told me, "Sure, honey, see you later. Be careful!"

However, being the youngest came with a price: either because of my immaturity, my oversensitivity, or because of some underlying resentment toward me, teasing from my brothers became a necessary cross I had to bear. With as much ingenuity as I could muster, I would try to overcome their taunts by pretending toughness, tattling, and even exchanging a few blows; that is, before my diagnosis ended this option. Nothing worked. And so, at six and seven, I frequently ran away. Or threatened to do so. Like a hobo who walked the train tracks in some old black-and-white movie, I would grab a scarf and fill it with a snack, a doll, and some underwear. Then, tying it to stick, I would sling it over my shoulder and dramatically shout to my disinterested brothers, "I am leaving!"

"Goodbye, crybaby."

Slamming the door, I plodded down our long street, weeping, feeling my life in the Miller home, too hard to bear.

My tragic exits came so frequently that on one occasion Mom finally asked, "Can I help you pack, Sarah Bernhardt?" Her reference to the theatrical, silent-film star did little to stem my outrage.

Over time, I realized my suffering did not remain a private matter. With each new bone break, Mom and Dad, as well as Don, Beth, and David, also bore the weight of my disease. Children often compete for attention in a family, and given the steady stream of drama resulting from my bone breaks and surgeries, my brothers and sister might have thought it a losing battle. As the years passed, Beth took on many responsibilities for my care. Often in the middle of the night, while in pain or in need of help, I would just as soon call for Beth as for Mom, though she was only two years older than I.

But if my siblings wrestled with it all, Mom and Dad struggled far more. In addition to juggling work, kids, meals, housework, and the tasks of raising us, Mom and Dad also had the rhythm of their lives interrupted by caregiving or by daily visits to the hospital. Inherent in their trips to see me were hours spent in rush hour traffic and the scheduling conflicts of an active family. One or both of them would come to the hospital every day to keep me company: we'd watch TV together or play cards. They walked with me through it all—the pain and the boredom, every step of the way, doing what they could to love me through. They watched me suffer and bore my tears and fears as only loving parents can.

Did my mother ever feel resentful? Did my father ever feel frustrated that his hard-earned money went toward medical bills instead of much-needed items like shoes, car repairs, or saving for our college? That's likely, though they never expressed it. Back then, we had no guidebooks to give directions, as you would have when traveling in a foreign country.

Despite the pressures on our family, I knew my parents loved me, but the guilt of being a burden to them felt like a weight both hard to bear and confusing. I knew Mom would just as soon relax with a book than get me a drink. Often I would debate with myself, "Shall I ask, or shall I wait?" But eventually, I would shout out from my hospital bed, "Mom, can I have some water?" The weariness in her response often seeped through. This is the life of a child with special needs. For Mom, this was now her life, too. Though always my mainstay and best friend, she also made sure I did my chores like everybody else. Since the toilet sat low enough to the ground for me to reach while in a body cast, I had to clean the john. Her training made clear that I had to contribute, that having a disability didn't earn me a free ride. I did not recognize it at the time, but this lesson would serve me well.

Apart from sibling tensions, a part of everyday life and no little matter to my sensitive heart, our home seemed like the center of a party. As young, upbeat parents, Mom and Dad made every holiday an opportunity to be together. Mom hosted family, friends, and every stray cat that didn't have a place to go. Our noisy Miller holidays always included my grandma and grandpa Daughberger, my great-aunt Dorothy and her husband, Uncle Joe (from my dad's side), and newcomers who seemed to fit right in no matter what their age or reason for being there.

Pockets of activity happened throughout the house: a sports show on one TV, a holiday movie on another, and a talk over munchies in the kitchen, or a Pinochle game at the dining room table. The cacophony of shouts and sometimes cursing at the football team on TV, and teasing laughter over a card game, all competed for attention. Not only did we argue easily, but we also spoke all at once, stomping over each other's conversations. In short, we were not a serene group given to relaxation.

Mom and Dad had a way of making Christmas merry and extravagant. I felt this derived from Dad's upbringing in an orphanage. Sitting around the dinner table each Sunday evening, enjoying the aftermath of pot roast and German chocolate cake, Dad told of his life as a kid in Detroit, Michigan. "I remember when I was eight and I didn't get anything for Christmas." The hubbub at the table quieted.

"Really, Dad. How come?" I said.

"My mom, your grandma Dottle, had to go away to find a job in another city and left me with my aunt. Then she couldn't take care of me any longer, so my aunt placed me in juvenile hall. Grandma searched for me but couldn't find me."

We figured if we kept asking questions, then he would keep talking. Often, he did.

He told how he won a yo-yo contest, wanted to be a professional baseball player, and how after living six years in foster care and orphanages, he at fourteen came to live with his mother again. He described Christmases in the orphanage that would come and go with little in the way of gifts or holiday cheer. Dad made sure his kids would have it better.

Like a symphony of harmonic notes rising to a dramatic crescendo, our Decembers had many happy moments escalating to a glorious Christmas morning. The opening note of our festivities began around December tenth when we bought our Christmas tree. We never picked the tall, stately Christmas tree, but each year we chose a short, plump fir. It dawned on us over time; we always selected a tree that bore a striking resemblance to our family. Except for Don, all of us had a small stature, and a few looked quite pudgy. It seemed that a short, fat evergreen inspired unwavering affection, and so Dad would bargain for a reasonable price, and that night we would all decorate the most magnificent tree in the world.

I spent several Christmases in body casts, but I was never so unfortunate as to spend Christmas in the hospital. When I was four, each night in December, Dad would gently lift me out of my hospital bed in the family room and lay me on the floor next to our Christmas tree. One night, he carried me out to our station wagon. With the promise of a surprise, he packed me in the far back. and my brothers and sister piled into the middle seat.

"Dad, where are we going?" David asked.

"Wait and see."

"Moooom! Tell me! Where are we going?" I said. A smile played about her mouth, but I couldn't get her to spill the beans.

Rarely did I leave home while laid up, so I could barely contain my excitement. I was not disappointed. Mom and Dad had brought us to see Santa Claus!

I resembled a stiff mackerel in the photo as I sat on Santa's lap in my body cast, and I looked a little scared of the white-bearded man with the red hat. But today the memory brings a smile when I consider how my parents made childhood as normal as possible for their little girl in a body cast.

CHAPTER 4

Humiliation

ALTHOUGH I DREADED THE hot, rotating saw that burned my skin and cracked open my cast like a walnut, I counted down the days, hours, and minutes until my release. Confinement and boredom were reason enough for my eagerness, but the daily strain of being encased in plaster was, at the least, awkward and often mortifying. I could not dress my stiff, cement-covered frame in standard attire, so I wore what looked like a diaper. As I got older, I found this demeaning garb hard to bear when visitors arrived, and with three siblings, lots of intruders came in at awkward times.

Lying down and being incapacitated meant I needed help with emptying the bedpan and disposing of my toothpaste spit and sponge bath water. All my bodily needs depended on the help of nurses or upon Mom and Beth, and the fact that I burdened them also burdened me. Freedom from a body cast would restore my dignity.

In the hospital, humiliation took on cosmic proportions. Pressing the buzzer for the nurses' station might or might not bring immediate results, meaning I would sometimes sit in warm, then cold urine that made my cast smell. The odor of a body cast after some months of ownership is worse than a boy's football locker.

One day, I lay in a fresh-made body cast, suffering from the effects of too many drugs, too little movement, and lying horizontal for a month. Tears streamed down my face as I lay on my side, clothed in a cast, but exposing everything that counts of my young womanhood, the stiffness of the plaster causing one leg to stick up in the air like the mast of a ship. In that helpless state of wrenching cramps awaiting the medication that would help me go to the bathroom, facing the door, curtain wide open, the young lunch server walked in the door. For the past week I had noticed the cute guy. He was stunned. I was horrified!

Such is life in hospitals and body casts. Dignity flies out the window.

Being poked and prodded, having no say and having no control, are atmospheric weather conditions for abuse—like when a white-coated man sneaks into your room to touch places mommy always called "private." And the kind that a nurse did when she pulled my bed into the middle of the room, away from the call button, so that she could shine a heat lamp on the back of my damp cast. Writhing under the fierce temperature, without a fan or even a cup of water, I cried out into the empty hallway, "Nurse! Help! I'm *hot!*" *Surely they can hear me? Wouldn't a nurse come if she could hear me? Where is the nurse? Why has she left me?* All evening I called, "Help! Somebody help me!" No one came for hours.

I never thought to complain to my folks or seek their protection because suffering had become routine.

Then, there was the pain. I never liked taking drugs, but at times, only the sting of a needle could bring release. I knew the disgrace of begging for drugs—crazed and screaming for a few hours of oblivion with that sweet, horrible prick. As I waited for the next shot, I agonized, "You can send people to the moon. Why can't you take away my pain?"

When I was eight years old, in 1969, Neil Armstrong landed on the moon. Dad had his four children seated in front of the TV and said, "Kids, this is a moment in history you will never forget. When I was a boy, I used to watch science fiction movies about going to the moon, and now we are doing it."

His sense of wonder about outer space proved infectious. The lunar landing made me feel like anything could happen. In the light of such significant scientific breakthroughs, I could not understand how no one could quiet my throbbing leg.

At such times, I was beyond comfort—hysterical with unyielding stabs in my femur. The aftermath of those storms? Pools of shame.

Becoming fiercely self-sufficient became the only way I could maintain what little control I had left. While receiving help from others horrified me, I soon realized that I needed more than independence to face the battles before me. I needed God.

CHAPTER 5

Why Me?

"SHHH! LET ME SEE if anyone is here first." I held up my hand like a cop stopping traffic and ducked my head through the doorway and looked around. "Okay, we're clear."

In whispered tones my five friends and I giggled, dipping our fingers in the holy water, and then making the sign of the cross as we genuflected before the large crucifix. We all knew the church was off limits during lunchtime at St. Patrick Catholic School in Largo, Florida, but these recruits, being an adventuresome bunch, willingly joined in on my caper.

Pointing to a pew in front of the altar, I directed my first-grade choir to their positions. "Now everyone, open your hymnal to, *Ave Maria.*" The girls dutifully obeyed, whether they could read or not, and our voices joyously rang out in the empty sanctuary.

If any of the nuns ever stumbled across our presence, we never knew, but the undisturbed quiet brought greater reverence to our weak song. Often I would sneak away with friends or by myself during lunch recess and sing to Jesus in our church with stained-glass windows.

Simple worship of innocent faith created holy awe. I started my lunchtime rendezvous shortly after having a dream.

Some dreams fade away with the sunrise and are quickly forgotten. Others stay with you for a lifetime. At age six, I had one that I remember just as vividly today as the morning when I woke up. While walking in a foreign land, upon dusty, red dirt roads, I trailed behind Jesus. He caught my gaze over the mob crowding him and smiled at me. I felt drawn to him by an irresistible magnetism. In my dream, I followed Jesus wherever he went, captivated by his love.

When I awoke, I tried to re-enter the dream and stay close to Jesus but could not. Awakened hunger caused me to look for Jesus in the face of bearded strangers. Although singing to him brought me joy, I could not put into words why going to church didn't satisfy me.

Aching to have an experience like one of the saints, I'd ask him to appear to me like when Mary came to St. Bernadette (a young girl who saw a series of apparitions of a beautiful lady). When he didn't, it affirmed my cursed unworthiness. I was too rascally to be a saint. Even as far back as kindergarten, wherever I went, trouble followed. Enamored of one little blond boy with blue eyes, I chased him around the classroom until the teacher said, "Stop bothering Drew, or I will have you sit in the corner!"

Mostly, she yelled at me for talking. I thought myself a bad girl, indeed, for she seemed to do that often. When the class went on a field trip to McDonald's for lunch, my teacher said, "No, Lynn. You are not going with us. Only those who have been good can go on our field trip." No one else had to stay behind, so I decided early in life that I was an unusually rotten kid.

For my crimes, in first grade, Sister Immaculata often sent me to stand in back with all the coats. I made a few visits to the principal's office, too. In second grade, my teacher gave me poor marks in conduct, and I missed most of my third-grade year because of broken bones. But my fourth-grade teacher, Miss Gressil, had other ways of dealing with my socializing: she tied me to a chair, slapped my hand with a ruler, and threatened to tape my mouth shut.

I figured murderers and evil people like Adolf Hitler went to hell, so maybe I would escape that, but a disobedient girl like me would have

23

to go first to purgatory, where I would be purified for most of eternity. I found this to be disheartening and not sufficient incentive for living a holy life, but I desired to honor the Jesus of my dream and to please my parents. My spirit was willing, but my flesh weak.

During my third-grade year, a girl with a learning disability named Katie died in a car accident. (At the time, in the 1960's, before society thought of kinder words, they called her retarded.) Katie hadn't been a student at St. Patrick's, but the whole school went to her memorial service. As the funeral procession passed by, I whispered to my friend, Rita, "How come there is a white cloth over her casket?"

Ever since day one of first grade, Rita was my best school chum. Sister Immaculata had told her new students to line up at the door, and Rita noticed me standing there, wide-eyed and nervous. "Hey, Girl!" she called from the back of the line. "Can I stand next to you?" Our immediate bond blossomed into eight years of friendship.

With a swift, stealthy look toward the teacher, she leaned closer and in hushed tones whispered. "The white cloth means Katie is a saint. She is going to heaven because she was retarded."

She got to go straight to heaven. No detours through purgatory. I badly wished that I could be retarded like Katie so that I could go to heaven, too.

Despite my character flaws, I still longed to know God. I searched for him in religious films and by reading books about saints, but as my condition worsened, so did my faith.

After closing his men's store, Dad worked Monday through Friday driving all over Florida selling Farrah slacks to department stores. Though not a wealthy family, Dad allowed himself this one luxury, a Cadillac Eldorado. It sparkled impressively, with its olive-green exterior, leather bucket seats, and a camel-colored dashboard. He kept his Caddy pristine, so one day when I climbed on the trunk to observe the street and gaze out on the quiet neighborhood from its enormous height it felt like desecrating holy ground. I felt blissful, but also guilty perched up there, my world deceptively peaceful.

A few stolen moments of forbidden pleasure battled with my fear of being caught. I jumped down, thrusting out my hands to brace myself on the ground. Crack! My left arm crumpled under the impact. The grotesque protrusion like a camel hump frightened me. The pain was familiar. Already, at eight years old, I diagnosed broken bones like an expert.

I cradled my arm to protect it from the slightest bump, while mom drove to the emergency room (ER). Confusion and agony erupted in a loud cry to my mother, to God, and to the universe, "Why me? Why always me?"

Mom remained silent, probably asking herself the same question. What could she say to her daughter, undergoing a spiritual crisis at such a young age?

"How did it happen?" she asked.

I could not endure the pounding in my arm plus recriminations. At that moment, truth took second place to the fear of punishment. "I fell off Don's bike and hit my arm on the car tire." A small lie, I reasoned — close to the facts. My oldest brother's bike stood near the scene of my fall so it would make sense.

The X-ray confirmed it: a compound fracture.

For an entire year, everyone accepted my lie.

Time together at the local baseball field added to the rhythm of our family life. My older siblings, Don, Beth, and David joined teams, and aside from the occasional thrilling tournament, I rarely watched the whole game. And so I became a Little League orphan wandering around the field looking for spare change to buy a snack, or a log on which to tightrope walk.

One night, as the game wore on, I played catch with another of the loose-change girls at the ballpark. We lazily tossed around conversation along with the ball. We played a smooth game until she threw out a hard truth. She said, "You know, anyone who lies commits a mortal sin and is going to hell."

Conviction hit me like a punch in the stomach. I remembered my deliberate fib — now a part of medical records and family conversations accepted as fact — but not accurate. Had I committed a mortal sin? Would I go to hell? Guilt drove me to Mom's bedside that night. "I need to talk," I said. Tears filled my eyes and she sat down, recognizing the gravity of my tone.

She drew me close, ready to comfort before hearing my crime. "What's wrong?"

"Mom, I lied. I didn't break my arm falling off Don's bike — I jumped off the trunk of Dad's car."

"You know it isn't right to lie, Lynn." She didn't shame me; no need for severity given the heavy weight of regret I already bore.

"I know, Mom." Then I added, "What are we going to do about the medical records?"

"It's all right," she said. Then absolving me of my trespass, she added, "We'll just let it go."

Mom's exoneration felt sincere, but I wondered about God's. Guilt plagued me, and my monthly visit to the confessional at our Catholic school did not silence the inner accusation. For two years I confessed the same sin, unsure of the pathway to forgiveness, with the parish priests not seeming to recognize my struggle. I did not understand the spiritual conflict growing in proportion to the trauma of my broken bones. I had spent much of my young life in hospitals, enclosed in body casts. "Why me?" was the only way I could articulate my sense of injustice and inner confusion. Since no one could answer the question, I came to my conclusions. I figured God hadn't blessed me, so I must be one of the cursed in life. This could be the only explanation as to why I broke one bone after another.

CHAPTER 6

Wrestling Fear

OLDER SIBLINGS HAD GONE out for the afternoon. Saturday boredom drove me to the garage, where I scrounged from its recesses my sister's roller skates. Plopping down on the driveway, I turned the key to shorten the metal boot so it would strap onto my shoe. As I fumbled with the mechanism, the possible danger settled on me like a shroud. Although only eight years old, I reasoned, *If I go roller-skating, I could fall and break a bone.* I stared at the footwear a long time. Wrestling. Longing.

I put the skates away.

Several months later, on Christmas morning, I eagerly rushed out of bed and into the living room, searching for the bike Santa had surely left me. To my utter grief, he delivered the game Kerplunk, instead. I got the message. No longer would enjoyment be determined by my dreams. I could see that life would be, must be, restricted by fear of breaking bones.

Having broken my shoulder early in third grade during PE and my hip later that year when, at recess, I slipped on some water by the fountain, my family had decided playtime had proved too risky. For the

27

next four years, like Rudolph who couldn't join in any reindeer games, I could not participate in the fun of recess, PE, and lunch with my peers. Once again, fear diminished my life.

At first my girlfriends seemed delighted with the privilege of lunching in our room or sitting outside under the stairs in our pretend fort. But one by one, they tired of my company and joined in on the playground hoopla. Some part of me knew not to take it personally. But it hurt. I felt rejected.

After that, my teacher, Miss Gressil, remained in the classroom to keep an eye on me. She relaxed at her desk, and I parked at mine. Sometimes a colleague would join her. Other occasions she would sit alone, grading papers while I quietly ate. Every day she asked, "What are you having for lunch?"

"Chicken." Most days, Mom put a single chicken leg in my lunch pail.

Miss Gressil joked, "One day, you're going to turn into a chicken."

"Yeah, I guess so." And that would be the extent of our lunchtime chats.

The following summer, early in July, I had corrective surgery to put a pin in my right femur, and spent four months in another body cast. During my recovery, while we built our new family home in a nearby city, my family moved into an apartment for a few months. My rented hospital bed sat at the huge front window. From there, I held court each day while kids and neighbors came by to visit "the girl in a body cast." When one of the kids had a birthday party, Dad carried me up the stairs of the complex and laid me on our neighbor's couch. I won a prize for tossing the most clothespins in a bottle.

After getting out of my cast, and only a few months after we moved into our house, I stood up at the kitchen table to look inside my mom's pink sewing box. As I cleaned it and removed tangled threads, my femur snapped like a wishbone. Then a few days after surgery, while at St. Petersburg Children's Hospital, I lay in the activity center, utterly enthralled by making flowers with colorful tissue paper. Abruptly, a piercing pain stabbed my heel. I screamed, and continued wailing, with no reprieve from the persistent cutting sensation.

Nurses endeavored to shut me up but could not. My nurse friend, Sandy, the one who gave me her nurse's cap, spoke firmly, "Lynn, you have got to stop this ridiculous screaming right now!"

Sandy? You, too? Don't you know me better? Her words hurt.

Then Mom arrived and tried to comfort me, "Come on, honey. Settle down. You need to stop this now. They are sending for a doctor." Despite their efforts to quiet me, I continued to scream, inconsolable.

After two hours of hysteria, a doctor came and cut off my cast below the ankle. Immediately I felt relief. A scar the size of a dime remained for years, the only evidence of the mysterious sudden pain in my foot.

Learning that a broken bone could occur just because I stood up, or that the feeling of being amputated with an ax could arise without warning, underscored the capricious nature of life with a bone disease. My parents could not protect me, and this realization added to my fears. Terrors, whether realistic or bizarre, plagued me. After viewing the sci-fi movie *The Andromeda Strain,* I worried that infectious disease would come from outer space to destroy the planet. For several months, I obsessed about some alien bacteria spreading. Then one day, after noticing that I had not once thought about the world coming to an end, the phobia abated.

My fearful outlook on the world, however, lingered, though I could not yet perceive how it would hinder me in the years to come.

CHAPTER 7

My First Wheelchair

WHEN THE LOCAL FUNERAL parlor closed, my mom got the deal of a lifetime—a wheelchair for a penny. It was wide and puke green, and I imagined it being used to cart dead people to their caskets. Though only nine, its gruesome history didn't bother me at all. More important, I needed the chair during that stage of recovery between body casts and traversing with crutches or a walker when my knee was stiff, my muscles weak and my equilibrium shaky from months of lying down. At such times, my funeral home discard came in handy.

Most people think of life in a wheelchair as a great tragedy, but I thought of it as freedom. Instead of being cooped up in the house, playing it safe, my green metal fortress made it possible for me to be out and about in our new neighborhood. Having a wheelchair gave my extrovert personality an outlet for expression as I strolled along the street, making friends, selling products, and socializing. I rolled all over town in that chair, celebrating its extra-wide girth by having my dog, Keyon, share it with me. My shaggy, blond, ten-pound schnoodle probably thought the contraption belonged to her. She danced excitedly around the chair, her soft Oreo eyes begging me to hurry, anticipating our outside excursion. She fit perfectly, tucked in beside me, her long tail hanging out the back, wagging as we rolled along. My first wheelchair adventures had Keyon by my side. As I went for strolls with my puppy, I learned how to maneuver up steps and through doorways, and in the process, I discovered that being in a wheelchair could be fun.

IN FLORIDA, IT IS common to have not only hurricanes but also intense storms. Before the weather got too dangerous, I would open up my umbrella and let the wind carry me along down the street—kind of like windsurfing. On my trips around the block, I often stopped and visited with neighbors, especially other dog walkers. I remember one day when I came across Mr. Lopez and his dog Frosty.

"Hi, Mr. Lopez. How's Frosty today?" I petted the large Samoyed as he licked my hand. Frosty's calm, friendly demeanor did not match his scary, wolf-like appearance. He always seemed out of place in our semitropical state, and I wondered if he felt, through some innate sense, homesick for Alaska, not knowing as a child that it would be Russia from which his breed hailed.

"Frosty's fine. He just had his daily grooming and is ready for a walk."

Frosty endured my hug as I buried my face in his thick, white fur. "I feel sorry for Frosty. He must be hot with all that fur."

Mr. Lopez chuckled. "Oh, he sheds his coat this time of year. We find it all over the house, so that's why I groom him every day."

Mr. Lopez installed pools for a living and once invited my brothers and sister and me to his house for a dip. Aztec tiles of blue, orange, and yellow lined the entire pool and made his home seem the most elegant place on the planet. My idea of a perfect abode would include a small shack with a huge pool. Mr. Lopez's oasis raised the bar.

I continued my trek around the block to my tutor's house. "Hi, Mrs. Jones. I came by to see how your husband is today." Having recovered from cancer of the throat, Mr. Jones now had a metal voice box that he could press, allowing him to converse.

"Come on in," she said. "I think I might even have a homemade cookie lying around here somewhere."

Perhaps Mrs. Jones knew me well enough to suspect that my visits had an ulterior motive. After saying hello and collecting my cookie, I didn't stay long.

Arriving at the furthest end of the block rewarded me with an affectionate exchange from our neighborhood dreamboat, three years older than me, who looked like the blond version of my favorite teen idol, Keith Cassidy. For years he warmly called out to me, "*Que pasa!*" as I rolled past. This fleeting interaction felt sufficiently affirming until I learned that he had asked my older sister out on a date.

Many other neighborhood citizens became a part of my childhood play and education—the elderly couple with an indoor pool delightfully placed in the center of their living room, and the somewhat full-figured, gregarious Carol who threw a block party with square dancing. Coronel Miller shared his secret popcorn recipe with me and taught me chess. Mr. Henson grew corn in his backyard. From him, I learned that if I immersed the ears in boiling water within one minute of being picked from the stalk, it would not become a starchy vegetable.

Grasping every excuse possible to go around the block and socialize, I began selling Easter Seals, a fund-raiser for kids with disabilities, which proved a lucrative endeavor for a little kid in a wheelchair. In fact, selling just about anything door-to-door turned out profitable. Eventually, my brothers sent me off with their World's Finest chocolate bars—a fund-raiser for their baseball team. I only asked the small fee of a little chocolate for myself.

One drizzly day, Mom waved goodbye with concern as I departed in my chair to take orders for painting ceramic figurines. She sighed watching me hobble down the street, pushing my wheel with one hand and holding a large box of painted samples with the other, brimming with the hope of earning some cash. Mom worried aloud to Dad, "Bob, poor Lynn is going off in the rain. What if no one buys anything?"

Several hours later, I returned with so many orders that she had to help me paint the decorations to finish them in time for the holidays.

EARLY ON IN LIFE, I had begun to think of every activity with a view of how much walking it would require, always choosing the most direct route.

Thinking ahead, I gathered all my materials to minimize going back and forth: back to the house, back to the classroom, back to the car, even retracing my steps back to the bedroom from the living room were trips I strived to avoid. Far too often, I declined to participate in some junket or other because I would have to walk. A wheelchair broadened my horizons. Though I didn't know it at the time, this would be another answer for surviving my minefield. Adaptive equipment could improve my mobility and allow me to better enjoy life.

In time, my big granny vehicle became part of the family. After coming home from the grocery store, Mum would open the door and yell, "Lynn, I need your wheelchair."

"Okay." I sat at the dinner table and gave my "legs" to Mom. A few minutes later, she returned with a chair-load of groceries, taking five more trips to complete the job.

Each year after Christmas, with bags hanging from my chair handles and a stack of boxes on my lap, we made our returns to the mall. On one occasion, Beth said, "Thank God we have Lynn. I don't know what we'd do carrying all these heavy packages."

"Yeah, Lynn sure comes in handy." Though she walked behind, pushing my chair, I could hear the wink and smile in her tone, fostering in me a kind of pride in helping out the family. Although in actuality I couldn't take credit for my replacement legs becoming a handy wagon.

Nothing compared to the perk we enjoyed in getting on rides at Disney World in Orlando. Other families stood in long lines in the hot Florida sun, dripping with sweat from the sticky weather, but not the Millers. We would scoot through the exits and hop right on the boat or car or tram—even going around twice sometimes. Our privileged status allowed us to visit the whole park in a day. On those occasions, I felt like a hero.

IN NOVEMBER OF FIFTH grade, I got out of my body cast and attended Holy Family Catholic School in St. Petersburg, only a couple of miles from our new home. I had never gone to school in a wheelchair, but after shedding my cement cocoon, I longed to make new friends and become a social butterfly. It did not occur to me that my disability would define me, nor did I foresee the ostracism that accompanied being different.

For the first time, having friends didn't come easy. Other kids got presents from their Secret Pals at Christmas. I didn't receive fun cards, little sweets left on my desk, or a gift on the last day before holiday vacation. Kids stashed mean notes in my lunch pail; labels like ugly and fatso stuck like Post-its in my heart. Practical jokes added to the abuse. Two girls pretended to welcome me over to their house for a visit but snuck out the back door before I knew what had happened. Mystified, I searched the rooms and called their names. Naïve to such cattiness, it took a while for me to grasp that they had ditched me.

I still did not go outside to recess, lunch, or PE, but now the teacher didn't stay behind to keep me company. Through the window, I observed my classmates on the playground, and it drove home all the fun I missed out on.

Leaving school after the three o'clock bell rang was the happiest moment of my day. Mom sat behind the wheel in her car, and Keyon waited with her, propped on top of the automobile like a hood ornament. Upon seeing them, the weight of the world lifted off my shoulders.

Perhaps starting a new school in a wheelchair determined my fate. Maybe it was the next two-and-a-half years after I left behind the chair and wore an ugly brace on my right leg. Two prongs at the bottom of the contraption hooked onto the heel of a saddle shoe; medical-beige straps belted the brace to my leg and waist. In addition to this unsightly protective gear was the embarrassment of squeaking when I walked and having to wear uncool, stretchy, old-lady pants.

Sixth grade with Sister Carlota developed into the worst year of all—and my first awareness of depression. Perhaps the nun sensed this. One day she called me up to her desk. "Lynn, would you like to read a Bible passage for our school mass Friday morning?"

"Really?" At twelve, I loved reading aloud and relished having such an important role. Always in school, I sat in the front row, raising my hand to engage in discussions. This assignment suited me. "Can I go practice in the church?"

"Yes, but come back before lunch," said Sister Carlota.

Yeah! I get to read for the school and also get out of math. Taking advantage of this opportunity to bend the rules, I popped a piece of gum in my mouth and rushed over to the sanctuary. I had already visited the principal's office twice for chewing gum, and I didn't want a repeat performance. Getting out of class allowed me the added luxury of enjoying my great vice—Doublemint Gum.

I flipped on the speaker and climbed the steps to the podium. True to my word, I practiced the gospel of Luke chapter one, enjoying the sound of my voice magnified throughout the empty church. This was fun!

An elderly lady intruded on my sanctum when she entered through the side door. I didn't mind. I continued to read, "And the angel of the Lord appeared to Mary…" As I read, she lit a candle and came over to sit in a pew directly in front of me, a willing audience.

When I concluded my eloquent oratory, she commented, "You did very well." Then she added, "It must have been quite hard for a young girl like Mary to travel on a donkey when nine months pregnant. She was probably only a child about thirteen years old."

"Wow! I didn't know that," I said.

"You know, dear, if you want to do a good job, you should get rid of the gum. I'll tell you what. I will give you a dollar if you throw it away."

"Okay." And I flicked it into the trash.

I passionately reread the passage, and she listened and praised my efforts. Afterward, she said, "Come on over here. I will give you your dollar."

I climbed down from behind the podium and limped over to receive my pay.

My elderly friend began to cry, deeply moved when she saw I wore a clunky leg brace. Her tears wet my cheek as she clung to me. She said, "I came here feeling sorry for myself—and look at you…"

While not understanding why I'd made her cry, I felt good that something about me healed her heart. She let me go, then scrounged in her purse for a hanky and her wallet. She said, "Here you go, honey. Take this." Instead of the dollar I expected, she pulled out a five. I felt bewildered but thrilled at receiving such a high price for tossing out my gum.

THAT SUMMER, MY FAVORITE cousins visited from Michigan, and kid laughter filled the house. We had just returned from an evening dip in the neighbor's pool and were preparing for bed and our excursion to Disney World the next day. Mom shouted out to kids dispersed throughout the house, "Put your towels in the dryer everybody!"

Rushing to the front door to grab my discarded towel, I slipped on a droplet of water in the hallway. I broke my right femur.

Unable to postpone the trip to Disney World but a few days, my family and visiting cousins left for the amusement park as I recovered from surgery in our local children's hospital.

Sympathizing with my disappointment, Dad came back bearing treasures from the magic shop on Main Street in Downtown Disney. With this token gift from the Magic Kingdom to compensate for my loss, I became the best kid magician on the children's ward. On the Fourth of July, the staff at St. Petersburg Children's Hospital had me perform my tricks for all the kids and the visiting TV station, too.

I found fame to be a solace.

Having served my time recovering all summer and into the fall in what was now my sixth body cast, I joined my classmates several months after school started, once again donning my leg brace. Soon I caught up with my studies, but every day the now familiar heartache of loneliness plagued me, as I returned to the routine of lunching alone, missing out on recess and staying inside during PE.

Then one night at one of our school functions, I ran into my benefactor who had given me five dollars. She lit up when she saw me, and said, "Thank you for what you did for me that day. I want you to know I've been doing well ever since. I've gotten involved in life again, and I'm no longer feeling sorry for myself."

It made me happy to think that I had somehow touched this woman's life. I felt better about all those hard things in my life, too.

Then things began to turn around for me. Toward the end of seventh grade, in 1974, my parents allowed me to join the other children during recess and lunch. Reasons for the sudden change were not given; I assumed my folks thought seventh-grade girls wouldn't engage in active games. They were right, too. Mostly, we just hung out and talked.

Except for one occasion. Since toads resided always in

abundance in our swampish state, our science teacher, Mr. Moreno, ordered boys to collect them one recess. All the seventh-grade males hunted the critters and then slammed them up against the building to prepare them for dissecting. But the temptation proved too much for them. Soon boys chased after girls with the bloody remains. As I fled before one nasty guy with a good arm, one slapped me square in the back.

Later that day, I had a rather large amphibian pinned down with its skin peeled back for a good look at its innards. While I leaned in to examine its still-beating heart, the monster jumped off the tray into my face. The whole school heard my scream—a shrill so loud it would wake the dead or kill a beast. The toad died.

Mr. Moreno yelled at me, but my lab partner, Susie Gillespie, and I roared, sucking in deep gusts of air between snorts and chuckles.

A dear friendship formed with Susie—though shy, she was quick to laugh and a little too easy for me to tease. Off, we'd go to the mall; she pushed my chair, Keyon tucked in by my side. We'd take hours inventing ways to spend the dollar mom gave us.

Perhaps Susie understood my unique struggle. She had a glass-eye implant because of a brain tumor she'd had at birth. I always thought her beautiful. Fear and rejection may have invaded my life, but with Susie, I was wild, crazy—and free. Together we were mighty; my wheelchair only contributed to the fun. She would get on her bike and yell, "Hang on!"

Grabbing her cycle in the back, I'd shout, "Okay, ready!" Holding on tight, she pumped the pedals as we zoomed into the breeze until my chair shook so badly I thought the screws would pop out. Unable to hold on any longer, I released her tail fender, and Susie plunged ahead, while I slowed to a halt. Delighting in the speed and wind in my hair, I laughed and shouted after her, "Let's do it again!"

Susie giggled, too, then turned her bike around to start all over.

Though my social life began to improve, I still struggled with relating to God. The eminent, Bishop Sheen, officiated at my confirmation—since his niece was my classmate. Despite such a godly man giving the sacrament, I lay in bed that night, sharing my utmost disappointment with my Maker that nothing profound had happened.

Jesus's disciples got tongues of fire and a mighty wind when the Holy Spirit came, and several years earlier, at my sister Beth's confirmation, she got diamond earrings. I, on the other hand, didn't even feel a nudge from the Holy Spirit, and from my aunt Dorothy, I only got a little pink ring. I felt ripped off on two counts.

In the summer before eighth grade, the doctor performed corrective surgery on my right leg. By inserting a steel rod down the inside of my femur, he reinforced the weak, thin bone. Though I could not feel the improvement, Dr. Linebach said the metal made my leg stronger, so I no longer had to wear the horrid leg brace. On the day we tossed out my squeaky contraption, Mom took me to buy my first pair of jeans. I felt hip and enjoyed the ego boost of dressing like other kids. For the next three years, I only used my chair for long strolls. Everywhere else, I walked.

With Susie as a friend and my leg brace removed, my gregarious nature reemerged. The girl's group that had been an impermeable membrane began to open ever so slightly. Soon, they invited me to join them in school plays, which we did as often as possible in the guise of a book report.

Both Susie and I excelled in our studies. Doing homework provided an excuse for spending time together, so our grades soared — as did our imaginations. For our classroom projects, we conceived and constructed masterpieces. Then we had the madcap idea of organizing a school-wide talent show. After getting permission from the principal, Sister Margaret, Susie and I advertised, organized, oversaw rehearsals, and introduced each act during the show. My eighth grade at Holy Family culminated in a grand finale, with the talent show becoming a huge success and many students participating.

For my graduation ceremony, I wore a homemade, floor-length blue dress with a sash around my waist. I relished my first formal dress up, and basked in a bubbly kind of happiness about growing up, excited to join my siblings in high school.

My grandparents came to cheer me on, and Aunt Dorothy and Uncle Joe also attended.

Dad looked handsome in his navy suit, and Mom wore my favorite dress, giving the occasion due honor. I had watched my siblings graduate, and now I had my turn. In such a large family, being center stage could be a rare event. I reveled in the attention.

As I stood in the back of the church, waiting to begin the processional, I looked over at my family. The Miller entourage took up a whole pew. They seemed particularly animated as they read the evening program. *What's going on over there? What are they jabbering about?* When they caught me looking over at them, they all waved and grinned like cats who had just found a big rat. *Why is everyone smiling like that?*

The music began. I thought no more about my oddly behaving family but joined my classmates for our grand entrance.

Sister Margaret's speech inspired us to pursue our dreams. Then, before the ceremony came to a close, she announced, "This year, our girl's scholarship goes to...Lynn Miller!"

Me? Did I hear, right? Classmates poked me into action. Floating up the aisle in a daze, I shook Sister Margaret's hand and accepted my certificate. My family clapped and cheered heartily. Now I understood their grins. I felt their pride in my receiving such a prestigious honor, and I knew it would mean a lot to my folks to now have my tuition to a private high school completely paid for.

For the first time, I wondered if there was more to me than I thought—maybe I could accomplish something significant. Part of me also wondered if the scholarship committee had made a mistake.

CHAPTER 8

Teen Challenges

WITH THREE OLDER SIBLINGS as upperclassmen, I easily transitioned into high school. I already knew the cheerleaders and basketball stars and had attended numerous football games at Clearwater Central Catholic (CCC). Having such a head start proved beneficial. Within months, my classmates voted me student council representative. Now I awaited the results of our election for class president.

My campaign speech had been bold. "If you elect me for class president, in four years we will take our senior class trip in the Florida Keys." When I told Dad I had to address the student body, he gave me a few pointers, urging me to appeal to their hopes for the future. Practicing in front of my mirror allowed me to fine-tune my message. Then on the day of my speech, their standing ovation told me I had hit the mark.

Now I waited in homeroom for the results of our second election for class president. The first had been a tie between Bobby Peters, one of CCC's freshmen football stars, and me. Kids had polarized over the two candidates, and I felt the tension, knowing that in a few minutes, the freshman football team might stone me.

Principal Dion came on the loudspeaker. I held my breath. "Our new freshmen class president is...Lynn Miller." The class cheered and applauded. I stood up on my chair and bowed, not taking the grand news with much humility.

My ascent to popularity developed into a bumpy ride when Bobby Peters took offense at losing the election to me. His teammates on the football squad also turned against me. I nearly buckled under the pressure when he mocked me during my Shakespearean speech. But mostly, eager to discredit me, he made sure that everyone knew my failings and juvenile crimes. Many of his accusations were true enough. Just as he said, I cheated on my Algebra test. And for two weeks, I experimented with swearing, dropping F-bombs into my remarks. I decided, however, that I didn't like foul language; it just wasn't me— stopped as quickly as I had begun. And I never again cheated on a test, deciding instead to live with a clear conscience.

With my short stature at four foot four inches and my severe limp, the burden of being different plagued me. Despite our class elections and all those who voted for me, I battled rejection. Ostracism that came from defeating a popular boy became hard to bear. To kids who'd once liked me, they now made comments like "You're stuck up!" and it stung, reminding me of mean comments and lonely lunches at Holy Family School. Instead of focusing on all those who believed in me, I had an unhealthy fixation on those who did not. I retreated to a smaller life and felt the ache of rocky friendships and not being asked out. I didn't even run again for class president.

Moreover, new health concerns contributed to my teen angst. In my sophomore year, Dr. Linebach sent me to Johns Hopkins to consult with a medical expert. Flying alone to Boston, Massachusetts, gave me a taste for travel. Dad sent me to stay with one of his business associates, Larry Kouns, and his family in nearby Maryland, who took seriously the opportunity to spoil me.

First thing in the morning, we visited the specialist, Dr. McCullough. After measuring my limbs, taking X-rays, and asking me to move in various poses to assess my flexibility, he gave his prognosis. "Someday, you will probably break your neck or back."

I stared at my S-shaped spine on the X-ray and felt afraid.

Pointing with his pen, he tapped the screen and told me, "Your left leg is bowing. This will most likely break. Moreover, I suggest corrective surgery on your right leg to remove the rod."

Larry joined the consultation so he could offer another ear to the doctor's assessment and report to my parents. I sensed his dismay, more than I could feel my own. The implications went deep, a diagnosis that would roll around inside me for months.

Larry and his wife, Patty, then whisked me away for a short adventure before I caught my evening flight. How I marveled at the vibrant, autumn trees hugging the road on our drive to the state capital. Beyond all my imaginings of a fall forest, I now saw what I had been missing in Florida, and I vowed one day to return north and linger longer. We did not have a full day to sightsee, but my host took me to the Lincoln Memorial. Strangely moved, feeling close to God, I read, "Four score and seven years ago our fathers brought forth on this continent a new nation, conceived in liberty..." The words seemed holy.

My trip culminated in a visit to the Watergate Hotel, all the more appealing given its scandalous history. We ate lunch and browsed the shops. I dabbed a sample of Gucci perfume behind my ears, the loveliest—and, at seventy dollars an ounce, the most expensive—I had ever tried. The fragrance remained with me through the flight home, each waft of its scent reminding me of my tour of majestic memorials and autumn in Maryland.

By the next morning, its allure vanished. Under the weight of Dr. McCullough's diagnosis, I entered a dark depression.

Skipping school was easy. Our secretary, used to my frequent doctor visits—not suspecting my duplicity, readily accepted notes with Mom's forged signature. Each day I hid out in my friend's car parked at the school, crouched down, and read a book, with no one the wiser. My Algebra II grades suffered, but other than this symptom, no one knew of my stealthy behavior or despondent condition, except my English teacher, Mrs. Torres. She asked me, "Lynn, what's wrong? You don't seem like yourself lately. Are you okay?"

I thought it so kind of her to notice, but I didn't know how to tell her of my sadness or where it stemmed from. So I half lied, "I am fine. I just need to have another surgery soon." Mrs. Torres looked worried but said no more. However, the fact we read Edgar Allan Poe in her class that year seemed quite fitting.

Then, in the winter of my junior year, my cousin Gary and his friend Tom drove down from Michigan for a visit. Tom's mop of curly red hair handsomely framed is fair complexion with boyish freckles. Our relationship blossomed almost overnight, given a boost by our first date at the county fair. After a few wild rides and my clinging to his beefy frame, our romance solidified.

When he returned home, love letters fanned the flame of our fling, lifting my heaviness, creating a joyful diversion as I prepared for yet another surgery. Dr. McCullough's concern that my right femur would grow weaker if the steel rod remained brought me back to Johns Hopkins in the summer of 1978 before my senior year, so that he could remove the rod.

While under the knife, in a rash decision during the operation, he decided to replace the rod with a plate held in place by screws. Immediately after the surgery, Dad gently broke the news to me.

Stunned, I said, "How could he do that, Dad? I thought he had to get rid of the metal, and here he added pins and plate."

Dad shook his head, "I don't know, honey. I don't get it, either." Both of us knew, after so many years, that we were at the mercy of doctors, with no guarantees from their treatment and few ways to contest their actions.

I wanted to cry, but instead, when I returned home, I vented to Dr. Linebach, saying, "Doesn't he know I always break bones at the site of screws? Why did he do that?"

Dr. Linebach defended his associate. "I am sure he did the best he could for you. He is a good Christian man."

I didn't care if he ranked up there with Saint Francis of Assisi. He had made a mistake, and I felt a horrible foreboding.

Dr. Linebach went on, "When he got in there and saw the condition of the bone, I am sure he felt it necessary."

Though not convinced, I stayed silent, swallowing my anger, unable to change the facts by complaining. Adding some comfort to my botched surgery, I discovered that Tom had driven from Michigan to

Boston to visit me. But before he'd arrived, I had already returned to Florida. His devotion moved me, and throughout my recovery, our love letters continued.

I SPENT FOUR MONTHS in a body cast. Then one day, Tom called long distance. "Hi, Lynn. Your letter said you get out of your cast tomorrow." He sounded excited, as if he'd just won a lottery.

"Yes, I can't wait." Calculating quickly, I added, "I am exactly twenty hours, twenty-two minutes...and thirty-four seconds from my appointment."

"Well, after you get out of your cast, how would you like it if I came down there to see you?"

"You're kidding!" I laughed at the thought. "I would love that. When do you think you'll come?"

"End of the month. Would you mind if I stayed a while? Would that be okay with you?"

My thoughts reeled. *Wow. Tom wants to move to Florida for me. He must like me.*

And he did. An adventuresome romantic, he hopped in his car and set up camp in his vehicle. For the next four months, his car would be his home, apart from an occasional night at my grandparents.

Tom didn't talk much, but I appreciated his openness to undertake all manner of games like chess and gin rummy, even though he didn't stand a chance. Though it seemed a bit hard on his ego, I had decided in seventh grade, when I intentionally lost a swim race to a cute boy, that I would never succumb to earning a guy's love by pretending to lose. I found it humorous when Tom kept choosing different games.

One day, I sat in the front seat of Tom's old Chevy, browsing the movie section of the paper, while Tom had his head buried underneath the car hood, fiddling with the motor. Suddenly we decided on a show about to start. Tom slammed the hood shut, jumped in the car, and rushed us off to the cinema.

Only when we arrived did we realize we had left my wheelchair in the garage. Like a man carrying his bride over the threshold, he carted me into the theater. We both laughed, enjoying the game, and I switched my ring to my wedding finger, pretending we were newlyweds. At least, that is what we told the others waiting in line.

But in a few short months, I grew bored. Other than a love for smooching, Tom and I had little in common. Not only did he not attend church, but he expressed no interest in going to college or in reading books. Quickly, we ran out of things to talk about. Before returning to school in January, we broke up. I could not lead Tom along, despite the unfortunate timing, with my prom only two months away.

Returning to high school made me nervous. A lifetime had passed in six months. But to my delight, classmates were glad to see me again. At first, I felt awkward relating to my old school chums—in a way hard to describe, I felt as if I'd already graduated. The ceremony itself seemed almost meaningless.

That summer, in June of 1979, my girlfriends and I went to a disco. A handsome Venezuelan who hardly spoke English asked me to dance. I didn't mind. He was cute, and I wanted to boogie. About halfway through the first song, I felt a piercing pain in my right femur. I tried to get by with leaning on my left leg and wiggling less enthusiastically. It didn't help. The agony continued, so my friends drove me home, and Mom took me to get yet another X-ray.

Just as I had feared, the screw holding the new metal plate to my leg had broken all the way through the bone. Dr. Linebach confined me to a wheelchair until it mended. I looked forward to the time when I would be able to walk freely on my own two legs. I didn't realize at the time that my broken femur would never heal.

IN THE FALL I attended St. Petersburg Junior College, with the hope of going into medicine, believing my years of breaking bones gave me a head start into the world of hospitals and patient care.

Although familiar with navigating the neighborhood and amusement parks and shopping malls in my chair, I had never taken on the demands of adult life in one. I kept feeling caught off guard and hurt by my limitations and didn't recognize I grieved my loss of mobility.

At that time my brother, David, fell in love with Evelyn, a girl who served drinks at a bar he frequented. Within just a few months, they got married at Holy Family Catholic Church. Seeing my siblings partner up with others had become commonplace, but when David got married, my lack of a love life felt more painful than ever, as did using a wheelchair.

Moreover, my new friendship with a student, Faith, seemed to highlight the differences between my life and my siblings'. Faith also used a wheelchair and had OI, though her condition was much worse than mine. She needed help getting her food, picking up a pen off the floor, even going to the bathroom.

While it may seem odd to say, being with Faith made me aware of my disability. She thought of me as able-bodied because I could pick up a pen and heat up her leftovers. Though she thought of me this way, I felt more conscience of my disability than ever before, coping with being in a chair 24-7.

Whereas I had been around nondisabled students, she had attended a school for kids with special needs. One evening, Faith took me back to her high school for a '50s night, eager to share me with her classmates. That night, my popularity soared. Young men swarmed around me, boldly flirting. I laughed, overwhelmed by their eagerness.

Faith's school chums never treated me like a wallflower, and the implications hit me hard. This dance, compared to all the previous ones at my high school, were worlds apart. What I dreaded most seemed true. I never attended a homecoming dance or been asked on a date because I was crippled. Now I wondered, *Will I only be attractive in a place like this, among other disabled people?*

Chapter 9

Pushing Limits

FAITH AND I ENJOYED only a brief friendship. Within a few months of our getting acquainted, Horace Small Uniforms offered their top salesman (my dad) an irresistible promotion. He asked us, "How do you feel about moving to California?" He spread out maps and brochures of Mission Viejo, a community in South Orange County, giving us kids a preview of possibilities awaiting us. The new city nestling up against Saddleback Mountain seemed more like a vacation destination. Photos of a lake that offered fishing, a swimming area, and sailboats to rent clinched the deal. I was sold.

OUR FAMILY MOVED OUT to California. After we all settled into our new house, I transferred to a college close to home. Unlike any other school I attended, Saddleback Junior College in Mission Viejo had a disabled students' department. The director, Ron Hastings, immediately invited me to the Revels, a club on campus for those with disabilities. At the first meeting, they voted me treasurer. Now, for the first time, I hung around school chums with disabilities.

Soon, my responsibilities as treasurer extended to becoming scorekeeper for wheelchair basketball. We organized parties and several bowling events, but wheelchair tennis became my favorite pastime. Although I didn't own a sports chair, my natural athleticism emerged. I could even hold my own on the court with some of my nondisabled friends.

My new peers buzzed with all sorts of information. I heard about the intricacies of sex with a paralyzed lover. I learned about short-term memory loss when my date asked me at the end of the night, "What is your name again?" My new tribe also educated me on the ins and outs of collecting disability benefits. It had never dawned on me that I could receive money from the government for food and rent, but many of my pals in wheelchairs found it helpful. I worked two jobs, selling insurance quotes at Farmers Insurance and as a cashier at Gordon's Jewelers. The notion seemed tempting. I would never have to go to college or go to work. After giving it some thought, I decided to only accept government funding for college expenses.

With this decision, I became increasingly aware that managing adult life from a wheelchair would be the road less traveled. At that time, I never saw the wheelchair as permanent, but despite this, accessibility became an ever-present concern. For much of my life, my wheelchair had served as a luxury transport launched only on all-day outings and shopping trips. Now it had become my legs. Exploring its capabilities became a matter of survival.

During our first New Year's Eve after we moved to California, my family set off for the ski slopes in Wrightwood, in the San Bernardino National Forest, equipped with new gear and the latest winter fashions. I had never seen snow. The curving highway and a ride with jerking stops and swerves made me queasy, but I took pleasure in sheer cliffs above and thick pine forests. We drove upward for an hour before snow patches lay like puzzle pieces on the ground. By the time we reached our inn, white fleece had cloaked the landscape.

Mom and Dad went looking for the motel key. My siblings unloaded suitcases and my wheelchair. When my parents returned, everyone moved into action, carrying in our luggage. But I sat frozen.

Stairs!

I checked the restaurant next door, the shops across the street, and the offbeat buildings farther down the road. Stairs. Everywhere—stairs. All weekend long, I would not be able to come and go like everyone else, even to get a Coke from the vending machine. Reluctantly I surrendered my hope for independence.

That night the entertainment at the local bar lifted my spirits. My brothers and I teamed up against three guys in a game of pool. I hit a multi-cushion bank shot, landing the eight ball in the corner pocket, winning the game. Victory felt sweet.

The next morning Mom asked, "So, Lynn, what do you want to do when we go skiing? You want to come with us or stay here?"

Stuck inside our rental, unable to get outside, held no appeal. "I'll go with you."

Since my front wheels sank into the snow, Don pushed and partly shoved me through slush from the parking lot to the rustic chalet restaurant. It dawned on me: a town covered in snow with steps leading to every door, and a ski lodge set on a mountain of mushy ice might just be the most miserable vacation of all time for someone like me.

But it wasn't the inaccessibility that bothered me most. From my first glance at the ski run, I ached to participate like the others. Skiing looked like fun, and the pang of missing out hit like a curveball. After all, for most of my childhood, my primary mode of operation entailed watching from the sidelines.

I sat, drinking hot chocolate, and waved off my family as they headed for the slopes. A steady stream of enthusiasts clomping around awkwardly in plastic boots came in and out the door, either taking a break from sporting or on their way out to the slopes to begin another run. From the warmth of the chalet, I observed ski instructors giving lessons on the bunny run. I searched among skiers, who resembled insects on an anthill, looking for the familiar attire of a family member, itching to be a part. Receiving no reward for my efforts, I ventured out to the perimeter of the building, hankering for amusement.

Nothing. Perhaps I'll stroll toward the ski lift.

Underneath my thick coat, I wore jeans and a pullover top—in the layer below that, my fleece long johns. A stuffed sausage, I could barely bend my arms to propel my chair. Already from brushing alongside my muddy tires, my sleeves from elbow to wrist were black. Preoccupied with pushing ahead in this straitjacket, I didn't see the danger until I rolled onto a path covered in ice—and descended downward.

I lost control as if I were a roller skater on glass. The momentum at first caused me to slide; then my chair tilted to one side, about to tip over. Frantically, I grabbed the bars and shoved the weight of my body to the opposite side, bringing both wheels back down on the icy surface. Though upright again, my knitted mittens slid uselessly along the wet handlebars as I sped downhill. I put my feet down to brake, Fred Flintstone–style, but without cleats, my boots had no traction. Sure I would crash, I seized the muddy left tire. My "toboggan" swung sideways and stopped.

I sat perched precariously on the side of the hill, but I now had a clearer sense of how to proceed safely. To avoid sliding uncontrollably downhill, I began to move horizontally down the road in a zigzag by holding one tire and pushing the other until I arrived on level ground.

After inhaling the brisk mountain air and exhaling the tension of my near-accident in a cloud of white vapor, I returned to my original plan. Wheeling over to the cute, blond god working the ski lift, I asked, "Hey, I was wondering, can I take a ride on this thing?"

"Sure." He rewarded me with a grin that would melt a glacier, and added, "If you want, you can get off at the top and hang out for a while."

"How will they know I need help getting off?"

"I'll call up so he'll be ready for you." He held the swinging seat steady as I clambered aboard, then he folded my wheelchair and attached it behind me. His proximity as he buckled me in made me a little giddy.

Holding on tight, I ascended to the diamond run and people-watched from my superior perch above, happy to be alive, relieved to be in one piece. I contemplated the plodding novice poking along far below me and a crazy speed devil who looked suspiciously like my brother. David's idea of skiing resembled a kid on a slide—straight downhill as quickly as possible. He didn't care to slalom like everyone else. On his first run, he sped right past the lodge and landed on the blacktop of the parking lot.

The ski operator at the top of the run was even more of a hunk than the first. When my swing drew up next to him, he stopped the lift and untied my wheelchair. Then the hunk lifted me off the bench and carried me to my chair. Though I could have transferred without his help, I didn't bother letting him know.

Like a dolly that tilts back to transport a refrigerator, the ski attendant leaned my chair on its back wheels and muscled me over to a secluded spot, a safe distance from the edge. I stayed parked where the young man deposited me, sinking deep into the snow. The unexpected turn of events after my near mishap proved a worthy reward. I felt like a climber conquering Mt. Kilimanjaro. I sat on that mountain vista, feeling like a queen before her vast kingdom, relishing its splendor. I wondered at those brave, perhaps suicidal, souls diving off the cliff and dropping to the ground twenty feet below. My teeth chattered. My clothes grew damp. The afternoon faded.

This taste of freedom on what could have been a dreary day, rather than satisfying my hunger, gave me an appetite for more. A few years later, ignoring the barriers I would surely face, I joined my friends on a ski trip to Big Bear Mountain, also in the San Bernardino National Forest. We stayed up late, laughing and visiting together in the rustic cabin. The next day, they took off to go snowboarding, but I had no intention of sitting around.

The guy at the rental company gave me a skeptical look, "You're going to rent a snowmobile?" he asked. "Who's gonna drive it for you?"

I ignored him, annoyed by his ignorance. Does he think everyone in a wheelchair can't drive a car or a snowmobile?

Grudgingly, he handed over the keys, glaring at me suspiciously through his bushy eyebrows.

Motoring behind a trail of ten other snowmobilers, we snaked through town until we arrived at a clearing in a wide-open wilderness of chalky snow. Then, careening off in different directions like crabs scattering on the beach, we sped through open fields at sixty miles an hour.

My first family ski trip gave me the chutzpah to return to the snow, navigate icy roads on wheels, and return for a day of

51

snowmobiling. I could not foresee at the time that for twenty years I would face many of these same obstacles as I led winter youth camps in the mountains, making it possible for hundreds of kids to have adventures in the snow.

SAILING BECAME MY NEXT great love. When I first read through Dad's brochures of Mission Viejo, with its man-made lake and recreation activities, a seed germinated. With each visit to Lake Mission Viejo and each trip to our local marina, Dana Point Harbor, I felt teased by sailors cruising past, saluting hello to us landlubbers. I waved back in envy, pondering, *What is it like to be on a boat, looking toward shore? What is it like to be in their shoes?*

Having mastered the snow-covered mountains, my attitude shifted. I decided that my wheelchair didn't have to stop me. For most of my childhood I had been a fan watching my sibling's sporting events. Now I pursued a new agenda. No longer would I be a spectator. I might have to do it differently than others. I might even be a little slower learning and less accomplished. But no way would I miss out.

One afternoon, at Lake Mission Viejo, I left my wheels behind and awkwardly slid into the sloop, ignoring the attendant's anxious offers of help, pretending a confidence I did not have and that getting from my wheelchair down on the dock and sliding into the boat, dragging my butt, was a natural way to board. Didn't he know that?

After taking sailing classes at Lake Mission Viejo, it took a few more months of putzing around there before I advanced to the wilder waters of Dana Point Harbor. In the larger rental boat at Dana Point, shifting my body from port to starboard and back again as I tacked, proved hard on my legs. I could not stay put in one position as I did with smaller boats; I had to put weight on my legs to change sides. But the discomfort didn't deter me. With all the elements I enjoyed most, forceful winds, salt spray, and the sun on my face, I streamed down the harbor channel. My little dog, Keyon, now a lot older, sat at the bow, nose pointed to the wind. She enjoyed sailing as much as our earlier trips around the block in my wheelchair.

The harbor's westerly and swift ocean current made sailing up the waterway much trickier than the lake. I shifted my body to port (left side) and slid the tiller all the way over. As expected, the boat turned about and the sails emptied. But instead of the billowy cloth refilling with wind as I turned, the sails continued flapping. Powerful gusts caught the hull, quickly carrying Keyon and me toward boulders hugging the shoreline. Wind and waves bashed us onto the rocks.

I had seen others hop out of their boat onto the rocks and smoothly push their vessels away from land, then jump back in. Since I was unable to stand, I instead frantically pumped the tiller, hoping to steer us away from disaster, while Keyon paced anxiously.

I knew that this could develop into a real shipwreck, with a hole in the hull, water filling the boat, and a girl and her dog swimming for their lives. I reached over the starboard rail attempting to push away from the rocks and slipped, nearly falling out of the boat.

A man strolling the island, seeing my distress, hurried out to the rocky edge, and shoved my boat stern away from the jagged rocks. The wind filled my sails, and I continued my tack, saluting a thank-you to the Good Samaritan.

This incident left me shaken, and I thought, *Next time I go sailing at Dana Point, I better take a passenger other than my dog.*

CHAPTER 10

Spiritual Longing

LOOKING AT THE MILLIONS of stars in the sky and wondering about the galaxies beyond those stars, I thought, *Who am I that God would care about me? I'm a speck of dust in this universe.* I felt small and inconsequential. So in my teens and early adult years, my longing for God morphed into disillusionment.

My departure from faith began years earlier at fourteen.

APART FROM THE DAYS I spent recuperating from a broken bone, I went to church every Sunday of my first fourteen years. Yet my heart craved more, desperately. One night, I lay in bed, reading a romance novel. Then I closed the book and thought about God, and recklessly decided that I would force the Almighty to show up in my life.

After shedding my leg brace, I still used a walker and had a severe limp, but my right leg felt strong with my newly acquired steel rod supporting the bone. I made up my mind to go off into the night and keep walking until I found God—or he found me. Drama is the life bread of a teenager, and this search epitomized the height of my rebellion. I threw on some sweats, left a note on my pillow, and wandered into the night, beyond the familiar neighborhood streets, leaving the housing tract, and crossing the busy boulevard, until I came to a church.

As I rested on the dewy ground, waiting for God to show up, the night shadows of the unfamiliar churchyard made my quest seem dangerous. I counted the stars. I plucked the grass. Peace settled in my heart. I thought: *I must return home and search for another way to find God.* Picking up my walker, I headed back.

Mom had been combing the neighborhood in a fearful search for me. Halfway home, she found me. "Where did you go? Don't you know how concerned I've been?" Leaving me no room to answer, she continued heatedly, "Don't you ever do that again! I called the police — we have searched for you for hours."

My tears fell. "Sorry, Mom!"

"Lynn, why did you run away?"

Taking a stab at explaining my struggle, I said, "Mom, I need God. I don't know; maybe I just need to become a nun."

"Honey, you will meet a nice man and settle down someday."

Her consolation didn't address my need, so I remained silent. My heart's emptiness lacked words. I reasoned that becoming a nun might impress God and make him come to me. Now I know that ministry—whether being a nun or a preacher or a pastor, comes from having found God, not because you are looking for him.

At sixteen, my hunger drove me to attend evening services during Passion Week. I sat in the back of the church with tears pouring down my face as I contemplated the suffering of Christ. The Holy Spirit powerfully touched my heart, as he had the little first grader singing in the church at lunchtime. The message of Christ's Passion brought me into wonder and appreciation as I worshipped, but it did not bring the answer to my God ache or an end to my search. Religion seemed empty.

MOVING TO CALIFORNIA INTRODUCED me to a broader view of life. Many of my new friends experimented with drugs, lived with their boyfriends, and disdained religion. Finding it hard to fit into the Southern California scene, I began to shift my standards, thinking that perhaps I behaved too goody-goody.

After studying anthropology with a dynamic teacher at Saddleback College, I began to think that God wasn't real, and the only explanation for creation had to be evolution. In my limited understanding, it was either one or the other. And if God did exist, my going to church and not murdering somebody would fulfill my duty toward him. I invented my theology and told Mom, "I believe we all come from apes."

She looked at me for a long five seconds. "I think that is stupid," she said calmly.

Her conviction rattled me, but my heart was too jaded by disappointments. My childhood dream of Jesus seemed a long time ago and meaningless now.

CHAPTER 11

Cosmic Battle

ON JULY 9, 1982, I looked forward to my Calculus II midterm like a gladiator entering the arena for battle. Several years earlier, I had enrolled at Saddleback with much trepidation about math since I'd missed half the year of Algebra II in high school and slid out the door with a barely passing D. Knowing I would have to conquer my old nemesis, I took a basic math class my first semester. Just as I had hoped, something clicked, and math began to make sense, becoming more like a game of chess—analyzing options, determining moves several steps ahead, and enjoying the mastery of the universe as I conquered the enemy. Only, in this case, my opponents resembled equations, intervals, and page-long proofs. I could not compete in sports, and my skill in a body cast wouldn't land me a job. College became a place to shine, and academic tests were my playoff games.

With the confident anticipation of annihilating a foe, I smiled at the day, slowing my pace and savoring the warmth of early morning sunshine. Using a rental chair supplied by the company from which I had ordered my first brand-new wheelchair, I descended the ramp from our college library to the lower campus. I'd used this contraption only a couple of days, and as I rolled downhill, the chair began to shake violently. Before I could grab the handlebars or plant my feet on the ground to slow down, even while the thought merely glimmered, the wheels seized up, and my chair froze, propelling me forward.

For a person who breaks bones, falling is a feeling of helplessness and heart-pounding fear smashed into milliseconds. The momentum threw me into the air and slammed me into the unforgiving cement. My wheelchair, not far behind, landed on top of me, then continued tumbling downhill.

Snap! My knee hit concrete. My left hip gave way. A sharp, stabbing pain confirmed my worst fears, an agony all the more intense because I always called this my good leg. My heart sank at the implications: I would not have a good leg to stand on.

In the foggy space-time continuum of trauma, students, anxious college administrators, and paramedics seemed to gather around me instantly. "Are you, all right?" asked a concerned student passing by.

"Can you move?" inquired another.

"My hip hurts. I think it's broken," I said.

As the crowd gathered around, I felt the burden of being center stage. A humorous approach became my defense mechanism.

"How are you doing? Does your head hurt?" asked the paramedic.

"Oh, I am fine, just trying to write a report on aerodynamics." Everyone laughed dutifully. So long as I lay still without the slightest of movements, the pain remained silent, and my endless jokes seemed a good distraction.

Over the years, I had discovered that physical pain could be as diverse as the colors in a box of Crayola crayons. Whenever I broke a bone, I got to try out the whole carton. But when the paramedics lifted me onto the stretcher, the pain took on a whole new color. I screamed. And I continued to cry out all the way to the ambulance. Every step felt like malicious jerking. Even the subtlest movement of sliding me into the ambulance, knife cutting bone.

Mom and Dad were waiting for me in the emergency room. I drew strength from them, breathed in relief, and thought, *Oh good. I am not alone.* Mom hovered helplessly as the doctors examined me, her face ashen. Dad rubbed his nose with the palm of his hand, an endearing gesture I recognized whenever he was upset or frustrated. I felt sad for them and sad for me, but the unrelenting pain demanded my focus.

I longed for medicine, but first, they had to take an X-ray. With each movement inflicting deeper colors of pain, the radiologist transferred me to the cold table, aligned my body for the camera to zoom in on my hip, and returned me to the gurney. But I plunged into the blackest anguish when my leg muscles began to spasm. My body had turned traitor on me, convulsing and moving on its own. Insane with the fierceness of it, I surrendered all pride or decorum and cried and screamed and cursed, too. Thankfully, the relatively impervious medical staff moved quickly, and the medicine I had been begging for finally arrived.

The bone specialist referred me to Los Angeles Orthopedic Hospital, where they had a clinic for those with OI disease. Dr. Brown, the head of the OI clinic, took over my care. He stunned me with the news that I had only a small fracture. After a minor operation, I would be rolling around again in just a few days.

And what a relief. I thought, *Am I really going to be able to get back to college and continue my courses toward becoming a doctor?* I had never before experienced a mild break.

The morning after the procedure, while I still felt excited by my quick return to routine life, a nurse came by to change the sheets on my bed.

"All right," she said. "I am going to need you to roll over so I can change your bedding."

"Okay, but my hip isn't strong enough for me to turn over, yet." Pulling from my vast history, I suggested an alternative. "Perhaps you can change the sheets from top to bottom?"

"No. I need to have you roll on your side."

"Listen, my leg can't take that movement, but I can pull myself up on the orthopedic bar, which would allow you to change the bed from top to bottom."

"I am not going to do that. You need to listen to me," the nurse insisted.

"Many nurses over the years have done it this way." I felt afraid. *Why is she so obstinate? What difference does it make?*

"I don't care what they have done in the past."

When I refused her request, she enlisted the help of three other nurses. "Please!" I pleaded with them. "You don't have to do this. Please don't. . ." The foursome would not relent. "Nooooo!" I screamed as they forced me over.

Like a batter hitting a foul ball, I could hear the loud crack when my hip broke in half.

THE ORDERLY LEFT ME in the hallway outside the operating room. With the air colder than a morgue, I shivered under a thin sheet. I had been here only a few days earlier, but it was different now, my misery more acute.

I couldn't remember the aide's name or her face. I probably couldn't pick her out of a criminal lineup. Though, as my friends said, that's where she should have been. Never again did I see the woman who changed my life. Neither she nor the hospital offered an apology.

Early that morning, a nurse gave me an injection to dry out my mouth so while under the knife, I wouldn't choke on my saliva. Now the medication made me queasy and tired, but sleep eluded me. I swallowed, unable to quench my dryness. Waiting in the corridor was no child's play, like when I lay on a gurney in the hospital aisle, pretending to be a forgotten corpse, spying on the hubbub of the nurse's station. This place was desolate, and my heart heavy.

From a room down the hall, attendants clad in scrubs and white masks came to retrieve me. "We are taking you in now," said the voice of a male pushing the stretcher from behind my head.

A woman's kind brown eyes appeared at the foot of my bed. "How are you doing? Would you like a blanket?"

I nodded—my chattering teeth sending the message like a telegraph to her.

Placing a heated cloth over my torso, she said, "Dr. Brown will be here shortly."

With expertise, having done the maneuver many times a day, in one swift movement, they transferred my fragile body onto the hard, cold Formica. Quivering, I stared up at the immense round light above my head. *Why can't they just give me a drug to knock me out? Why do I need to endure this pregame show?*

The anesthesiologist took my left hand and within seconds inserted the IV into my vein. The green-garbed team buzzed around me, arranging my blankets, untying the back of my gown and placing a cap over my hair. "When did you last eat?" the anesthesiologist asked.

"Dinner last night. Around 6:00 p.m." I said.

"When did you last drink?"

"About midnight." He offered no friendly chitchat. Just routine business.

"We will need to give you an epidural. I don't feel comfortable giving you anesthesia since you had something to drink. That means you will be awake for the surgery."

An epidural! The last thing I want is a six-inch needle in my spine! "But the nurse told me not to drink after midnight, and I didn't," I said.

"That would have been fine, except now you've moved up the OR schedule."

I rolled over on my side and lay, deathlike, while he inserted the needle into my back, metal burning as it penetrated flesh. He probed, searching for the spinal cord, but since my back curves like an S, it was harder than he'd thought. He withdrew the blade and said, "I'll have to try again. Stay very still."

Stay still? I am hardly breathing! When will this be over?

His second attempt succeeded. He poked my feet with a pointed instrument and asked, "Do you feel this?" He traveled up my legs saying, "Do you feel this?"

Like a star quarterback on a football field, Dr. Brown entered the room. Everyone snapped to attention. The operation began. For the opening play, they covered my face with an oxygen mask; I felt suffocated and nauseous. Then I vomited.

I heard Dr. Brown say, "Wow! Either this bone is hard, or this saw is dull!"

At the scraping of saw cutting bone, I rebelled and flailed about, tossed my head back and forth, and mumbled under the mask. The anesthesiologist said, "Let's just put her out. She's already expelled everything in her system."

I entered sweet oblivion.

The pain after my second operation introduced a whole new array of dreary colors. Instead of the acute, sharp stabs when I moved, I now felt a constant pounding. Its intensity demanded my unswerving attention, making sleep impossible. When my medication wore off, the pulsating escalated and I received a heavy dose of Demerol. It brought no reprieve at all. Just breathing was difficult—reaching for a glass of water not worth the effort. A hiccup, deadly.

In the days following my second procedure, I waited for time to pass. Life ticked by slowly, moment by moment, breathing in and breathing out. Visitors were not wanted, but I welcomed Mom, my refuge in the storm. She didn't talk. She got the water for me.

In the wee hours of the morning one night, I called Mom on the phone, crying. "Mom, I hurt so badly. I don't know what to do. The nurses aren't very nice, either," I sobbed. Over the years, I realized there is a point during a patient's physical suffering when caregivers get irritated. Inconvenienced by neediness, they become emotionally distant. I had hit that impasse with the staff at LA Orthopedic.

In the middle of the night, I telephoned Mom just to complain. A fierce mother bear, she called the floor station and said, "Listen, you need to help my daughter! In all the years she has been ill, I have never, ever had her call me in the middle of the night, crying on the phone."

Having no idea what Mom had done, I felt bewildered when several caregivers surrounded my bed, asking me how I was doing, anxious to bring relief, and sliding a needle into my arm. Such attention pierced me more than the shot, and I couldn't choke back the tears.

In the morning, Dr. Brown said, "Let's change her meds to morphine. Perhaps she will experience less distress." But that night, hallucinating under the strong narcotic, I shouted and screamed about riding a motorcycle. He switched me back to Demerol after that. He also threw Valium into the mix.

In the past, even as a young child, I weaned myself off all drugs only a few days after surgery. Not this time.

I felt fractured, not just with a broken hip but with a shattered heart. What needless suffering because of a nurse's ego. What injustice. Like a foul odor, depression entered the room and filled my soul.

Food held no appeal. Dad tried to entice me with my favorites. "Would you like some pizza, honey? How about an Arby's? I will go get it for you."

Dad. Always the one concerned about my weight, now trying to get me to eat? I must be bad. Dark thoughts pinned me down. *Will I ever laugh again?* Days blurred together. Weeks passed.

One night, throbbing pain, unaltered by powerful drugs, kept me wide-awake. Too fuzzy to focus on a book, the babble on TV too jarring to distract, I lay in bed staring at the ceiling. Waiting. About 1:00 a.m., an LVN came in, pushing a massive metal machine. She moved briskly, not asking for my consent, just getting the job done. "We need to dry the plaster so you don't catch pneumonia," she said.

After two consecutive procedures, my body had severely swollen. But that day, fumbling interns wrapped me in a new body cast to fit my less bloated form. Lowering the rail of the bed, the LVN directed a dryer toward me, covering the mouth of the blower and my cast with a blanket to insulate the heat. Familiar with the routine, I lay there acquiescing to the inevitable. After setting up the instrument, she departed.

Why this in the middle of the night? Do doctors plan their torture? The pain kept a steady rhythm with the dryer's thrumming. The combination of heater and cast heightened my discomfort, like wearing a parka in a sauna. As the outside cement dried, sticky sweat soaked the inside, tickling my skin.

Why didn't I ask how long this would take? Tears escaped my eyes, wetting the pillow. *This is going to be a long night.* The blower hummed.

A while later, the attendant returned and checked on my cast.

"When can I have my next shot?" I asked. I knew the answer already, but complaining out loud seemed the only remedy.

"You have two more hours before you can have your Demerol. Are you hurting?"

"Yes. And I can't sleep at all."

"If you want the pain to go away, why don't you say a chant? Here, I will write one out for you. You'll feel better." She scribbled on a pad and tore out the page, propping it up on the hospital tray for easy scrutiny.

Everything in me resisted the idea of uttering the words. I refused to even glance toward the text. Faced with an alternative to Jesus, and an alternative to prayer, I knew to whom I needed to turn. For the first time during my ordeal, I looked heavenward. "Jesus, *you* are my God. *You* can take away this pain."

The zealous woman came back a while later. "Did you recite the chant?"

"No. I didn't read it. I believe in Jesus and the Bible." Somehow, in this dark moment of despair, my humanistic belief that I am descended from apes went out the window and this became my confession.

During those wee hours of the morning, the LVN and I discussed our beliefs. I asked, "Give me one word to describe the Bible." I thought, *Love.*

Her response, "Hypocrisy." Despite my struggle to believe, the Bible seemed to me holy and beyond reproach. Her evaluation shocked me.

We talked for some time, and she told of her involvement in a religious group, which I found out later practiced the occult. In my most vulnerable hour, evil tempted me.

As morning light arose, I felt genuine astonishment. After turning to Jesus, my night had passed quickly, and the aching in my leg had ceased altogether. *Did he hear my petition? Was he nearer than I thought?* With questions about God and faith freshly aroused, I turned on a Christian program and even repeated a short prayer with the man on TV.

My sister and brother-in-law, Beth and Bobby Rowland, visited me that very night. Right before they'd gotten married, they had started attending Vineyard Church of Anaheim. Though they were new to their faith, we talked for hours, and I heard story after story of God's involvement in their lives and answered petitions.

Hope fed my hungry heart like a Thanksgiving feast. After Bobby and Beth's visit, I felt clear again, like a dense fog had lifted. Something had changed, and the pain lessened. I refused to take any more Demerol and Valium. Within a few days, Dr. Brown sent me home to recuperate.

I had entered the hospital with a minor fracture that promised to have me up by the end of the week. I left, instead, with a substantial break that is still with me thirty-five years later. Although sentenced to yet another body cast for months, the depression that shadowed my hospital stay began to fade away.

Overview

Age	Event	Result
2	Fell	Broken Collarbone.
4	Tricycle accident.	Broken right femur & left hip. Surgery, traction and body cast.
7	Slipped on grease.	Broken right hip. Surgery and body cast.
8	Jumped off car hood.	Broke both bones in left arm. Surgery and cast.
8	Monkey bars.	Broken right collarbone. Surgery and sling.
8	Slipped on water.	Broken left hip. Surgery and body cast. Used walker.
10	Corrective surgery.	Put pin in right femur. Body cast.
11	Standing up.	Broke right femur. Surgery, body cast and wore a brace. Used a walker.
12	Slipped on water.	Broke right femur. Surgery, body cast and wore a brace. Used a walker.
13	Corrective surgery.	Put rod in right femur. Body cast. Used a walker.
16	Corrective surgery.	Removed rod and inserted pin. Body cast.
17	Injured while dancing.	Broke right femur. Surgery to insert rod. Wheelchair.
20	Wheelchair malfunctioned.	Hairline fracture of left hip. Surgery and wheelchair.
20	Nurses forced me over.	Severe Break. Surgery and body cast. Wheelchair.
21	Corrective surgery.	Electrodes and body cast. Wheelchair.

CHAPTER 12

The Decision

I HAD COUNTED DOWN the days and hours and minutes. The night before my unveiling, I'd hardly slept. On the morning of October 6, 1982, I washed my hair in a little bowl of water and for the first time in four months donned lipstick and mascara, spraying my body with Jean Nate because I fancied the lemon scent. Today I would finally lose my thirty-pound bodysuit.

The technician at LA Orthopedic failed at his first attempt at X-rays. I am sure my barely contained excitement distorted the shot. Dr. Brown needed this assessment of my progress before cutting me out of my cast. After the radiologist got a good shot, my doctor gave his prognosis, "Lynn, it looks like your left hip is not forming bone at the break. You see here," he pointed with his finger, "This darkness shows no bone is forming as it should."

A fist squeezed my heart as I remembered how hard it had been to locate the fracture when it first injured. Now, thanks to the caregiver who forced me over, there was no mistaking it, nor dismissing the enormous repercussions.

Mom looked almost as upset as me. She asked, "What do we do next?"

Dr. Brown said, "I want to place electrodes in Lynn's hip and around the bone in her right femur that has not healed. The electrical impulses will stimulate bone growth. Although a minor surgery, she must be immobilized for another two months in a body cast."

The countdown began again.

Over the holidays and into the New Year I played chess with my brother Don, or volleyed a Ping-Pong ball against the wall, or read romance novels to get me through the sleepless nights. While laying on my skateboard cart, I painted ceramics, made Christmas cookies, and watched lots and lots of TV. My confinement finally ended in February, seven months after my initial fall. The doctor decided to remove the cast because my left hip and right femur did not respond to the treatment.

Both fractures are still with me today, the bones held together by soft connective tissue instead of hard bone.

I reveled in my first bath, a luxurious sensation of soothing coolness to dry, flaky skin. Then I got my hair done, celebrating my twenty-first birthday with dinner and my first 'legal' glass of wine. Each small pleasure affirmed my liberation from my plaster prison, although the effects of the body cast still lingered. I also had a new deformity. The fumbling attempts of two interns as they wound the toilet-paper-type plaster around my body had a lasting impact, which I only discovered when removed. Not sure how to make a body cast properly, they had made one with a huge bulge in the back. During my long recuperation, the contraption molded my body and severely curved my spine.

I could never stand up straight again.

Now that I returned to using my wheelchair, my parents took off for a short vacation in Tahoe. Lying horizontally for months had left me weak, so I had to stay with Beth and Bobby. As soon as I arrived, my sister said, "Oh good! You can go to church with us." Beth had an irresistible pull on all us siblings. Early in life, we had nicknamed her, Grandma. She hated that term, thinking we mocked her bossiness. But a fair amount of respect went into that honorary title.

Beth and Bobby claimed to be 'born again.' Concerned that their born-again church compiled a bunch of crazies, I wanted to stay far away. But then, who could say no to Beth?

Their conversation on the way to church didn't help. "Lynn, this will be very different than a Catholic church," Beth said.

"What do you mean?" At first, her warning amused me. I recollected standing in line at the grand opening of Space Mountain and the dire warnings over the loudspeaker before embarking on the roller coaster, "Warning, if you are pregnant or have a heart condition, this ride might be dangerous to your health."

"How is it different?" I said.

"Well, people raise their hands in worship..." Bobby said.

Heck, I had seen that in the Catholic Church. "Anything else?"

"Sometimes people get emotional and cry."

As they continued to talk, I panicked. *What have I gotten into?* From time to time, we saw weirdoes in the Catholic Church, too. During Mass I remembered sitting next to one guy who raised his hands while singing. I found his enthusiasm irritating. Occasionally, when the priest spoke, he would shout out a reverberating, "Amen." In my estimation, his behavior seemed bizarre. Still young enough to care about my image of being cool, I could not tolerate demonstrative praise unless it celebrated a touchdown or a home run.

Despite their forewarnings, Anaheim Vineyard dumbfounded me. They held the Sunday service in a gymnasium at Canyon High School, no cross on the building, no long wooden pews, no stained-glass windows, just hardwood floors and stadium bleachers. The gathering didn't wear their Sunday best but jeans and cut-offs. Churchgoers, mostly under the age of twenty-five, packed the place. Beth and Bobby ushered me up to the front, and I sat sandwiched between them, wide-eyed at the sheer multitude gathered for an ordinary church service. It looked more like a crowd for a basketball playoff game.

Before the second song ended my fears were conquered. God-inhabited heavenly music poured over me like torrential rains as voices joined in simple songs of love. The congregation sang with abandon as I listened, their hands raised in worship; some people knelt on the floor. Expressions of faith that once scandalized me didn't even prompt a smirk. Nothing had prepared me for the immensity of his presence. I sobbed uncontrollably. Beth and Bobby cried, too ... and passed a tissue.

God is real! And these people know Him. My months of agony culminated in this grand finale. God filled this gym, and the reality of His nearness overwhelmed me.

Because the pastor, John Wimber, took a trip out of town, Bob Fulton gave the sermon that morning. As he preached, he unveiled secrets from my heart. "You look to money and romance to fill you," he said. "You think, if I just get a good job then life will be okay. But there is only one thing that can meet your need. You were created for God. Nothing will satisfy you until you have a personal relationship with Jesus Christ."

Bob preached a message tailor-made for me. Looking for the path to heaven has inspired many toward faith in Jesus Christ, but that didn't motivate me. Being free of the burden of guilt has also drawn many to Jesus, but I had no awareness of my need for forgiveness. The day I rolled into Beth and Bobby's church, love-hunger fueled my search. An accessible God summed up my Good News. My most desperate need was friendship with him. Had Bob Fulton, then and there, asked me to accept Jesus as my Lord and Savior, I would have eagerly responded. But he did not.

Several weeks later, I returned to the Vineyard with Beth and Bobby. John Wimber led the evening service on Sunday night, March 6, 1983. Once again, the electric atmosphere created a feeling of anticipation and young adults crammed into the gym scrambling for seats. With bewilderment I thought *Where are all these people coming from? Do they all know Jesus?*

After the sermon, John invited people to receive prayer for healing. He added that Jesus wanted to heal scoliosis of the spine. My having an S-shaped back made this offer applicable to me, so they told me to go to an area behind the stage, where the ministry team would pray for me. I had heard of healing services in the Catholic Church but had never attended one. This church seemed to *live* the Bible, not just *read* it. I burned with excitement at the possibilities.

As I waited in the room behind the bleachers, a man walked up and theatrically pointed at me saying, "In the name of Jesus, rise and walk."

I sat frozen. The doctor had warned me not to put any weight on my left leg because I could easily tear the weak connective tissue stabilizing my hip. When the man saw me hesitate, he got aggressive, "I said stand up and walk!" Like a bear about to attack, he towered over me menacingly. "If you don't stand up immediately, you will lose your healing."

Confused by his tone, and scared of missing out on healing, or making my leg worse if I stood, I started to cry.

Bobby and Beth ran for help, returning with their Bible study leader, a young man named Bruce. Standing protectively beside me. Bruce questioned the wannabe healer. "Are you on the ministry team?"

"No."

"Are you a member of this church?"

"No." The aggressive man seemed to deflate.

"Then you need to leave here immediately. Only the ministry team and those receiving prayer are allowed back here."

The man slithered away.

Afterward Beth, Bobby, Bruce and their friends offered to pray for me. Each one reached out a hand, one on my shoulder, a few on my back. "Lord, come heal Lynn's back..."

Although they prayed fervently, after a while, I stopped listening and silently spoke to the Lord about my longing for something more than healing. I ached for him. Silently I said, "Jesus, I don't want to know you as some distant God out in the universe somewhere. I want to love you from my heart."

Even as I prayed, while my eyes remained still closed, I could see a ball of light from high up in the corner of the room move closer and rest on me. I sat in the warm heavenly glow, afraid to move lest it fade away. A lifetime of religion had not prepared me to encounter God. The light was not merely wattage, but the radiance of his glory. Love rested on me, surrounded me, and penetrated my skin. Like Sleeping Beauty awakening from death with the affection of a kiss, this tangible embrace both filled and enlivened me. The light seemed to move inside, then it shined out of me, and I knew an intense love for Jesus.

I began to cry with joy and relief, as if I had crossed a barren desert and crawled over my last dusty mound to find a stream of water running to a broader ocean. The expanse of my most essential need overwhelmed me. A good job, a new car, or a kiss from a friend would not sustain me. Only one thing could help this desert wanderer survive — a Presence both tender and powerful, a love I had never, ever known.

God's touch in the back room of the gymnasium catapulted me over the barricades of unbelief. The mysterious, far-off Jesus became a living flame inside me. Later, I noticed a more intense appreciation of nature and music felt more exhilarating. I had found what the Bible calls "first love," when the Spirit of God breathed into my heart. Jesus said, "Very truly I tell you, no one can enter the kingdom of God unless they are born of water and the Spirit. Flesh gives birth to flesh and Spirit gives birth to spirit." (John 3:5-6) Now, for the first time, Scripture became personal, as God's Spirit brought life to a place that had been dead inside me.

My parents had taught me right from wrong, and Catholic school had told me of the cross. But I missed this essential unwavering truth. I could not have intimacy with God until his Spirit entered me. The baptismal waters as a baby did not save me. This alone was my destiny changing moment. I didn't quickly lose thirty pounds. My back didn't straighten. My problems didn't disappear. But a change occurred: never again would I be alone, and never again would I work out life on my own. Everything about me now belonged to him — good, bad, and ugly . . . forever. All I had previously known of religion had not prepared me for the reality of being consumed by a divine love affair.

CHAPTER 13

Love Letters

I HAVE A FRIEND named Kathrin who fell in love with her husband while they lived 5,800 miles apart. When she told me they planned to get married, I shared my skepticism. "How can you know each other just by writing letters?" With conviction derived from my practical nature, I added, "Why don't you spend time together so you can see if you are compatible?"

Kathrin and Thomas had attended the same church, but they barely knew each other. When Kathrin's visa expired, she returned home to her native Switzerland. Thomas asked if he could write her. I had waved Kathrin off, thinking I would never see her again, but a few years later, after Thomas and Kathrin married, she moved back to California. I had originally thought that a letter would only reveal oneself in the best light and therefore could never foster an authentic relationship. But I had forgotten that Kathrin and Thomas were sincere and honest people with themselves and others.

Similarly, the sincerity of such correspondence nurtured my romance with God. Before this, I never kept a diary, but everywhere I turned, a friend, a stranger, or a pastor's sermon would mention how keeping a journal could help my prayer life. Believing the Holy Spirit guided me, I bought my first spiral-bound notebook. I did not know how to talk to God, but when I wrote, pouring out my thoughts came naturally. Each day I visited the pages of my journal, and began with "Dear Jesus..." Then I shared everything with him, as if he sat beside me over a cup of coffee.

After writing in the fresh pages of my new notebook, I used up a whole roll of toilet paper as I cried and forgave. In writing letters to my Savior, I unearthed unhealthy thoughts and attitudes and gave them over to God.

The conversation didn't flow one way either, for God chatted with me all about himself through the Bible. Some passages I found hard to decipher, but it didn't matter. As long as I had a willingness to hear, I found it uncanny how I would be struggling with an issue in my life, only to discover the topic in God's Word.

Since God commanded his people to put him before money, I took a grand leap of faith and sent off to a radio show, *The Bible Answer Man* with Walter Martin, a whopping thirty dollars. The following weekend, I attended my first women's retreat. When I arrived in my room, I noticed an envelope on my pillow. I discovered later that a kind soul had sought the Lord for a timely, meaningful Scripture passage. My card read: "Bring the whole tithe into the storehouse, that there may be food in my house. Test me in this," says the Lord Almighty, "and see if I will not throw open the floodgates of heaven and pour out so much blessing that there will not be room enough to store it" (Malachi 3:10). Out of the thousands of verses, I might have received, this obscure Old Testament promise flashed like a neon sign—more than a funny coincidence. I wondered, *Is God telling me he saw my offering and would bless me financially?*

When I returned home after the weekend, I had an unexpected check waiting for me in the mail for twelve hundred dollars. I said, "Thank you, God, for pouring out this enormous blessing." With such a powerful lesson on honoring God above money, giving became a natural part of my devotion.

I also found that following God's Word sometimes required

other kinds of sacrifice. A family member drove my cherished, baby-blue Chrysler Regal while I recovered in my body cast. I'd purchased the hand-me-down from Mom for eight hundred dollars a few months before my tragic tumble down the hill. Caring for my car had not been a priority, so my blue beauty got trashed as the months went by. When I first started following Jesus, I read a Scripture in Luke 6:29–30: "If someone slaps you on one cheek, turn to them the other also. If someone takes your coat, do not withhold your shirt from them. Give to everyone who asks you, and if anyone takes what belongs to you, do not demand it back."

I did not know everything God meant, but I decided to go all in and determined to follow even this advice. Since I still recuperated, I did not ask for the car back. When the doctor cleared me to drive again, the vehicle could not travel down the road without overheating. Dad and I set off to the Nissan dealer owned by one of his golfing buddies, Gary.

Dad enjoys few things in life more than wheeling and dealing for a good price, but that day he didn't have much to work with. Only one set of wheels fit into my budget, their cheapest Nissan Sentra—a mere shell of a car with no upgrades, and battleship gray. Though I preferred a red auto, my baby-blue Chrysler would be sorely missed now that my only option was this homely heap.

"How do you like the car, honey?" asked Dad.

"Good, Dad. It will work out great." Knowing I couldn't afford anything else, I didn't bother contesting our pick.

"Okay, let me go talk to Gary and see what we can do. You wait here."

I sat gazing at the gloomy replacement vehicle, trying to bond with the stranger. Silently, I prayed, "Jesus, I know I should be grateful for this Sentra, but it's blah. Could you finagle a better one? I would sure be obliged. I am sorry if I sound unappreciative. Still, it would be nice."

Dad returned. "Lynn, what do you think about that little Pulsar?"

"Which one is that?"

"You see those three cars on display? It's the red one in the middle."

Set on a raised platform above all other cars sat a sporty red racecar with a black line along each side. I had drooled over the interior with its corduroy red-and-black stripes and cherry-red dashboard. I had no doubt; this dazzling star outshined every other car on the lot. "It's amazing, Dad,"

"How would you like to own it?"

"Dad! Don't tease me. That's not nice."

But he smiled broadly. "Now, don't get your hopes up. It all hangs on the Regal and how much we can get for it. We have to get it detailed. Then drive back here for their mechanic to assess what it's worth."

"But, Dad, we can barely take the car two miles down the road without it overheating."

Undaunted, he said, "We'll bring lots of water."

So my dying blue-baby got a facelift and shined as it had the day I had bought it. Unfortunately, the motor could not be camouflaged. On the way back to Gary's dealership I prayed, "Oh Jesus, please keep this old car running." No steaming explosions interrupted our drive.

Dad and I watched from our air-conditioned seat inside the showroom as the mechanic hovered over the Regal's innards. Occasionally I shot up a silent plea to heaven as if the fate of lives depended on it.

Gary joined the mechanic, and in his dress shirt and tie, he searched the engine. Pulling his head out from under the hood and standing upright again, he looked at the motor and shook his head as if he eyeballed the carcass of a dead horse. He glanced our way and then circled the remains, tapping the tires with his foot. After a few minutes of what seemed an intense discussion with his mechanic, Gary joined us inside.

Reaching out a hand to Dad, he said, "You have a new Pulsar." Then he added, "And, Miller, you owe me one!"

As I drove home in my red dreamboat, the sunroof opened wide, a carload of cute guys beeped their horn and gave me a thumbs-up, approving of my wheels.

I laughed. Never would I have thought I could own such a prize, or had I ever thought to ask for one. God began to teach me how he faithfully fulfilled his Word and how lavish his answers could be.

Now that I followed Jesus and read his love letters, my walk of faith took on new dimensions and bigger risks.

One Sunday evening service, John Wimber gave an invitation after his sermon, "If anyone here is struggling with sexual sin, the Lord wants to restore you. Come forward if that is you." Young men and women flooded the altar and filled the aisles.

The sight upset my sense of privacy and embarrassed me. I said, "Oh God, please don't ask me to do something like that."

As young people stood at the front of the worship band, many wept. The ministry team swept in and blessed the young adults as they turned to God. Putting hands on their shoulders, they leaned their heads in to pray, but I didn't hear English. It sounded like gibberish, and I didn't like it at all.

Often my questions would get addressed as I studied the Bible, and within a few weeks, I read how the Holy Spirit gave the gift of tongues to believers (1 Corinthians 12:10), and the apostle Paul said that he spoke in tongues more than anyone. (1 Corinthians 14:8) With such a strong endorsement, my desire to praise and pray with a secret language grew.

One day, while spending time with Jesus, I saw a word written out in my imagination. I began to pray the funny little phrase, "Shaun·dra·sha." In the quiet of my home, with no one around, I prayed that peculiar word over and over. All at once other sounds I did not understand flowed rapidly from my mouth, like a well gushing up out of hard ground.

I doubted, *Am I making this up?*

As with the disciplines of prayer and fasting, I questioned why God valued my speaking an unknown language. How could it build up my inner person? (1 Corinthians 14:4) I did not understand that prayer, fasting, and speaking in tongues did not earn God's acceptance but provided a means to overcome distractions, unbelief, and other pulls interfering with hearing and following Jesus. These were on-ramps into intimacy, not hurdles to perform for God's acceptance.

One Sunday, at the Saddleback Valley Vineyard, the congregation began to sing in tongues. The melodious mix of foreign dialects brought heaven to earth in an exquisite symphony, and I joined in with my own spiritual, mysterious song. After this holy moment, I readily accepted the Spirit's gift.

In the years ahead, God's Word, which was his love letters to me, did more than guide my decisions or introduce me to prayer, fasting, and speaking in tongues. They showed me his face and exposed his passion. What jewels I unearthed as I beheld his unrestrained affection toward a wayward son (Luke 15:20). I feasted on the revelation of God as a lover ravished by the devotion of his people (Song of Solomon 4:9). And, of course, I saw him wild-hearted in Jesus who wept over a city which would in a few short days brutally kill him (Luke 19:41).

How could I have ever thought him stoic?

My ignorant view of God as unmoved by my needs had hindered my prayers and perverted my reading of Scripture. Now I looked for his kind face in the stories I read, and shared my thoughts with him in the cozy place of prayer as I wrote, "Dear Jesus..."

Bible study and gathering to worship with others became lifelong strategies for nurturing my spiritual walk. Unfortunately, I did not perceive my weakness, nor did I have enough history with God to grasp his great passion in our relationship.

Nothing is more defenseless than a baby. As a new Christian, I, too, like a newborn, entered a vulnerable stage in my development. Years of confinement had carved into my soul a deep well of loneliness. Little did I know about the landmine beneath my next step. Unaware of my brokenness, the emotional pain and unhealthy thinking, I built my Christianity on precarious footing.

CHAPTER 14

The Detour

"Lynn, you are deceived." Beth had finally said it. For months I had sensed her disapproval and had avoided getting together. *She doesn't understand my situation. I guess she is just too religious and rigid. Poor Beth. How can I explain?*

A warm end-of-summer sun beamed brightly as we sat on a bench in Dana Point, overlooking the yachts and the island side of the marina. Locals and tourists lounged at the outdoor tables, sipping coffee or eating ice cream. Their noisy chatter had driven us to this isolated spot by a gate leading down to one of the docks. A seagull landed on the railing next to us, begging for a handout. I knew the place well, having spent almost every day of the last four months down at the harbor.

Beth continued, "Chet isn't right for you, and I think he is taking you away from what the Lord has for you. You haven't been to church in months. Mom and Dad say you don't seem like yourself lately."

I could outtalk Beth, and out-argue just about anybody, just one of the blessings and curses of being like my father. I explained all the reasons why she was dead wrong.

Always the romantic in our family, to me marriage seemed a natural course of events. Even as a child, I collected funds from my siblings and arranged dates for Mom and Dad's birthday or anniversary, because this seemed like my idea of a perfect present. I had chased a blond-haired boy in kindergarten, wooed a fourth grader by challenging him to a spitting contest, and anonymously called up my brothers' friends on the phone just to flirt. High school had stifled my youthful expectations, with few crumbs to cherish. Now at twenty-one, with my hip still broken despite the corrective surgeries and months in a body cast, from here on, I would roll through life in a wheelchair. But in my mind, I lacked only one thing for complete happiness—a boyfriend.

After I got out of my cast and before I could get behind the wheel of a car again, I took an access bus down to Dana Point for a change of scenery. As I sat on my beach blanket, a man much older than I, with an athletic build and ocean-blue eyes, came over and introduced himself. During my post-cast recuperation, I had nothing much to do, so my visits to the harbor came more frequently, and I spent lots of time with Chet. I thought of him as a renaissance man, and I found his conversation stimulating after being cooped up for so long. At heart he was a sailor, with a passion for the sea, and whenever we spent time together, this kept us close to the water. While I read, Chet sat for hours, gazing out at the Pacific. His leathery face and the way he stood, with legs apart and knees slightly bent indicated he was a man more comfortable at sea than on land.

When I started driving again, and between visits with Chet, I resumed my college studies. Soon enough, I discovered my heart was no longer in it, and I found it impossible to overcome the physical barriers in my organic chemistry class while handling carcinogens. To avoid inhaling the hazardous fumes, all the students needed to work under a chimney-like hood while setting up their titrations. This required that I stand, but my legs did not have the strength. Instruments fell. Glassware broke. Within the first few weeks of class, I owed the department a whopping one hundred dollars. As the debt rose, my plans for medical school quickly faded.

Mom, always ready with an idiom for every circumstance, would have said, "Well, Lynn, you're caught between a rock and a hard place." And I was.

A year earlier, my anatomy professor had indicated that the science department would not adjust to my needs. While I dissected the corpse of a cat, he came by to both check on my progress and put me in my place. He said, "Don't expect to get any preferential treatment from me just because you're in a wheelchair."

Astounded at the mere thought, and annoyed, I said, "I never even asked for any help from you!" And I made sure I never did. He had pricked my pride. He had also thrown down a gauntlet.

I became the top student in his class.

At the end of the term, I felt vindicated when he apologized for misjudging me. But his underlying point taunted me—don't ask for help no matter what. I got the impression my anatomy professor felt taken advantage of by disabled students who'd used their disabilities as excuses. Unwilling to be seen as needy like them, and unaware of my rights in classes that didn't accommodate my needs, I lost my drive to attend college.

Chet proved a welcome distraction, saving me from organic chemistry mishaps and my lack of motivation in pursuing medicine. Our relationship developed quickly. About that time, my parents decided to buy a boat. It seemed appropriate, given Chet's vast experience, that he would step in to help. And Dad needed it. For years our family had teased him about his infamous fishing disasters. He always had good intentions when he took us fishing at the pier, but his luck did not match his intentions. Since we were children learning the sport, our clumsy attempts at casting kept Dad busy disentangling lines or replacing hooks because we caught more of the bottom than anything alive. Myriad costly mishaps became the norm. For Father's Day, we gave dad brand-new fishing pliers. They fell through the planks of the dock. He once bought a bucket of live shrimp, but all went lost when David threw it in the water with the lid open. Then Dad bought a new pole. As my brother Don reeled in the line, a pelican nabbed the juicy bait and flew off with the rod. All evening, the bird taunted us from a distant perch, our new fishing pole dangling from around his throat like a necklace.

One night, a school of fish hit the pier, and we couldn't reel in the whiting fast enough. Dad worked for hours filleting the skin and removing the guts. He would be feeding his family for weeks with the catch. But a visiting cousin didn't recognize Dad's treasure, dumping the bucket of meaty trimmings into the sea.

Then Dad suffered various accidents. While he removed the hook from an ornery sail catfish, its venomous spiny tail whipped around and sliced open Dad's shin. Next, he suffered the wrath of a stingray when he stepped on it. After a Sea-Doo had gouged into his calf, the paramedics asked, "Hey, don't we know you? Aren't you the guy we brought in last year when you stepped on a stingray?"

And, of course, he was.

When Mom and Dad decided to buy a boat, they did not take this unhappy history into account. Now, I say Mom and Dad, but truth be told, Dad bought the toy and Mom, the easygoing one, went along with it. So my dad bought the 1965, forty-two-foot, double-cabin cruiser christened *Sea Horse*. After his purchase, introducing Chet to my folks came easy. He even came along to help Dad motor down the coast from Marina del Rey to Dana Point Harbor.

Dad, Chet, and I pulled out from the dock and set out to sea, in our brand-new old boat. Given the midday hour, no other family members could join us. For months I had wondered how it felt to cruise around on a yacht, now I sat aboard one, having a first-class adventure.

But I didn't know the half of it. Only an hour passed before the starboard engine sputtered and then expelled its dying breath. Dad took the wheel while Chet opened a hatch in the middle of the living room floor and jumped down to check out the engine. After a few minutes, Dad yelled over the throbbing of the remaining engine, "Can you fix it?"

Like a groundhog popping out of his burrow, Chet's head emerged from the hole. I peered into the underbelly of the boat. *Look at that! There's a whole world down there. Gee, if it wasn't for that god-awful smell, you could sleep down there. Almost.*

Chet wiped oil from a screwdriver in his hand. "No way to fix it now. She's blown a hose." Using his forearm, he mopped perspiration from his brow. "Listen, Bob, this is a twin screw. We can get home on one engine."

Dad shook his head as if he couldn't believe it, saying, "Damn it! What the hell!" Annoyed that his expensive purchase could disappoint so quickly, he threw in a few more expletives.

With nothing else to do, we continued. I returned to enjoying the salt spray and sun, sitting in my chair by the rail. Chet stood with Dad by the wheel. Now and then, Dad could be seen shaking his head, frustrated at the turn of events. *Poor Dad. He still can't believe his bad luck. I hope this boat isn't a lemon.*

For thirty minutes, we chugged southward before all became ominously quiet. Waves slapped against the hull. The whir of the motor ceased. We had no engines. Chet, once again, descended into the bilge to check hoses and the oil gauge.

Now we floated in the Pacific with no land in sight. Without the power to cut through the choppy water, we became like a fishing bobber caught in the swells and trough of each wave. *Wow! If I don't get seasick now, I never will.* I stayed in the fresh air, keeping my face to the wind. Dad kept the bow pointed into the waves as best he could, and Chet my heroic "groundhog" sweated over the engines below.

Then Chet shouted, "We're starting to take on water down here. There's a leak in the exhaust. Turn on the bilge pumps, Bob."

Dad flipped a switch. Nothing.

Chet's voice wafted from the boat's bowels, "Did you turn them on?"

"Yes." Dad flicked the knob off and on again. Nothing.

Chet climbed out of the engine room to check for himself. Nothing. He hurried to the electrical board and fumbled with breakers. No bilge pumps turned on.

So now we had no engines and no working pumps. And with no land in sight, we were sinking. Dad looked seasick. He picked up a handset, "Mayday. Mayday. This is the *Sea Horse*…" The radio worked. It was the only thing that did.

On my first ride in our new yacht on my first voyage out to sea, the Coast Guard towed us into San Pedro Harbor.

We came to refer to the *Sea Horse* as "The Money Pit," an apt description. For three years, every time my family went out for a joyride something broke. Now that my parents owned a not-so-seaworthy sea vessel, Chet and I had another interest to draw us closer. Soon, he moved onto my parent's boat to oversee repair projects. Not long after, he joined in our family functions.

Beth always treated Chet kindly, but she secretly prayed I would wise up and leave him. I may have outtalked her, but she never changed her opinion of my boyfriend.

Although Chet had known the Lord a long time, he never went to church. I dismissed his lack of interest, not wanting to judge him. Ignoring what might have been a warning sign, I made him the center of my life.

One day I drove to a secluded park near the harbor and sat in my car. The Bible told of a man named Gideon who put a fleece before the Lord to test his will (Judges 6:37). I decided to do the same. I said, "Jesus, if you want me to be with Chet, I pray he will be standing on the corner when I drive home." Foolish as it sounded, I didn't know much about discerning God's will, so I asked for a fleece.

About forty minutes later, I headed down the hill. Chet stood on that exact corner. Shocked at seeing him, I asked, "What are you doing here?"

"The Lord told me to get up and start walking. I stopped here, wondering what to do next."

I figured this equaled the sky parting and a voice thundering from heaven. I didn't know how deception worked back then. My desire for romance, more important than my relationship with God, left a door wide open for the enemy to steer me off course.

Only months earlier I had begun to believe in God. Accepting the reality of Satan seemed too long a leap. I refused to believe he existed or that a malevolent being could influence my decisions. With a dangerously selective theology, I chose truths to embrace and truths to toss out.

In the wee hours one night, I abruptly awoke. A dark, menacing being pinned me to the bed. It enclosed me like a coffin. I lay frozen, my screams trapped in a chokehold. For a long time, I did not know what to do, unable to call out for help. Then, I cried out in my thoughts, a desperate "Jesus!"

In the name of Jesus, the release came immediately. The frightening weight lifted, and I could breathe again. This was the first moment I accepted that evil existed. But like Eve, in the garden entertaining the snake, Chet and I were deceived and tempted toward compromise.

Assuming the answer to my fleece must have been from God, I decided Chet had to be the right guy for me. Before 1983 ended, we discussed getting married and moved in together, living on the family boat. I easily dismissed college as a distant memory, but I ached for the worship gatherings I had once known. One night I talked Chet into going to Vineyard Anaheim. God met me extravagantly during worship, but after the service when Chet observed me talking to an old friend, he became jealous, believing I liked the man romantically. Though I denied it, Chet wouldn't accept the truth. He said, "We are never going there again." And so Chet became my whole world. God, Christian community, and family gatherings relegated to the back burner.

After living on the boat together for several years, I sensed dullness in my heart toward the Lord, which confused and worried me. *Jesus, will I lose you if I stay with Chet? But then again, Lord, didn't you answer my fleece?* And for the first time I wondered, *Could that reply have been the enemy deceiving me?*

I would learn how deceitful sin could be. I justified my behavior, resisted the Spirit's guidance, and ignored words in Scripture directing me toward a godly path. And I ignored my own restless heart, which also signaled my need for a change. Jesus remained with me, so I assumed he validated my choices—not realizing his kindness merely wooed me back and did not affirm my lifestyle.

In time, my despair escalated. And I gained forty pounds. I learned few are more miserable than lovers of Christ who ignore his lordship. One day, I got down on the edge of a cement dock; the act was more than an empty gesture. Now that I had a broken hip, a fractured femur and extra poundage, I didn't know if I could get back in my chair. Obscured by boats, I sat in a hidden corner of the marina, holding a rope in my hand, contemplating suicide. *Shall I tie myself to my chair and roll it into the water? The weight will surely pull me down. Will I go to heaven or hell if I kill myself?* For a long time, I stared into the water, wrestling my fate.

I got up off the dock. No searing pain shot through my hip. But with fresh resolve, after being with Chet for four years, I knew something needed to change.

Soon after this incident, I took an overnight trip to my parents' house because of business I had in the area. I left a note for Chet in the fridge, saying, "I love you, honey." While I drove, the strain of my life's drama seemed unbearable. In a desperate search for peace, I decided to seek counsel. Before I lost my nerve, I drove to a Christian ministry located near home, the Full Gospel Businessmen's Association. I wheeled up to the receptionist and asked, "Is there someone here who could advise me?"

Carla, one of the leaders on staff, listened to a blow-by-blow rendition of my romance with Chet. Her response sounded like Beth. "Lynn, I think you are deceived. I know what I am saying may change the course of your life, but I believe you must leave Chet."

My attempts to avoid the all-too-familiar pain of loneliness had kept me by Chet's side. Now I had to make a decision. Would it be God or Chet?

With surrendered obedience, I called my fiancé. Through sobs, I spoke. "Chet, I won't be returning. I care about you, but I am not happy. My relationship with God is suffering, and I no longer think he is in our being together."

He argued with Carla's counsel, but I would not budge. My decision seemed miles away from the sentiment in the note I left in our fridge. Yet I did not waver.

Mom and Dad had never liked Chet. Mostly they did not appreciate who I had become because of my association with him. Already they were disappointed in my leaving the Catholic Church. Though they didn't treat me differently, and we never argued about it, my dad said plainly, "I don't like that you are not going to Catholic church. It is the real church instituted by Saint Peter." In my dad's eyes, at the time, my nondenominational Christian fellowship did not qualify as church. But when I chose to move in with Chet, they could see my life did not match up with my profession of faith. I had grown more distant and critical than Christlike and loving. Despite all this, they had long since decided to accept him into the family since he treated me well.

Mom responded with enthusiasm when I asked to move back home. Wanting to console me, she said, "Beth told me Blaine Cook is going to be starting a church in the area." And a few days later she added, "If you want to host a home group, you can meet in the bonus room upstairs."

I had always admired Blaine, who had taught classes at Anaheim Vineyard when I'd first attended there. At the news, my heart leaped with joy. I called him that very night, and within a few weeks, he began teaching a Bible study in my home. Like the prodigal son when the Father kissed him, put a ring on his finger, and threw a party at his return, I also felt the undeserved welcome of my heavenly Father's blessing (Luke 15:11–32). Each Wednesday night, as God breathed on the new church and poured out his mercy on my life, young people from all over the region packed into our upstairs game room.

Astonishingly, Chet was easy to get over. I could only attribute it to the grace that comes when one obeys. Or, in this case, *finally* obeys. Although I felt humbled by my detour, I saw more clearly the face of a kindly God. I came to believe since he foreknew my failure when he first touched me so profoundly, then surely his provision would be there to restore me. I had no idea, at the time, how much I had blessed his heart—that, out of my failure in choosing to move in with Chet, I now could offer the gift of a more wholehearted devotion. His embrace, and his mercy on my return, won my love.

That which had been denied me with Chet became central to my life—community. The thrill of being in a young, growing church seemed like a satisfying replacement. It became the hospital, school, and extended family I needed to recover. In Christian fellowship, which Scripture refers to as "the body of Christ," I continued to encounter God. I discovered he shines through individuals, but he is glorious in the midst of his people. The church was Jesus with skin on.

Not content to stick my toe in the water, I dwelt in the community, making friends, mentored by others further along than me. Within just a few weeks of leaving Chet, I volunteered at Open Doors, helping to stuff envelopes and send off books to those praying for persecuted Christians around the globe. Doing a small part to help this ministry rally prayer and bring Bibles into closed countries connected me with believers all over the world. I made new, like-minded friends. Then a year later, at twenty-six, I joined a crisis prayer team, answering phones and praying for those who suffered. After several years on the phones, I transitioned into feeding the homeless in Santa Ana.

No longer did I live my faith separated and alone, like a stray cat scrounging for food in a dark alley. I feasted on God in gatherings of praise, in compassionate prayer and ministry, in restaurants, while playing board games, and at numerous other events. And because I had a community of young friends on a similar spiritual path, we enjoyed rich times in prayer as well as all manner of fun. We put on a play, we fed the poor, we visited the elderly, and we attended conferences together. We celebrated weddings and attended funerals that felt personal because church felt like family. When a baby developed a heart disorder, we all gave blood and prayed. When a child got leukemia, we prayed, brought meals for the family, and grieved when he passed away. Whether I faced a mound or a molehill, friends helped me through all manner of terrain, especially my minefield. And I made a difference for them. In this healthy environment, rich with love, I grew in faith. The body of Christ proved to be the catalyst for all that followed in my life.

Hidden Scars

SMACK! THE IMPACT HIT mere inches from my body. Car metal crumpled but effectively halted the oncoming vehicle at my driver's door, like a catcher's mitt stops a ninety-mile an hour fastball. Random thoughts collided in unnatural slow motion. *What did I do wrong?* I looked up at the traffic light, feeling guilty for being the source of my demise. Green. *Oh good, it isn't my fault!* My relief gave way to anger at the injustice of being hit. *This crash isn't right!*

Frightful questions came burst upon me: *Am I going to die? Will I be maimed? Is somebody else going to hit me?* Within milliseconds of the impact, I cried out helplessly, "Jesus!"

An old man, the negligent driver of the car that had hit me, emerged at my driver's window, "Are you okay?"

Trying to register his anxious flow of words, I stared at him blankly.

"I was lost and looking around and didn't see the red light. Are you okay?" the man asked again.

I wasn't sure. But like a flickering match in a dark room came a flash of clarity. Broken-bone pain always intruded on a mind in shock, and I experienced none of that now. "I think I'm okay."

"Can you get your car out of the intersection?"

The engine still running, my car limped and groaned as I drove it a few feet to the bike lane.

A Hispanic woman ran up to the passenger-side window. "Are you okay?" Concerned, kind eyes searched for an answer, but no words came to me. Her black hair, pulled back in a ponytail, with escaping tendrils, gave me the impression she had been working hard. Deep lines around her eyes indicated it had been a tiring day. Her hands juggled a cold, sweaty Coke and a bag from McDonald's. It appeared she had been nibbling her meal as she walked home. My mind was in a fog, but these irrelevant details registered.

I felt no jarring pain. "I think I'm okay." *What am I supposed to do now?* My thinking slowed, as if swimming through mud. Not sure if I had the idea or the woman suggested it, I grabbed my cell phone to call the police. I stared at it, waiting for my mind to jump-start. I couldn't remember how to get the number.

The woman reached out her hand and said, "Here, let me make the call." As I passed her the phone, my fingers trembled.

I Googled it later and discovered my reactions were quite common. Our bodies respond to trauma by releasing a substance in our systems that will either help us fight or flee. If we can't do either, the chemicals wash over our brain and create confusion that lasts a few minutes or even a few weeks, depending on the severity. My trembling hand and slow thinking were classic symptoms of this fight-or-flight rush of adrenaline. It also reawakened a long-forgotten memory: While I rolled away from the wreck without an injury or even a scratch, the incident reminded me of what breaking bones felt like—unexpected and violent, with an aftermath of shocked confusion.

AS A CHILD, I did not know how to process or even articulate the inner scars left behind by trauma. I could not perceive how they shaped my view of life, my opinion of God, my ambitions, my sense of joy, or my wrangles with depression. These attitudes had become part of my life as much as my looks and height, my family, and my education.

One night as I'd sung worship songs at a Bible study group in my friend's home, Jesus had let me know his plan. As the music ended, a holy silence filled the living room, and a thought had come to my mind. I'd recognized the Lord speaking to me, "Lynn, would you let me come into every room in your house?" With instant insight, I'd known I had places inside that represented the sum of who I was. Some of those darkened rooms did not have Jesus's truth inhabiting them.

Despite my utter fear of what opening those doors would unveil, I'd invited Jesus into every part of me to do a renovation, and the warmth of his love had filled my heart, making anything but obedience to his voice anathema. But how good-hearted of him to ask for my permission. Having already received Jesus as my Savior, this work of sanctification happens in due course by the Holy Spirit. In fact, I took great comfort from a song inspired by Scripture, "He who began a good work in you will complete it" (Philippians 1:9). That night, Jesus asked for something more than mere consent; he wanted my partnership. I had two ways to travel down this healing pathway: kicking and screaming, or hand-in-hand with my Savior. He wanted a more companionable journey for me.

In many ways, I did well, given all I had to overcome. But like dull, dreary gray paint, trauma oppressed my life, dampening my dreams. Lies blockaded these darkened rooms; untruths I believed through prolonged suffering: God can't be trusted. I'm cursed. Something is wrong with me.

If a thief had come into my home, I'd have screamed, shouted, and called the cops, desperate to restore safety and keep my belongings. By asking me to attack these familiar lies with the same fervency, Jesus handed me a stick to put in the ground next to a dangerous explosive. How could I dream freely, embrace a grander view of life, or live with a sense of adequacy? My past held me hostage, like a chain around my neck, yanking me to the ground with each attempt to forge ahead. Lies had entered my front door like a menacing thief. They didn't sit nicely in the parlor, but snaked under closed doorways to dwell in nooks and crannies.

I didn't know how to talk to Jesus about my breaking bones. I wrote him letters about my longings and daily hassles but never about my life of breaking bones. Discussing this elephant in the living room inevitably made me feel rejected or that something must be wrong with me. Before I walked with Jesus, I had no sense of being upset with him about my bone disease. I had stopped asking, *Why me?* I had figured, if God existed at all, he was far off in the universe and not involved in the daily affairs of my life. Maybe a holy saint like Saint Francis of Assisi got his attention, but not an everyday person like me. And if God chose to be distant why get mad at him? After all, everyone had problems.

A faith that believes in a mysterious, distant Savior is less likely to expect anything from him and less likely to get offended. Only after I had given my life to Jesus and gotten deeply involved in church life had my anger intensified. Had I attended a church that never expected God to move, which kept to a safe philosophy that dismissed the supernatural, it may have been more comfortable. Instead, I had landed in not only a community of vibrant worship but also a fellowship where God performed signs and wonders. Legs growing out, deaf ears opening, and cancers disappearing were manifestations of God in our midst. While these healings were not commonplace, the fact that they happened at all created hope for change. People traveled from all over the world to experience God's power and learn how to pray for the sick, but my expectations spiraled into disappointment again and again.

While I never heard teaching on the subject, I thought harboring negative feelings toward God bordered on blasphemy—the worst kind of sin. So I ignored the long-suppressed emotions burning inside me like a subterranean volcano.

My pastor at Saddleback Valley Vineyard, Blaine Cook, had an international healing ministry. Since he led a fiery home group each Wednesday night in my upstairs game room, my hope revived. And each time I went to Vineyard Church Anaheim on Sunday night, I looked for a miracle that would change my life forever. I wanted to be free of my wheelchair, able to walk without pain. I longed for simple pleasures, like a stroll on the beach and digging my toes in the sand. Eager, faith-filled believers often prayed for me. Unfortunately, my exploding joy in worship was an antithesis to the dullness of healing prayer. After some months of this tension, bitterness boiled. In the biggest problem of my life, God did not intervene.

I had yet to discover the depth to which the Lord desired intimacy with me. Like any great lover, he wanted authenticity more than my ability to be a good girl. My closest friends got the real me, but with Jesus, I pretended there was nothing wrong at all. In my letters and while in prayer, I never even talked to him about my despair.

About that time, Mom developed a hiatal hernia, severe enough to resemble a heart attack. Because of the intense pain, on several occasions, she ended up in the emergency room. Longing for mom's recovery, I shyly placed my hand on her shoulder and uttered my best prayer. Her symptoms left—for a good two weeks. Then one night, before I left for the evening meeting at church, Mom informed me her hiatal hernia had flared up again. I received the news like an earthquake. *I don't get it. Why didn't God heal Mom?*

During the service that night, John Wimber said, "There is someone here with a problem in their left hip. God wants to restore you." Eagerly, I raised my hand to receive prayer. *Wow Lord. Is this it? This offer surely has to be for me. Yippee! I wonder what it will be like to walk around again?*

A couple sitting in front of me turned around to pray. After Janet and Larry had introduced themselves, Larry asked, "What's wrong, Lynn?"

"Five years ago, I broke my left hip, and it hasn't mended."

"Okay. Let's pray," said Janet.

I didn't know whether to keep my eyes open or shut them. I was a little confused about my part. *How do I receive a miracle? Do I pray along with them? Maybe I should just sit here and listen. What do I do while they pray?*

Janet interrupted my thoughts and said, "Lord, if it is your will, please help Lynn."

If it is your will? Don't they know? What do they mean, "If it is your will?" Didn't the pastor just give a word for my condition? My anger rumbled.

Larry continued, "We know that your ways are not our ways, Jesus, but Lynn would like to walk. Please have mercy. Please come Holy Spirit in Jesus's name. Pleeeaase, Jesus, touch Lynn. And if it isn't your will, then I pray you would give Lynn grace." They prayed with little conviction that God even wanted to heal me, and their requests sounded more like begging than faith.

Nothing happened. Disappointment flooded me. *Did I do something wrong? Maybe I don't have enough faith.* The volcano inside me reached cataclysmic pressure.

As soon as I settled into the long drive home, my molten fury erupted. "God! Why don't you heal people? If you did miracles, maybe more folks would follow you!" I poured out my bitterness loudly, with fist shaking and tears. I cried while I drove the forty-minutes home, and then I sobbed myself to sleep.

I never felt so enraged as I did that night.

In the morning, before I opened my eyes, memories of my rage the night before came flooding back. Guiltily, I wondered, *Will God ever visit me again?*

Before I could mutter an "I'm sorry," and before I could form words to explain or apologize, God's presence greeted me, filling my bedroom. An unusual heaviness thickened the air. Later I learned that the glory of God is called *kabod*, which means "weight" in Hebrew. The weight of his "Good morning" felt like pure love.

God's welcome after my madness the night before both astounded and comforted me. It also crushed my accusations. And I surrendered. "Lord, I don't understand why I can't walk yet, but no matter what, I will believe you love me."

At the time, I didn't recognize my leap forward. Even with my experience of disappointment, I had chosen to believe Jesus loved me. Every victory and joy that followed I could trace back to this moment. My decision became a stake in the ground for my faith.

Now I started down a new road. I had a different way of interpreting life—through the lens of his love. Oh, violins did not play, heaven did not open, nor did angels appear. Nothing dramatic indicated the enormity of this incident. Yet his tenderness shifted the course of my life. Whenever I found myself confused by life's setbacks, I would seek out the embrace of God to comfort me and take my pain.

I thought the morning's encounter with my Savior would settle the matter forever, especially when a few weeks later Blaine and Becky Cook prayed for Mom before our Wednesday night meeting, and her severe pain went away. I thought I would never doubt God's love again. I was wrong. He didn't drop into my world that morning and lift the elephant out of the living room. Instead, he began to invade memories where trauma had me stuck.

Studying anatomy in college did not enlighten me on the intricacies of brain science as it relates to inner healing, but later I discovered that the memory center located in the right hemisphere and the truth and reasoning faculty of the left hemisphere each play a part. Though ignorant of the mechanics, I appreciated firsthand that God became my holistic doctor. He did not just throw facts at me, but he visited by his presence old wounds, addressing memories as well as lies. I devoured the Bible because its contents applied salve to my unhealthy thinking. However, my experience of the living Word, Jesus Christ, also restored me.

It began one weekend in May when my sister and I decided to attend a women's retreat in La Jolla. Beth and I are a dangerous combination inside a car. Since conversation overshadows the more significant task of driving, our destination became secondary. As a result, we started off at three o'clock in Santa Ana and got to La Jolla through San Diego, which is much like traveling from Florida to Texas through New Mexico. We didn't arrive till eight o'clock at night. Given the late hour, only one Saturday workshop had room for us, "The Power of Forgiveness." Beth and I wrote our names on the sign-up list, disappointed in the slim pickings.

The next day, two women in their early twenties led our workshop. Although incredulous that women so young would lead, Beth and I joined about fifteen other women who sat on beds and on the floor, ready to hear a Bible teaching. We got so much more. We closed our eyes and together, in Jesus's name, asked for the Holy Spirit to come. I sat in peaceful silence, not sure what I waited for. Then one of the girls began to describe what she saw and repeated an incident that had happened in my life as it had exactly occurred. Now I had received little communiqués from God in the form of a picture, but this girl saw a movie.

She said, "I see a little girl in the pool playing. Your brothers come along and take your mask, and you try to grab it. They are teasing

95

you, holding it above your head out of reach, laughing at you. When you start to cry, they call you a crybaby and fatso. As you are walking away, you look back at them and say, 'I hate you!' The Lord wants you to forgive your brothers."

My memory of the incident, even the part about saying, "I hate you!" was not buried deep in my unconscious. I could have painted the same scene she described. Only this young woman had not even been there. Like removing a bandage on an old wound, the Lord exposed my unforgiveness. As though it were background music, the girls continued to declare their insights to women all over the room, while I sobbed. Childhood seemed a long way off, but the hurt surfaced as if it were yesterday. Then I, too, saw a picture. As I fled my brothers' mocking laughter by the pool, I saw Jesus walking with me, his arm around me.

Never again did I see that moment the same way. When I think back on it now, all I can remember is the way Jesus comforted me. This vision seemed to settle forever the hurt inflicted by older brothers, making it effortless to forgive. Since then, I have not felt anything but love for them, and we have grown closer.

Then God invaded other parts of my past. When one of my girlfriends had hurt my feelings, intense anger had me stuck in unforgiveness. Oh, I knew I needed to surrender my resentment, but I found that, numerous times throughout the day, I felt anger and imagined a scenario where, with a few choice words, I put her in her place. I was stuck—and since Jesus died for the forgiveness of sin, I knew I could not ignore my attitude. One day, as I discussed it with Jesus, he reminded me of an incident that had happened at eight years old when my dear friend hadn't chosen me for her team. Though it had happened a long time ago and seemed silly even to me, I wept over it. God came into that memory and directed me by the Spirit to forgive. Somehow, my present circumstance of rejection had a connection to this moment when I first believed a lie about myself. I could better deal with the adult dilemma by removing the one from childhood.

In time, I recognized a pattern. When mild brush-offs brought inordinate grief and offense, I knew that I dealt with historical issues. With some objectivity, I could own that the anger I felt toward someone who'd offended me, and my struggle to forgive, did not always match the crime. These were live wires to past, unresolved hurts. Jesus helped me grant forgiveness and get free of lies, both past and present. Having been with me every moment of every bone break, having seen every rejection and every sin committed against me, I discovered how God cared about it all, even those wounds long forgotten.

CHAPTER 16

Hope for Healing

As I WHEELED THROUGH the doors, I noticed the heavenly charged atmosphere, but I hadn't expected God to tackle me. It was as if he waited for me.

Vineyard Church Anaheim had hosted a healing conference all week, but I could not attend. The guest speaker, Francis McNutt, provoked my interest not only because he was oddly out of place, a Catholic priest speaking in an evangelical, charismatic church, but also because he had a well-known healing ministry. I arrived at the church, coming to the evening service as I usually did.

As soon as I walked in, God's forceful welcome felt urgent and even heavy. I didn't receive a warm, friendly greeting—a king apprehended me, demanding my attention. Quickly, I wheeled over to an inconspicuous spot in the back of the sanctuary. I closed my eyes, blocking out the loud singing. I heard, "Lynn, I want you to give me your hope for healing."

He did not speak audibly. Nor did his words descend like a feather gently floating in the air coming to land softly. Neither did his message appear as a fuzzy picture. It loudly intruded on my thoughts over the crowd's boisterous worship, breaking into my consciousness.

What? This request couldn't be God. "Lord, surely this isn't you?" I asked. But I knew the answer already. I knew it because of the weight of glory engulfing me. I knew it because I recognized him as the one who loved me and saved me—the God I prayed to every day. My rational mind wanted to resist, but my spirit recognized I tread on holy ground. God drew too near to entertain unbelief.

I heard again, "I want your hope for healing."

"But, Lord, how could you ask me to give you my hope to walk again? You are the one who promises to heal, and you can't lie. How can you ask for such a thing from me? I don't get it? Jesus, I can't."

On and on, I reasoned with the Lord. And in some way hard to describe, we had a conversation. I lost track of time. I lost track of the crowd around me. God and I wrestled.

Tears poured down my face. His request cut me to the core. Now I knew not everyone gets healed of their sicknesses in this life, but I came to faith in the midst of a revival. Young people swarmed into the church, the Holy Spirit set people free of their addictions, and anything seemed possible. Just that year, I had gone to dinner with Jessica, a gal who had been in a wheelchair and now walked after receiving prayer from Blaine. This miracle had flesh and bones and a name—a person with whom I supped. I thought God needed to live up to his Word and heal me, too. "God, if you love me, you should heal me," I said.

The extravagant gift of his sacrifice on the cross didn't factor into the equation. It is almost as if God said, "Lynn, isn't my dying proof of my love?"

My attitude said no. Even though he had awakened love in my heart, I often got offended at him. I welcomed the companionship of his presence. I felt alive with the joy of relationship, but I would go on detours—sometimes for a week, sometimes for a month. Nagging doubts and anger at God for not doing what I wanted interfered with my spiritual walk.

All through the songs of praise and adoration, I argued with him while his Holy Spirit rested on me. Relentlessly, he requested I relinquish to him my heart's desire. Defiantly, I refused. Still, he wouldn't let go.

And in my heart, I knew he deserved my surrender.

Forty-five minutes of worship came to an end, and as the final notes played, I raised my white flag. With a profound sense of loss, I lifted cupped hands up in front me and gave up to God my hope for being healed.

No heavenly chorus sang. A bright light didn't appear saying, "Well done, good and faithful servant." What did happen caught me off guard. As soon as I raised my hands to give him this invisible offering, he gave it right back to me.

The gesture disoriented me. I thought, *What? I don't get it? What just happened?* Then I recalled the story of Abraham, who'd offered up his son, Isaac, to God. The Lord stopped Abraham from going through with sacrificing his boy. He told Abraham, "Now I know that you love me, for you have not withheld your only son" (Genesis 22:12).

The Lord spoke to my heart, "Lynn, your hope for healing has been about your way and your timing. Why don't you hope in me, and I will hold onto the dream for you?"

Apparently, God didn't want me to put my life on hold. He had many blessings ahead that I would never perceive if I only obsessed on this one demonstration of his love. He saved me from getting stuck in a smaller life, like some single friends I knew who waited for a husband before going on the mission field—who couldn't shop furniture without a spouse, so they lived with garage-sale discards—who didn't save and didn't travel, waiting for marriage to come along.

Years of rest followed my surrender. Instead of becoming stuck on the one thing not happening, I could move on and embrace God's plan. New priorities emerged. Soon after, he addressed my aversion to children, which had started in my early teens.

CHAPTER 17

Children

HOWEVER UNLIKELY, FROM THE home of Mickey Mouse and Donald Duck emerged my phobia toward youngsters. For several hours, I decided to walk around Disney World in Orlando. I tired quickly and lagged behind my family as we meandered from one attraction to another, but I didn't mind. Though my legs ached, it felt good to blend in with tourists and forgo the stares of strangers. It was 1975, and at fourteen, I hoped walking would be my new custom, making my wheelchair obsolete.

Chains connected to metal stands cemented in the ground kept everyone in the queue as we waited to board Pirates of the Caribbean. "We'd skip the lines if Lynn would use her wheelchair," my brother David reminded everybody.

"You want to use your wheelchair?" Dad asked. "We can go back and get it, honey."

Sweat dripped down my back, my once pristine white shirt now a wet gray. Clinging to normalcy came with a price, but I would not cave in. "No. I'm good."

Heat and boredom competed for attention. We moved along in

a mindless daze, paying little attention to each other, willing to wait in misery for ten minutes of entertainment.

Then a girl, about kindergarten age, cried out in front me, demanding everyone's attention. Onlookers zeroed in on the child and followed her pointing finger. Shrilly she yelled, "Mommy! Mommy! Look at the midget!"

Instinctively, I looked at her.

But she pointed at *me*.

Even at age fourteen, I never thought of myself as unusually short. With little resistance, I could own the truth of my looks: not so pleasantly plump, curvature of the spine, and a severe limp that made me look contorted when I walked. From first grade on, my height made me the shortest in the class; "midget" never occurred to me. My teenage desire to fit in suffered a severe blow.

Thanks to a child, I discovered another deformity that would mark me forever.

I found that the little ones, always honest and forthright, often mentioned my most unbecoming features. Why are you short? Why are you fat? Why are your legs so skinny? Sometimes they didn't say a word; they just gawked. To them, I was freakish.

"Why are you in a wheelchair?" started the conversation rolling.

When this first happened, I acted friendly and direct, "I broke my leg."

The child's response to my reply often insulted me. Contorting their faces as if they had just eaten canned peas, they might add, "Eww, yuck!" before running off.

I got used to bruising stares from adults, but the reactions from kids left me bleeding. I decided I hated the little urchins. Avoiding them was key. If children stood in one line at a grocery store, I would go in another. If dining at a table in a restaurant, I planted myself across the room, out of eyeshot. Dodging children was symptomatic of my fractured self-image.

Now, with divine wisdom, God targeted my kid hang-up. After service one Sunday, a leader asked me to paint faces at the family picnic. I said, "Sure," glad to be of help. Only as I pulled in to park my car did I belatedly realize I would have to be around *kids*. Panic seized me. I plunged into an abyss, reliving years of wide-eyed, fearful stares, and words that stripped my dignity. I wept hard, wept over hurts, long ignored, and I grieved my deformity. I cried out, "Jesus, I need you. I can't do this without you."

It never dawned on me to ditch the picnic.

Two other girls worked the face-painting booth with me. My eyes were still red and swollen from crying, but I decided to put on a brave face. I pushed up to our table, organized my supplies, and prepared for the firing squad. Kids began coming.

A cute little guy stepped up close, ready to be my canvas. "What would you like?" I said.

"I want a frog right here." He pointed to his cheek.

His devotion to frogs amused me. With stillness uncommon to a six-year-old, he stood frozen, determined to get the best tattoo possible. I had never before painted the green amphibian, but his grin beamed in appreciation at my masterpiece. I smiled into his eyes, immediately liking this kid and wanting him to know it.

As more youngsters drew close, an intense tenderness emanated from me, and we chatted like old friends. Often they would sneak in a hug before scurrying away. I painted kid faces all afternoon, and God filled my heart and flowed through me. I didn't just feel Jesus nearby. I felt as if *I* was Jesus.

Children gobbled up my affection like chocolate candy; butterflies, unicorns, and snakes became secondary. Hours of child smiles followed one another, and their faces became familiar as kids returned over and over. I thought, *My goodness, am I the only one painting faces now? How many kids are at this picnic?* Casually, I looked over my shoulder at the other artists. Two children stood waiting their turns. My line had seventeen.

Parents stood on the periphery. They didn't know my story but marveled at the scene before them. "Lynn, it was as if we watched Jesus bless the children," said my friend the next day. "The kids were drawn to you."

Whether I donned Jesus's skin or he mine, I have rarely felt as one with my Maker as on that day. Having lived the Bible verse, "Perfect love drives out fear" (1 John 4:18), I discovered that one of the greatest joys in my life could be found in serving children.

Soon after my day in the park, during an evening service at the Vineyard, John Wimber asked anyone who felt called to work with kids to come forward and receive prayer. I wheeled my way up front, still not sure I understood God's will for my life. Certainly, if my future included children then a supernatural enablement would be necessary. Responding to this invitation to receive prayer felt like undressing in public. My body quaked, and tears flowed. But God's profound presence rested on me, as did his passion for his little ones, and the hard walls of self-protection around my heart crumbled.

After that, kids popped up everywhere. Not because they saw me as an oddity. They wanted to talk to me and showed more interest than fear. Despite my trepidation, God continued to change my attitude. But was he drafting me for a job?

Ever since Chet and I had broken up, I had lived at home and directed my time toward the new church and my relationship with Jesus. Now, after three months, I needed a new direction and a job. In a quest to resolve my questions, I fasted for three days and sought God's will. I said, "Jesus, please don't let me knock on a hundred doors looking for work. Show me what is next."

On the first day of my fast, I met Cristina, a new teacher who spoke of her high school students with such contagious enthusiasm I wondered whether I could become a teacher. I wanted to dismiss the idea. After all, working with kids seemed far less noble than being a doctor. But that is not how God saw it. In an honest heart-to-heart with my Maker, the Holy Spirit convicted me for not valuing the ones he treasured. I asked for his forgiveness and a new heart. And from that day on, my perspective shifted. Never again would I think of working with kids as a lesser calling.

During my fasting and prayer the next day, I recalled how my high school class gave a rousing standing ovation when I ran for election. I remembered my college speech class. Students welcomed my talks with enthusiasm, and some even cried when I shared a motivational message about helping needy children. As I thought of these affirming responses, I believed Jesus said, "Lynn, I have given you the gift of communication so that you can impact many lives."

On the final day of my fast, I had spent my evening volunteering at a crisis prayer line. Overwhelmed by joy at seeing many lives touched that night, I stood in the middle of our kitchen while my family slept, and praised the Lord for his goodness. I said, "Jesus, I love you!"

Immediately, I heard a loud thought interrupt my worship, "Feed my lambs."

Not registering the enormity of his response, I repeated more fervently, "Jesus, I love you!"

A thought echoed more loudly, "Feed my lambs!"

But my words seemed inadequate, and my heart too full of joy to take note of his reply. I reiterated with as much passion as I could muster, "Jesus, I love you!"

"Feed my lambs!" With this third command, I recalled a passage in John, chapter 21, when three times Jesus asks his disciple, Peter, "Do you love me?" After Peter proclaims his love, Jesus replies, "Feed my sheep."

I accepted my assignment and set my priorities toward caring for God's lambs. When I dated Chet, I would drive by the college and say, "Oh, thank you, Jesus, I don't have to go there anymore." Now, surrendered to his will, I headed to college to get a teaching credential. In 1986, I enrolled in the social ecology program at University of California, Irvine.

Despite my new attitude toward children, my call reminded me of a stuttering Moses being sent to speak to Pharaoh (Exodus 4:10). Kids were my pharaoh. I still lacked confidence in social settings and battled depression. It would take God's touch and truth in regular, powerful doses to keep these anxieties at bay.

CHAPTER 18

Zorro Dream

I FELL ASLEEP QUICKLY, as I usually do. While I did nothing but sleep, God spoke to me in a dream: I picked through a disheveled display of Halloween costumes. No longer hanging neatly on the racks, ransacked by eager little hands, the outfits would not have drawn me except one that captivated the playful, child-hearted adventurer in me—the Zorro guise.

I love Zorro. While in a body cast, old black-and-white reruns on TV occupied many of my late nights. Several times I watched both movies, the old rendition and the new. Zorro—brave, reliable, mysterious—always a benefactor of the poor and downtrodden. A real hero.

In my dream, I brushed aside princess paraphernalia searching for the black garments that were Zorro's trademark. I found a hat. Too tight. I found a mask. It slid down my face. Only one Zorro costume suited my frame—Zorro, the Gay Blade.

Now any Zorro enthusiast could tell you about *Zorro, the Gay Blade* also a movie, and a spoof of the original. *Zorro, the Gay Blade*, acted as a comic version of my dashing hero. Since this black hat with the long, red plume fit perfectly, in my dream I became Zorro, the Gay Blade. As I donned my feathered hat and flamboyant persona, joy bubbled up in my heart.

I awoke laughing into the morning air, enjoying Zorro humor with a broad smile and a fresh lightness of heart. All through my day, I giggled at the memory of my sleep-time shopping excursion and sensed its significance. At seven years old, my encounter with Jesus while I slept had drawn me toward God. Now that I read Scripture and learned how God spoke, it gave me a new appreciation for his voice in dreams. Although these night visions were rare, I had a growing respect for them, having received both guidance in decision-making and forewarnings of dangers to my family. I knew late-night pizza didn't cause this dream, but discerned the Holy Spirit had visited me with something important to say.

That evening, I went to home group at Mike and Janiece Hudgin's house. Each week I came to their home; Janiece led worship on the piano, and Mike led the meeting. That night, after a long, sweet time of singing praises to Jesus, Mike asked, "Is the Lord showing anybody something?"

Still ruminating on my Zorro revelation, I recounted my dream. Maybe it sounded like an odd anecdote to share, but I felt compelled to solve the riddle. Everyone laughed and continued to chuckle.

Then Mike said, "Lynn, that is the weirdest dream." Smiling and shaking his head, probably wondering why I'd told the tale, he added, "What do you think it means?"

"I don't know," I said. But instantly the interpretation became apparent. "I believe the Lord is saying, 'Lynn, you want to be this dreaded warrior dressed in black, but I have clothed you with joy—a joy that will disarm the enemy.'" With conviction, I knew I had ascertained the dream's true meaning.

That day God made me a profound promise. He had already begun removing unseen scars from my childhood trauma although depression still made up my interior world. Now I received some hope of a radical shift, a life with joy as my new identity. I wondered how he would to do it.

WITHIN JUST A FEW months of hearing, "Feed my lambs," I began classes at the University of California, Irvine, home of the Anteaters. With its sprawling campus and considerable hills to traverse, I broke down more than once in frustration, because I forgot a book in the library and had to circle back or, for the third time that day, push up an Alpine slope to the social ecology building. Although challenged by terrain and tests, plus writing lengthy research papers, I enjoyed using my brain and relished seeing God in all aspects of life.

I had thought I'd needed to go to a Christian college so I could merge my passion for Jesus with this new season of learning. But when I prayed about it, I sensed a strong urging to attend UCI. I asked Jesus, "Why do you want me to go to UCI? Don't you want me to learn theology?"

His answer came in a whispered thought, "Lynn, all truth is my truth, wherever you find it."

I discovered in my three years at UCI that my deepening knowledge of the Word brought abundant reward to all my coursework. In psychology and psychotherapy, I could see grains of biblical precepts in its theories and methods of counseling. Thrilling tidbits from Scripture proven by scientific research and longitudinal studies were like unearthed rubies found in a child's sandbox. In my history class, I savored stories of the Reformation and saw God at work in the account of a slave, Equiano.

Spending time with Jesus between classes, parked under a shady tree in various parking lots around campus, gave me time to chat with my Maker. Often in these unlikely sanctuaries, parked under a shade tree, I wept.

One day, a thought intruded on my monologue-like prayer. "Lynn, what are you going to talk to me about when you are no longer depressed?"

The question caught me off guard, but the comment brought a smile. I thought, "Yippee! I guess I won't always feel down in the dumps." Until then, I had no idea that my inner life could be void of sorrow. Easily triggered by the ups and downs of my day-to-day life, relief came as I unburdened my troubles to the Lord. More importantly, a torment I could not articulate, seemingly linked to years of hospitals and rejection, found expression. Crying became a part of daily life when I spent time with Jesus. Emotions long suppressed and issues I'd never talked about with anyone poured forth in the safe space of my college days. This resulted afterward in a new lightness of heart.

At times, in these solitary places, a knock on my driver's side window startled me. "Excuse me, ma'am," said a cop one day. "I noticed your car parked here. Are you okay?"

Perhaps my wheelchair license plate drew attention. These interruptions happened often enough that I formed a canned response, "Oh, I'm fine, Officer. I just came to this secluded spot to pray to Jesus."

They seemed okay with that.

The Bible taught me to accept the gift of tears. In the backdrop of signs and wonders, I saw Jesus spending nights in prayer. And as the writer of Hebrews tells it, he wept with loud cries and supplications (Hebrews 5:7). I followed Jesus into these places, too.

My laments seemed a countercultural remedy, but I found peace because I didn't grieve alone. Jesus drew near. As a child, bravery meant keeping my feelings locked tight, but God became dear to me as I cried in his arms the grief of years. Joyfulness began to emerge in my life, and my college acquaintances grew inquisitive.

Jana and I both used wheelchairs. She studied counseling theories with me at UCI; our mode of transportation was a mutual bond between us. Although we met several times on campus for lunch, I found her company hard to bear. Jana didn't just seem unhappy. Bitterness seeped into our conversations, and negativity emanated from her. I arrived at our final exam early, and so did she. As we sat waiting for our professor to open up the room, she asked, "Lynn, why are you always so joyful? Your face seems to shine. I don't get it!" She seemed annoyed.

"It's because of Jesus," I said. "It is hard to believe that someone invisible could be so real. I used to be depressed and feel rejected all the time. Now he romances me with his love and fills me with joy. I am awed by the way he speaks and…"

"Stop!" She interrupted my rambling and put up her arms as though defending herself from an attacker. "Stop! I can't take any more."

Her plea silenced me. For days, embarrassment over my lack of reserve gave me a good beating. My fumbled attempt at telling Jana about Jesus squelched my passion for sharing my faith, leaving me with a feeling of being inept at evangelism. When I befriended a new coed in my history class, Karen, I decided that I would not talk about God, ever. I would have no other agenda except being friends.

For three months, Karen and I went to lunch twice a week after class. She told me about the boyfriend she lived with and her desire to get a business degree. I yakked about everything but Jesus. When our class ended, I sat across from her at a familiar restaurant. I set down my fork and began my goodbyes. "It's been wonderful getting to know you." I figured we would now go our separate ways, taking different classes. "I hope we meet up again—"

Then Karen interrupted me. She seemed frustrated, maybe even perturbed. "Okay, Lynn, we have gone to lunch for months now. When are you going to tell me about Jesus?"

I could not have been more shocked. *I never mentioned Jesus. How does she know I am Christian? I guess I must have let it slip at one point.* Though I had religiously tried to avoid being religious, it dawned on me that Karen had been hoping to hear about Jesus.

For two hours, we sat drinking coffee and babbling theology. Mostly, I shared about how Jesus continued to change my life. Finally, she addressed the issue that hindered her from following Christ. "So Lynn, if I give my life to Jesus, do I have to move out from my boyfriend's place?"

My reply was not typical, but my relationship with Chet had taught me so much about God's grace. While a holy life is God's high call for all his children, I hesitated to create a roadblock for Karen. Often people think they need to get clean *before* coming to Jesus. But I knew that God's kindness had conquered my resistance. His love put the "want-to" in my spirit.

Karen longed for a Savior, but his lordship made her afraid of being alone. Gazing at her, sensitive to the tussle inside her, I sought inspiration, remembering how quickly I had gotten over Chet. I said, "This is what I know, Karen: If you follow Jesus, he will guide you. His love shifts everything, even desires of your heart."

Karen and I never saw each other again.

But a few years later, I ran into Jana. We both waited in line at the admissions office at UCI. Jana smiled and waved me over. "Hey, Lynn, I've been looking for you. I want to tell you something."

"Really? What's up?" Her countenance told a story before she spoke. She looked happy and alive, having lost her usual sour expression.

"After our talk," she said. "I decided to start reading the Bible."

"Jana, I am so glad to hear that." I was shocked, too. Who would have thought that a woman who had cried out, "Stop! I can't take any more." would have felt drawn to God?

"I wanted you to know I am going to synagogue again." Like a child looking for approval, she told me of her reach for more and her return to faith. My joy in Christ had shined a light on her path. In exchange, her breakthrough gave greater meaning to my suffering. Once again, life with Jesus brought another unexpected, delightful twist. And the promise of my Zorro dream would become more and more evident as my UCI days rolled along.

CHAPTER 19

Facing Firsts

FLUCTUATING BETWEEN BOTH PRIDE and relief, in May of 1988, I earned my degree in social ecology, with an emphasis in psychology. My family attended the honors ceremony and cheered when, in cap and gown, I left my wheelchair and limped up the stairs with my Canadian crutches, to receive my diploma. In the photo commemorating my accomplishment, like a drunken sailor clutching his treasured bottle of whiskey, I blissfully grinned, hoisting my certificate.

After straining through four finals and a goliath research paper, the teaching-credential program appeared daunting. My brain, having crammed into it colliding bits of data, now heaved with exhaustion. I welcomed summer break for a much-needed reprieve.

As a graduation gift, my parents paid for a cruise. Before June ended, my friend LeAnn and I embarked on a Caribbean tour, stopping off at Cozumel, the Cayman Islands, and Jamaica.

From the ship's railing, I gazed at Grand Cayman, a modern city built on prime beachfront property. Its white sandy coast, so unlike the dirtier-looking brown seashore in California, reminded me of my childhood play in Florida, how the white crystals had clung to my body after my brothers buried me up to my neck. I remembered how I had swum out past the waves to undress and shake out the sugary granules from my bathing suit, delighting in a few moments of skinny-dipping.

As we disembarked from the massive ship, two muscled seamen lifted my chair, with me in it, down several sets of stairs. After that, we hit the beach and snorkeled for most of the morning. My bathing suit, with its glittery fringes that hung down from around my cleavage, lured tropical fish closer, allowing me a unique, up-close encounter few enjoy. At lunchtime, LeAnn and I sat eating lobster and having a glass of wine just a few feet from where the waves gently curled at the shoreline. The scene seemed nearly perfect, especially when two young men decided to buy us drinks. Like me, Alan and Bruce had just finished college and were decompressing on our cruise ship. Alan still needed to pass the bar exam; Bruce intended to go into business. LeAnn was the employed vacationer of the group. She waitressed at the Ritz-Carlton Hotel.

In the Caribbean, my friend LeAnn looked exotic with her striking Asian features. All week I had noticed men admiring her and had felt pangs of jealousy. But now this was different. With two men, we had one for each of us. Quickly enough, Bruce expressed interest in LeAnn, leaving Alan and me to pair up. Bruce looked like a California surfer, blond and tan. Alan had a dark complexion and thick black hair. I thought him the more handsome of the two. We flirted freely, talked nonsense, and laughed. Before separating, we made a date to meet up for dinner.

Our cruise ship quickly became a Love Boat. For our dinner, I sported a pink miniskirt with a leopard-print top; LeAnn donned a red dress and high heels. We met at a local bar, and although not fond of beer, I found the foamy draft with a slice of lime resting in the chilled glass heavenly. Conversation flowed easily, with no uncomfortable lulls. But one thing began to dawn on me: Alan had expectations. I thought, *Oh Lord, how do I let him know I am not into a casual fling?* When we returned to the ship, Bruce and LeAnn wanted to hang out alone together, so Alan joined me in the digs LeAnn and I shared. The small room left no space for comfy seating, so we settled on a bed. At first, the awkwardness was palpable.

Then Alan brought up a peculiar topic. "Do you ever get jealous of LeAnn?"

I searched his face, wondering why he would ask such a bizarre question. Relaxed, he reclined against the pillow; his muscled body filled the room. *Man, he really is handsome! Sort of a male version of LeAnn—exotic, but swarthy.* I said, "Yes, I guess I have been jealous. It's not a feeling I am proud of, and it's tripped me up on this vacation. Just this morning, I spent some time praying about it. I am doing a lot better now."

Casually, he shoved another pillow behind his head. "I don't believe in God. I am an existentialist."

"Oh really?" I always thought this view about as sad and hopeless a set of beliefs as could be. "What does being an existentialist mean to you?"

"I believe everything in our lives is futile—that we all live and die. There is nothing after that."

"Before I met Jesus, my life felt meaningless. I used to be depressed because I broke bones and felt ugly and rejected. Now, God is changing that by helping me accept how he sees me." I shook my head in awe. "I love how kind he is."

For hours, Alan and I discussed God, and I thought it odd to have this conversation with a guy, lying on a bed in a small cabin, suggestive of a different kind of intimacy. As we talked, I realized that a man with a philosophy is at the mercy of a woman with an experience. I did not share with him about mere ideas. I spoke of a real person. He asked lots of questions—not about theology but about how Jesus touched my life. Then, before LeAnn walked in the door and we had to say good night, Alan took my hand. "Lynn, promise me you will never stop sharing about Jesus. People need to know. Will you promise me?"

His request and our surreal conversation gave gravity to my answer, reminding me of my school pal, Karen, who had waited months for me to share about Christ. "Yes, Alan. I will always tell others about Jesus."

I didn't realize at the time that it would turn into my life's work.

The next morning, LeAnn and I left the ship early and caught a taxi to our morning scuba diving class. I questioned, *Can I even take an underwater tour? Oxygen tanks are too heavy for me to carry. How will*

I get in the water? Still, I figured I would face that hurdle once I got certified. I paid my money.

After the training, right there from shore, we set out for our under-the-sea excursion. Rather than putting on the equipment before wading in, our instructor helped me attach all my gear while we stood in the shallows. Buoyed by the water, the tanks on my back felt quite light. Although I usually took to water like a fish, I found it hard to swim, and I kept plummeting to the ocean floor. Seeing my distress, the instructor quickly detached the lead weights from my belt, allowing me to float instead of thud along.

Now that I could move more freely, I glanced over at LeAnn to determine if she was ready to head out. But LeAnn panicked, thrashing like a drowning child. Grabbing hold of her, the instructor drew her toward the shallows until she calmed down. After he'd guided her again through the steps of breathing underwater, she and I continued on our dive, descending deeper and deeper into the unknown. Sucking air through a hose, and the sound of loud gurgling with ascending bubbles,  made the unconscious activity of inhaling and exhaling through the mouthpiece awkward. Both the breathing apparatus and the mask closed me in, creating temporary claustrophobia. Soon, however, discomfort dissipated, and I became lost in a magical world of tropical fish. The vibrancy of colors and artistry of design filled me with wonder. Stripes, polka dots, and long, feathery fins created as much diversity as might be seen in animals of a rainforest. Only this was an entirely different part of the planet.

Our guide took us out twenty-five feet below the surface, where we came upon a sunken ship. Creatures of all kinds claimed the dark, shadowy wreckage as their home. Inspired by the scene, I could imagine myself a pirate searching for sunken treasure. And jewels I did find, but not the sparkly kind. I gathered gems of underwater photos and cherished memories. I came to consider this under-the-sea scuba dive as my favorite adventure, an appropriate and extravagant reward ending my days as an undergraduate.

My cruise and my scuba dive were two happy firsts. In the year that followed, almost every area of my life took me deeper into the unknown as I faced many new beginnings and tackled one of my oldest foes.

AN EPIPHANY IS THAT sudden, often unexpected, revelation of insight, which many people say comes during mundane tasks like taking a shower or driving the car. Mine happened as I stood in front of the refrigerator searching for a midnight snack. The quiet house rested in shadows. While I stood in the dim light, it was not the chilled air that left me trembling; it was the cold truth. I was terrified.

Beginning student teaching in the fall, when I would be assessed continuously on my performance, loomed before me. And fear's friends—insecurity, worry, and foreboding—had been with me a long time. I expected things to go haywire, because, after all, things seemed to always go wrong. If my days flowed smoothly, I saw it as the calm before the storm.

During my childhood, with one small shift or one subtle action, my life could turn into Disney's Mr. Toad's Wild Ride. My big brother, Don, always cracked me up by screaming like a banshee and pretending to be terrified as the car on that ride careened out of control (it seemed) through walls and dark tunnels and screeching demons and flames of fire, only to collide with an oncoming train—almost! Events out of my control made life like Mr. Toad's Wild Ride. My experiences of suffering tainted my outlook.

Harboring negative expectations can be a powerful spiritual reality that invites history to repeat itself. If believing leads to eternal life, then what I think is powerful. Hopeful thoughts are essential ingredients to success, but trauma had put a kind of unbelief in my life. A door had opened to negative expectations—one after the other. Believing only God could help me with such a giant-sized "personality flaw," I prayed, with the refrigerator door open, "Jesus, please forgive me for agreeing with my enemy. Take this fear from my life."

I knew God had a mammoth job cut out for him. I doubted he could handle it. Within a month of that late-night revelation, I had a face-off with my childhood enemy—fear. I had been testing the waters to see if working with high school kids, rather than younger kids, better suited me. But I felt intimidated by them. Since these anxious feelings were, for me, commonplace, I needed more to go on, some additional time with teens before making my decision.

IN ORDER TO EXPLORE working with teens, I began attending Young Life meetings. Each week young people from our local high school gathered at a house near the campus; they played a crazy game, ate a yummy snack, and heard a short Bible message. Afterward, the Young Life leader invited youth to commit their lives to Jesus Christ. As summer approached, the leader asked me to be a Young Life counselor at Woodleaf Camp in Challenge, California. I thought the city aptly named. My hanging out with young people for five days could be compared to an agoraphobic shopping in a mall at Christmastime.

Though I had never been to camp and had no idea if stairs led up to every cabin, I got up early Tuesday morning and met the kids at Mission Viejo High School for the ten-hour bus ride. I believe this first portion of the trip settled matters once and for all. When I became a teacher, I preferred teenagers to be nowhere in sight. I had forgotten how being "bad" inspired youths to respect each other. I had forgotten how being accepted was far more critical than being oneself. I had mostly forgotten how adolescents strived to like themselves, and, as a result, often showed disdain for others. One brash girl with an ego as big as her hair sat next to me on the long ride up. For the entire drive, she held her ghetto blaster against her chest like a shield and played music incessantly at an obnoxious level. I couldn't stand her. God, always being in the business of character development, made sure she slept in my cabin. Each girl fiercely clung to her self-image and often spoke of the motivating passion by which she derived her identity—cheerleading, dance, a boyfriend, and so on. Too late, I concluded that teens were not my niche, given my mountain of insecurities. Unfortunately, the bus had no intention of leaving till the end of the week.

Arriving late afternoon, we settled in our rustic cabin, nestled alongside a lake ideal for swimming and surrounded by hundreds of acres of pine trees. Within a few hours, more stars than I had ever seen canopied us. Young Life Clubs came from all over the Los Angeles basin, a thousand teenagers from different backgrounds and races. Our busload of Orange County adolescents looked small next to the mass of youth arriving and running around with luggage and camping gear.

The first day started with silliness at breakfast. Impersonators of the Three Amigos entertained us with announcements. Afterward, everyone gathered outdoors for a team game that involved shaving cream and getting wet. In the afternoon we ended up at a mud track with go-karts. Each kid got a chance to drive the go-kart around the track while leaders hosed the dirt road to make it slippery. Cars whirred past with such speed my wheelchair shuddered. Drivers swerved onto a curved wall, apparently defying the laws of gravity, almost sure to tip over. With such little traction, they would often slide off and spin out of control. It looked dangerous, and with all my heart, I wanted in on the fun.

After ten years, my wheelchair no longer hindered me from traveling and enjoying the outdoors. But this struck me as different. Go-karts were unsafe. How could I dare do something jarring and bumpy when my bones broke so easily? I watched intently. The force of the six-horsepower engine shook both vehicle and driver. The ride would be rough. Cars careening off the bend sometimes spun and abruptly halted—it could give a person whiplash—or a broken neck. Still, I observed, fascinated, assessing the risk. Our turn at the track came to an end. Every teen and counselor had gone for a spin. The car sat empty before of me. Taunting me. Daring me. I got in—heart thumping as though to the beat of death metal. Visions of being carried out on a stretcher by paramedics had kept me paralyzed for an hour. Now I strapped myself into a go-kart, taking a genuine Mr. Toad's Wild Ride.

Its vibrating engine rattled my body. The flag waved me off. Swerving to the right and then to the left, the car slid along the track. Skidding into the curved wall, I hung perpendicular to the ground. Instinctively, I tightened my hands on the wheel in a moment of panic as the cart pulled away from the curved turn and floated in the air. *Oh no! Will I flip?* I landed with a hard thud. My body jerked in a tailspin with mud flying everywhere. Like Mario Andretti winning the Indianapolis 500, I accelerated quickly and sped to the finish line. With a rush of exhilaration, after conquering my qualms and remaining in one piece, I exited the vehicle out of breath and laughing. I had overcome.

That night, the girls and I talked into the wee hours, and I heard stories about their struggles. We laughed and cried and prayed together. I even softened toward Ghetto Blaster Girl.

On the second morning, fun continued with the Three Amigos and more hilarious games. For the main event of the day, we went to a ropes course.

Before I saw her, the camper's screams echoed through the forest. We came to a clearing where a group from Los Angeles traversed a series of obstacles up in the trees. A tall, lanky girl, standing sideways on a single tightrope, wobbled precariously and clutched the support rope in front of her. Tears of panic wet her cheeks. She pleaded, "Let me down! I'm scared!"

Climbers stacked up behind her, stalled by the roadblock.

Even from our distance so far below, I could see her body tremble. No attention-getting drama instigated this holdup. Only hysterics. We pulled for her, willed courage into her, and probably sent up a few prayers, too. Most remained silent; others shouted, "You can do this, Shanna!" Shanna inched along a few steps and then grabbed onto the rope hooked to the belt at her waist. Since it offered no support, she dangled upside down in midair about fifty feet above the ground, flailing frantically, and screaming as if death imminent.

"Grab the rope in front of you!" yelled the guide. It seemed as if she didn't hear. "Shanna! Shanna, listen to me. Grab the rope. You can do this."

Reaching out a tentative hand, she grasped the line, pulling herself upright again.

The guide's calm voice continued to nudge her along. "You can do it. Only a little farther now."

Having found her foothold, she slid along the taut rope and climbed a rickety ladder to the last hurdle—a platform at the top of a tree. About four feet away from her perch, a metal bar dangled from a tree limb. She had to jump out and seize the bar while the guide held onto her lifeline, keeping her from crashing to the ground. My heart went out to the inner-city youth more comfortable walking the streets of LA than lodged in this tree. Watching Shanna combat the ropes course emphasized to me that this afternoon entertainment posed more of a threat than go-karts. What if the guy holding her lost his grip?

Shanna clung to the platform for a good thirty minutes, shaking and crying. She begged for rescue. Instead, the guide continued to encourage her, "I've got you, Shanna. You can do this. Trust me." Finally, with all the bravery she could muster, Shanna made the leap, clutched the bar, and floated gently to the ground, held firmly and safely by the Jesus-figure guide.

Everyone cheered. Girlfriends flocked to hug her, while Shanna raised her arms in a hallelujah. With the ropes course freed up for the next group, our turn arrived. As my girls ascended the gangway, a crazy idea took hold. *Can I do this?* And with temptation, followed the far more logical feelings of apprehension. *I would be nuts to do this!* Though I waffled between desire and danger, the longer I watched, the more determined I became to reach past my limits and confront the voice that always said, "You will break a bone." I wanted to live. And, yes, I even wanted to do something risky. "Give me a harness," I told the assistant.

Because of my broken hip, my fractured femur, and the pain I felt from standing, I did not know whether I could make it. I worried, *What if my legs start killing me? Will this moment of independence result in months of anguish with twinges of pain in my hip? Worse yet, will I end up back in a body cast?* With each step up the log to the ropes course, I wrestled.

Before reaching the first obstacle, my legs already throbbed. *If I could just sit down and rest...*I looked for a branch or something to support my weight. Then my legs trembled involuntarily signally they would soon collapse. In desperation I leaned back into the harness, which formed a kind of sling. Relief came immediately. *Thank God! I can rest in the harness when I get tired. Maybe I can go farther.*

After my legs stopped shaking, I proceeded ahead past the log onto the ropes, taking frequent rests in my makeshift swing. I navigated each new section, designed to create increasing difficulty for the climber. By the time I'd progressed to the last obstacle, resting in my harness would not reenergize my quivering legs. But I had to finish. Forging ahead to the most arduous hurdle, balancing on a single tightrope, I stepped out.

Immediately, the twine slipped out from under me. Now facedown, I swung back and forth, my stomach in my throat. *You can do this Lynn! Just a little farther. Grab the rope. You're okay!* I swayed, gazing upside down at spectators below. My legs appreciated the rest. Grasping the line attached to my belt, I pulled myself upright, steadied my feet onto the wobbly cord, and turtled along the swaying rope until I arrived at the final platform.

Though the course had been tricky, I recognized the foolishness of jumping out to the bar. The inevitable, sudden jerk of the rope on my falling body could crack the screws holding together my weak hip. I recognized the need to draw the line. Instead, I asked the guide to lower me to the ground.

Like in the film *Rocky*, when Rocky Balboa finishes his training on the steps of the Philadelphia Museum of Art, I danced around in my chair—twirling a victory dance. Perhaps I was adapting to teens; maybe they were getting used to me. Woodleaf seemed like the most fun I'd ever had—up there with scuba diving.

On the third day, the camp leaders sent us to the zip line. The zip line could have potentially been the most exciting stunt of the weekend; for me, it looked like suicide. A steel cable stretched over the lake—one end anchored underwater near shore, on the opposite side of the pond, the other end connected to a high tower built on a hill. Enthusiasts ascended the slope and climbed up the lookout. Then, strapping themselves into a harness, they zoomed at forty miles per hour between trees and over the lake, splashing into the water below.

I watched. Some kids landed smoothly; others rolled on the surface like a bowling ball. I knew my body couldn't do that. *It would be insane for me to attempt this.* I sat all day, watching youth play. As the hours passed on our last day at Woodleaf, I made up my mind to do the craziest stunt of all.

I circled the lake, leaving my wheelchair behind when the rocks became boulders and the pathway inaccessible. My legs quivered from strain. Muscles burned. I stopped every few feet to rest. Exhausted but

121

determined, I hauled myself up the ladder. Now that I had arrived and stood peering over the glassy lake from the tower's great height, I felt no sense of accomplishment, only terror. *Oh God! What have I done? This is stupid!* But I couldn't make the trek back. Instead, I prayed for mercy.

I didn't linger. I leaped.

In those few seconds of recklessness, rushing through a blur of trees, I worried. *Will the water feel like cement when I land? Will I tumble around like bramble in the desert and break my back?* The lake came up fast. I closed my eyes, dreading the impact.

Then nothing. With a smoothness entirely anticlimactic, I landed in the water, gliding to a stop.

I never went on the zip line again.

In time, I saw that the obstacles I overcame provided object lessons for how to confront the future. My face-off with fear in Challenge, California, established steel bolts in the rock face I climbed, creating the capacity to go higher. Now I knew, when fear taunted me and attempted to paralyze me, I could still go on. Surmounting physical hurdles did not comprise my only achievement. It was the joy I found on the other side of fear: the late-night laughter with teens, the love the girls had for me, and the positive influence I had in their lives.

I was only twenty-seven when I visited Woodleaf, but in the years that followed, I endured many uncertain moments as I entered student teaching, interviewed for jobs, stepped out into new areas of ministry, squeezed through financial losses, underwent more corrective surgeries, traveled foreign countries, and preached before congregations. The go-kart, the ropes course, and the zip line taught me that fear would no longer dictate my life.

Now and then, an admiring friend says, "Lynn, you are so brave. I am amazed at what you do."

I have to smile with the secret knowledge that I haven't always been courageous. I recall how an appropriate caution to protect myself from breaking bones, created unnecessary fears of all kinds, trapping me in a smaller life. And I remember tears pouring down my cheeks as I cried out to God, with the faith of a pea, "Lord, please help me overcome the fear!"

Within a month of my conquest at Woodleaf, I met my first test when my support system disappeared. After three years, the church that had welcomed me after I left Chet suddenly closed its doors.

IT HAPPENED ON MY first day teaching the third-grade Sunday school class, but the morning had only just got under way when a woman rushed in the door, irritated. "Where's my daughter? We're leaving."

I sat in my chair near the chalkboard. "Is everything okay?"

She searched the room and then grabbed her daughter's arm, almost dragging her to the door. "They just closed the church, so we're going."

I assumed she misspoke. "You mean the service is already over?"

"No. I left because the pastor is telling everyone that they won't be meeting anymore."

"You mean the church is shutting down? It's ending forever?"

"Yes."

God had warned me, after all. Earlier that summer on a Sunday morning during worship, I had an awareness the church I loved would not be around much longer. I'd discussed my concern with some friend but they had talked me out of it.

I'd desperately wanted to believe them. Instead of receiving God's warning, I had thrown myself into building the church community, doing what I could to keep it from going out of business. Each week after the service, I'd gathered young adults to join me for lunch, making sure everyone had felt welcome.

Rather than being ready for change, the loss of my church hit me hard. My community of friends soon scattered.

After that morning, I thought I never wanted to step into a Vineyard church again, and I searched out congregations all over my city. Nothing fit. I went to one gathering, and the people acted unfriendly. Another seemed more focused on pointing out sinfulness than God's power to transform; it didn't feel balanced. So, I started the credential program at UCI and worked hard in my methods classes, even while my support system crumbled to pieces. I grieved the loss. While I searched for a new community of faith, I came to understand that my relationship with God would endure transitions and a big upheaval. He didn't disappear or even seem more distant.

My friends began to make their way into churches all over south Orange County. After several months of visiting various congregations without finding a place to land, I finally caved in and followed one of my old friends, Susan Blackburn, to the Vineyard Christian Fellowship in Mission Viejo. I'd first met Susan three years earlier. She had shown up at my parents' house to attend the home group in our game room. On that first night, when I'd opened the door to welcome her in, she'd handed me a package of toilet paper, saying, "Here, you will probably need this." Considering the fifty people packed into the room upstairs, I had laughed at the humor. Then one day I'd heard a knock at the door. Susan had popped by to say hello and she'd stayed for dinner. I am not sure if Susan adopted me or my family took her in. But after that, she could drop by anytime.

And so because of Susan, one Sunday morning in January 1989, I stepped into Eddie Piorek's church. God's overwhelming presence welcomed me home.

After the sermon, Eddie invited people to receive prayer. That's when I got an unexpected shock. That morning, the ministry team had met before church started, to ask the Lord about those he wanted to touch and what conditions he intended to heal. I found out later that a small gathering of about five people had written down what they'd sensed from God and had given the notes to Eddie. While in prayer, Mark Lorenzo had seen a picture of someone whizzing by in a wheelchair. So after the sermon, Eddie read from the paper, "There is someone here in a wheelchair that the Father wants to touch today."

Like a deer in the headlights, I came forward to respond to the Word. Mark and the assistant pastor, Bob Tremonte, laughed and chatted with me before they prayed. Their friendliness seemed like an oasis after my desert wandering. As Bob prayed, he said, "Lynn, I see the Father putting a mantle of love upon your shoulders."

I thought of the coat of many colors the patriarch Jacob had given to his son Joseph (Genesis 37:3). I cried out to the Father silently while they blessed me, "Yes, let me know your favor more fully. I keep forgetting it. My heart is like a sieve; I can't seem to hang on to the truth for long." The warmth, sincerity, and power of their prayer settled it. I knew where I belonged.

My experience that first week accurately reflected the community. Like Mark and Bob, the people possessed a genuine friendliness and a spirituality that prioritized prayer, listening to God's voice and receiving his love. I soon came to accept the favor God did for me when he ended the old church and brought me to this new home. Each week, God revealed himself to me as a loving Father through Eddie's biblical teaching and by ministry times in which one could respond to the sermon and receive prayer. Eddie not only led the church but also preached all over the world, carrying a dynamic, healing message of the Heavenly Father's love. In this atmosphere devoted to intimately knowing God as Father, I thrived.

CHAPTER 20

The Voice of Love

BEFORE I GAVE MY life to Jesus, I contemplated the vastness of the universe and felt insignificant. Although older now and further along in my faith, I sat on the edge of my bed, debating with Jesus about it. "Lord, why do you love me so much that you would die for me? I am nobody, not able to give you anything. I don't get it!"

Right then, my four-year-old nephew, Michael, burst through my bedroom door, calling, "Aunty Lynn! Aunty Lynn!" eager to share some tidbit from his simple life.

Looking at him, with his eyes lit, swinging on my doorknob, my heart swelled with affection for his dear face. It was as if the Lord had responded to my question. "Lynn, your nephew is too young to do anything for you, but love makes him significant. That is how I feel about you."

Conversations like this didn't happen before I met God. The prayer had always gone one way, with me doing all the talking. I could never sense his heart or his voice, and I always came away empty. In my new church, where listening to God had more value, I tasted more fully a potent love potion—the voice of God. It began in little ways.

One day as I lay in bed, talking to Jesus, looking up at the ceiling, I became intensely aware of my selfishness and unbelief. As I prayed, I saw a picture in my mind of laying myself at Jesus's feet, a bunch of dented pots and burnt pans in a heap of rubble. Instantly the scene switched, and I saw a red rose planted in fertile soil growing straight and healthy. In this way, God spoke to me, "Lynn, how you see yourself is not how I see you. To me, you are lovely inside and out, rooted in good soil and growing in faith."

Where once I had a famine for his voice, now God spoke through Scripture and, in subtler ways, through pictures, impressions, and dreams. While I longed to hear far more than I did, even a morsel from God proved richer than volumes of books.

After I left Chet, because of my disastrous fleece and detour, I didn't trust myself to hear God. Also, I didn't trust God. In the immaturity of young faith, I felt mostly afraid to hear him, terrified that he would ask me to move to Africa, witness to a stranger, or sell all my possessions and join Mother Teresa in Calcutta. Now that was changing.

I accepted that God might speak in order to release a miracle. Such as the time I prayed for a woman at church, and sensed the Holy Spirit moving down her back. I asked, "Do you have back problems?"

She pointed between her shoulder blades. "Yes, I have pain in my spine, right here. It's bothered me for years."

"I think the Lord is going to heal you today," I said. And he did! After we prayed, all the pain left her back. Hearing God for big things like this seemed appropriate, but speaking into the mundane things of my life is what felt so dear.

One day, I went down to Capistrano Beach hoping to spend time with the Lord and resolve a problem I had. Leaving my wheelchair parked on the sidewalk, I took a few steps onto the sand and plopped down on a towel—not having the stamina to limp to the water's edge. Since the day had a wintery chill, I enjoyed a bit of solitude rarely found on Orange County beaches. Only a few people could be seen: a little four-year-old built a sand castle while his mom read a book. A jogger strolled by at the shoreline. Absorbed in thought, he didn't notice the larger swells of an incoming tide; a wave splashed his ankles and soaked his shoes. He made a slight course adjustment, hardly breaking stride as he continued his run westward. I sat on my beach blanket having a heart-to-heart with my Father, "God, I have nothing to wear Friday night. I can't afford something nice, but I don't want to look like a frump at this gala event. Would you help me?"

Complaints warred with prayer as I sought advice about my attire for dinner at the five-star hotel, Ritz-Carlton in Laguna Niguel. A handsome friend, Bill, had offered to rent a tux, though lack of funds dampened my enthusiasm about this near substitute to the prom I never attended. The Lord interrupted my babbling with, "Walk over there, and I will show you something."

First, I argued. Then, hobbling over to the mound of rocks and seaweed with more skepticism than faith, I looked at the ground and said, "Okay, what is it, Lord?" Hidden in the debris, shined a black-and-white shell, which reminded me of a vintage shirt with sequins buried in the recesses of my mother's closet. I could wear that!

And I did. I felt gorgeous in my regal attire. Daddy God found me a prom dress.

Though he spoke kindly and mended hurt bodies, it did not mean that his voice would not correct or direct. In fact, I believe obedience to his more trying words broadened my capacity to hear. He is more likely to speak to one who listens. One day, as I drove by Mission Viejo Mall, I briefly noticed a woman sitting at a bus stop. As I passed by I heard, "Pick her up." I found myself wrangling with the thought. *I am not going to welcome an unknown person in my car. She could be crazy.* In time, I learned that arguing with oneself over a kind action is usually a squabble with God. But I wasn't there, yet.

After resisting for a few miles, I turned my car around. When I got back to the bus stop, the poor woman no longer sat alone, but now looked harassed by a creepy-looking man. I rolled down my window and yelled, "Hey, you want a ride?"

Relief swept over her face, and she hurriedly piled into the front seat. "Thank you!" she said, taking a deep breath. Obviously the guy had given her the willies.

For a few miles, we chatted before I dropped her off. Having completed my mission by the prompting of God, I peeked up at the sky through my windshield, smiling, and said, "Lord, thanks for including me in on your rescue operation. You sure make life unpredictable."

As long as I didn't have screaming kids in the car, a drive was my Mount Mariah for hearing God's voice, especially in the beginning. I found being still in prayer much like the shackles of a body cast. God invaded my quieter moments, while I looked out over the ocean or some mountain vista or as I drove along in my car. One Sunday morning, I took the I-5 freeway and whizzed past a car pulled over by the side of the road with what looked like two men checking under the hood. Again, I heard, "Turn around!"

I debated. *I'm already running late for church. Besides, I'll miss worship altogether if I exit the freeway and return to that spot.* I said, "God, you know I am not in the habit of stopping for men. I can't imagine you asking me to do something so foolish."

Still, the Holy Spirit continued to pressure me; for a few miles, I tried to ignore him. Impossible. I pulled off the highway at the next exit and retraced my route. Back at the stalled car, I didn't see the two men I expected, but a mom and dad worriedly inspecting the engine. A carload of kids, which I could not count in my brief glance, popped their heads out of every window. Big, round, curious eyes looked at the odd lady in a wheelchair. I didn't know how I could help, but I asked, "What's wrong?"

In heavily accented English, the man answered, "We got some bad gas down in Mexico."

"You know, I might have something for that." A few months earlier, before getting my auto repaired, I had gone through the daily ritual of spraying my starter with a can of ether, now discarded somewhere in my trunk. After scrounging through clothes and schoolbooks, I pulled out the ether can. "Here, let's try this."

While he turned the ignition, I sprayed the man's starter. Immediately the engine roared to life. Minutes later, the young family waved thank-you as they slid onto the highway with the gift of an ether can to help them make it home.

I also made it to church on time.

Jesus said, "The Father loves me, so he shows me what he is doing" (John 3:35). I felt the same affirmation. Like a hose that transports water to a thirsting flower, I enjoyed God's affection for me as he flowed through me. And I always rolled away feeling God's heart for others.

God amazed me most when he spoke about the inconsequential things of my life. I will never forget when I drove down the freeway and heard—not an audible voice, but an urgent thought, like a shout, "Slow down!"

This time I didn't haggle. Though late for a hospital appointment in LA, I immediately slowed my car. Seconds later, a police officer pulled onto the freeway behind me. I laughed aloud and said, "God, though I surely deserved it, thank you for saving me from a ticket. I appreciate your mercy."

And I believe God has spoken to me in humorous ways, too. One night my friend Cathy and I visited the city of Julian during the apple-picking season. We had gone to a dinner theater and enjoyed the play *Steel Magnolias*. Afterward, we went for a drive, pulled off onto a dirt road, and parked the car. Then we set out a blanket so we could sit down and ogle the stars. October not only ushered in the apple harvest, but also we hit the time of year when we could see the Milky Way with the naked eye and observe shooting stars streaking across the sky—far surpassing the showing of *Steel Magnolias*. Inspired by the heavens above, Cathy and I prayed and wept together as we gave over to Jesus the longings of our heart. As our prayer ended, Cathy cried out into the night a heartfelt, "Jesus, we just need to hear you. We need to hear you, God."

Right then, we heard a loud, "Moooo." We nearly jumped out of our skins, and then we began laughing till we snorted. Unbeknownst to us, we had parked in the middle of a cow field. Instead of a meeting with the "divine," we called this our "bovine" encounter. Though it was a funny moment, both of us knew our prayer was heard. God has conquered me with words that had nothing to do with a fruitful ministry, and, oh, how I have enjoyed his sense of humor. His voice has romanced my heart.

WHEN I WAS LITTLE, I felt like a princess whenever I wore my favorite green dress with white polka dots. I twirled around in that dress until it billowed around me, spinning until I got dizzy. But at age eight, while I rushed to our carpool with an older boy, Tim, he turned to me and yelled, "Hurry up, fatso!" I stopped and stared at him as if his words had thrown mud on my green polka-dot dress.

Because of my more sedentary lifestyle, Grandma Daughberger worried about my weight. In my hearing, she often mentioned her concern to Mom. Now Tim had called me fatso. The lie took root. I thought, *Oh, no. It's true. I am fat, and ugly as well.* The two words seemed synonymous.

Pictures of myself at eight don't show me as heavy, but I believed the boy's comment. Now that I wrestled with my weight as an adult, I could have easily lived out ugly. With extraordinary zeal, God attacked my negative self-image. One night at Bible study, we broke into small groups to pray for each other.

As my friend, Steve, blessed me, I felt the warmth of God's presence. Then he said, "Lynn, the Lord wants you to know how beautiful you are to him." As he spoke, God came as close as my skin, my lungs filled with God glory, and a wave of electricity swept through my body. I had no idea what happened. Through a fog, I heard laughter from far away. The chuckling got louder—closer. A familiar voice spoke in the distance and slowly drew nearer. I recognized Steve still praying. Then I realized, the laughter came from me. With tears streaming down my face, and joy flowing through my veins, God's love washed over me.

After that night, God continued to expunge the lie of being ugly. I heard from friends and in whispers from the Holy Spirit, "Lynn, you are beautiful." Even passersby stopped me to say that I was lovely—radiant—joyful. The words varied, but in time I learned from these encounters that beauty emanates from a woman well-loved. When he spoke of my appearance with such convincing tenderness, I began to know him as a lover, one who looked at me intimately, face-to-face. And although he knew my secrets, and extra poundage, too, he delighted in me. I think we all need the voice of a lover like this. Each communication of his heart sows a seed of transformation.

At the time, I could not foresee that I would someday teach those in my church and in other congregations, to listen to God. But as I plowed ahead into my career, his voice added to the adventure and proved helpful in getting to the other side of my minefield.

CHAPTER 21

Double Whammy

IN 1987 MY BROTHER's wife, Evelyn, asked for a divorce and returned to Florida with their three kids. Within a few months, because of health reasons, she returned the children to David and gave up custody. My brother's dependence on drugs, which took a turn for the worse after Evelyn left, affected his ability to care for the kids. So refusing to have their grandchildren grow up in foster care as Dad had done, my folks stepped in to raise five-year-old Michelle; little David, who was a year and a half younger; and two-year-old Laura. When my nephew and two nieces came to live with us, I dove with enthusiasm into being an aunt. And since Bobby and Beth had three boys, Michael, Daniel, and Joel, family gatherings were often rowdy and competitive, with card games, family softball, bowling, or laser tag. Having been called to kids, I knew that wisdom dictated I teach Sunday school. But my nieces and nephews led me by the hand into a child's world. Because of them, working with young people became not only a job but also fun.

As a college student, I could not afford to take the kids to Disneyland or the zoo, so we visited city parks, and I took them roller-skating—a benefit of my already being on wheels. We flew kites and attended beach barbecues, church picnics, harvest festivals, and holiday pageants. It did my heart good to laugh and sing silly songs together. Shiny-faced kids who joyfully shouted, "Aunty Lynn's home!" and welcoming hugs that clung, or snuck in a tickle, dismantled years of child-fears.

Always in tow, they joined me at my friends' houses and played with my friends' kids. I took them to camps, and one by one, at my new church, they each went through my first-and-second-grade Sunday school class. They trailed along so often, everyone called me Aunty Lynn. Their freely given affection and need for love uniquely prepared me for the day when children would press on me all day, every day, eager for my attention—or for times when recess duty would not be a reprieve from being "on," but kids would swamp me in a playground huddle. My bold, articulate, raucous crew taught me how to arbitrate all manner of sibling fights—a tool that served me well when I hung the shingle on my classroom door. But most of all, they gave me the privilege of comforting their pains and attending to their heartaches.

As my fears dissolved, an intense compassion emerged. Yet I had trouble convincing others I could take care of children. A special program had planned to offer financial aid to cover my last two years of college, but when they heard about my ambition to be a teacher, they decided I would not be a good investment and turned me down. My caseworker said, "Typically people in wheelchairs do not become teachers. Our team believes your goal is unrealistic."

So I appealed the decision and underwent additional interviews and rigorous testing to convince them I had what it took. I got my funding. But their refusal spoke volumes. *Would people not perceive me as capable of caring for kids?* The idea had not occurred to me.

Initially in my half-day student-teaching assignment, I admired my master teacher, Mrs. Williams, especially after observing her firm, patient management of a third-grade boy who defined *boisterous*. When it came my turn to try my wings, I taught reading rotations. Mrs. Williams was not impressed. I thought, *Next time, I will do better and wow her with one of my lessons from the UCI Writing Project.*

It went well. Kids raised their hands, excited to share their similes and sensory descriptions. Forgetting about the nit-picking, Mrs. Williams jotting notes as she observed me, kids taste-tested cookies, designed advertisements, and wrote persuasive letters to their moms, trying to convince them to buy their favorite brand. But after the lesson, she said, "You need to learn that 'new' is not always what is 'best' in education."

No matter what I did, each critique got worse instead of better. As the quarter progressed, I dreaded going to school, wondering if, after all, I had made a mistake in choosing education as my profession. Like Swiss cheese, my confidence was shot full of holes.

Meanwhile, I still adjusted to life in my new church, so one Sunday morning I visited our information booth. On the table sat a brochure advertising a private elementary school in San Clemente. The mission statement on the pamphlet caught my attention, "At Orange Coast Christian School, we are building young lives."

I thought, *That's what I want to do—build young lives.* For the first time, it occurred to me that Christian school might be a good fit. The brochure inspired me to continue, despite my master teacher's unfavorable opinion. On my last day of the quarter, Mrs. Williams sat me down for a conference to inform me of my final grade. She said, "I have given you a B, but in my opinion, I have been generous." Then she read aloud to me the rest of my report card, detailing, one by one, a long list of my deficiencies.

Surely there had to be something good about me? Still hoping for a small morsel of encouragement, I asked, "Do you have anything positive you can add?"

"What can I say, Lynn? Some people are not meant to be teachers."

Years earlier God had urged me, "Feed my lambs." Had I not received such an obvious call, I would have quit right then.

One hurdle remained before I finished my credential program— completing my all-day assignment under the supervision of a classroom teacher. This experienced "master teacher" would give me increasing responsibilities throughout the quarter and then turn over her class to me for an entire week. My new master teacher, Mrs. Simons, young and vivacious, in her early thirties, had an impressive style, managing her fifth-sixth-combo class with the skill of an NFL coach.

Soon enough, mustering the bravado of jumping the zip line, I taught my first lesson—equivalent fractions. I waited to hear the criticisms that were sure to follow.

"Lynn, you handled that like a pro," she said. "You had their undivided attention, and more importantly, you kept it." Her praise overwhelmed me, and when she gave me an A, I feared I might cry. After each lesson, her compliments and high grades pieced me back together. Under her leadership, my creativity blossomed, and her classroom displayed my efforts: math mobiles dangled above each desk; at the writing center sat a treasure chest with jeweled writing prompts; peppering the table, collections of student publications. For the pièce de résistance, dangling from the ceiling around the room, each bone identified by name, hung thirty kid-sized skeletons. At the end of the quarter, Mrs. Simons wrote me an effusive recommendation, and I earned an A. I knew I hadn't drastically changed into a better teacher in the two weeks between assignments. Clearly, my previous instructor saw limits that Mrs. Simons never even noticed. Now that I needed to look for a job, I wondered if other educators would also see what I had to offer.

IN THE SPRING OF 1989, I searched for employment—my first stop, Orange Coast Christian School (OCCS) in San Clemente, California. A gray-haired woman, in a navy, collared dress sat at the front desk. Though she appeared austere, she greeted me with a friendly smile. "Hi there, what can I do for you."

"I came by to get an application and to see if you had any teaching positions available in the fall."

"Oh, that's wonderful. Just a minute." She headed off to a file drawer where she pulled out a packet. "Here you go. This has our application and gives you information about our rate of pay. Would you like me to give you a tour?"

"Sure!" My first impression of OCCS was the friendly receptionist, Nora Stewart, who I also found out did double duty as the school nurse. But my positive opinion ended there. At 4:30 in the afternoon, the place seemed more like a ghost town than a school—and without lively kids running around, it felt decidedly dreary. The dilapidated two-story building had a sad neglected air about it, and I felt slightly disappointed that the noble mission statement I read on the brochure, "We are building young lives," didn't match the dingy decor. As Nora showed me around she offered relevant bits of history. "DeLeon Abell is our principal and has been in charge for almost seventeen years now. His wife, Anna, teaches the sixth grade in here." She opened the door to show me a room with ten desks. "This is our smallest classroom," she added before continuing, "About twenty years ago, the Baptist church that owns this property decided to start a Christian elementary school...and this is our second-grade classroom." Poetry with brightly colored illustrations stapled to the bulletin board gave it a much cheerier feel. I quickly counted twenty desks.

The unappealing, lived-in appearance at OCCS might have deterred potential prospects looking for a job, but that is not what dissuaded me. Once I got back in my car and had a chance to peruse the packet, it was the low pay that squelched my enthusiasm, and I felt indignant. *I am a college graduate? I've paid good money for this education. How can they pay poverty wages?*

I decided to search elsewhere for a job.

Although I lived in Mission Viejo, I interviewed at the Moreno Valley School District, about sixty miles away. Since my sister lived there, I felt moving to the area a feasible choice. They offered me the job. My starting pay would be $26,000 a year, equivalent to making twice that in today's economy, with full medical and dental benefits included. But I loved my new church and didn't want to leave. I sent out more applications.

Meanwhile, I wrestled and prayed and fasted, seeking God's counsel, asking, "Should I move to Moreno Valley?" Though God's voice of love enriched my life, I thought it a great mystery how his words came so easily when I hardly payed attention, and when I felt desperate, he chose silence. And I couldn't quite shake the idea of working at that little Christian school. Months passed.

One night, a leader at a church meeting discussed Keith Green's book, *No Compromise*. Moved by his story of radical commitment to Christ, I said, "Jesus, I give you my offense at OCCS's low wages. I will no longer let it determine my decision." Realizing that if God called me to be a missionary in a foreign land, I would expect to earn far less and never sweat it. I added, "Just please show me which job is suited for me."

Within a week, while shoving my wheelchair in the car, it dawned on me. I longed to share about Jesus. Why wouldn't I work in a private Christian school where I got to pray with kids and teach the Bible? I decided to accept the job at OCCS and be a missionary to San Clemente, California.

One of my dearest friends, Susan Blackburn, lived down the street from OCCS. After I got hired, I moved out from my folk's place and rented a room from Susan in her home, a charming yellow cottage with white trim, situated close to the beach. From my cozy room, French doors opened onto a grassy backyard with several fruit trees and surrounding foliage.

Both of us, at the same time, finished the credential program and started our first-year teaching. I got hired on at OCCS teaching fifth grade; she taught English at Serrano Middle School in Capistrano Unified School District. Because we had much in common, each night she would sit on the floor beside my bed while I lay snuggled under my covers. Then we would debrief about our day and work through our stresses. Although I hardly slept more than six hours a night the entire school year, this nightly ritual brought me great joy and made my new life as a schoolteacher all the sweeter.

Having a home and many mutual friends, it seemed fitting to host parties at our place. From the rooftop lookout, on the Fourth of July, we watched fireworks over the water. On my birthday, Susan threw me a huge celebration. When her birthday rolled around, I threw her a surprise bash. Oh, how I enjoyed staging a fake fight with our friend, Joanne, while the three of us shopped at the grocery store. Finishing our phony argument in a huff, I said, "Please take me home. I don't want to go out anymore." Of course, hiding at home were a thousand guests, or at least enough visitors that it appeared to be a thousand in our small cottage.

Out on my own and having a career gave me the sense of having arrived into adulthood. Much like a snake shedding its skin, my past fears and grief slipped away. Now I belonged to a vibrant church community, which unlocked in me new rooms for God to dwell. After three years of college, I had achieved getting not only a job but also a life of fruitful ministry. I lived down the street from work, close to the beach, and I shared a home with one of my best friends. God had rescued me from my past horrors. He brought me through the Red Sea.

I soon settled in nicely at OCCS, and I appreciated the principal, DeLeon Abell, a man humble enough to teach and take out the trash at the same time. Not once did I ever fret about the pay. In fact, I felt a little embarrassed when I realized DeLeon's wife, Anna Abell, taught our sixth graders and did not receive a paycheck. I recognized that others thought of this as a ministry to the Lord—a kind of missionary endeavor. Perhaps that is why I never struggled with my small wages. Besides, despite the low income, I had everything I needed.

On my first day of school, my lesson plans looked like an encyclopedia as I wrote out everything I wanted to say. Soon enough, I could go a whole day without glancing at my plan book. Adding to my natural first-day jitters, I had several ominous conversations with parents and even the principal. Each one said, with slightly different wording, "This is the most troublesome class we've had in years. They are all chiefs and no Indians." *Dear God, what does that mean?*

I leaned on coworkers with more experience than I and found solace from one precious friend and prayer warrior, Judee Kreg, who had a son in my class. I owed that woman my right lung. While the challenges came like a barrage of bullets, I learned how to say no instead of getting walked on by people a third my age. And I experienced firsthand how tenacious "chiefs" can be in getting their way, which mostly meant they argued about everything. At OCCS, I taught all the subjects as well as the Bible. I had never been in a position to share with others my intimate journey with God. In the privacy of our classroom, my inner life found expression as I shared my faith. I felt liberated, able to be more myself than I had ever been before.

I was too inexperienced to teach well that first year. But even my mistakes had a humorous side. One night I dreamed I had finals at UCI, with exams and a ten-page research paper due on the same day. I awoke sweating, relieved to discover my scenario merely a nightmare. I said, "Oh God, thank you that I am not under that stress."

Then a thought, like a whisper from Jesus, intruded on my gratitude, "But, Lynn, that is what you are doing to your students."

Unaware of the possible consequences, I had organized my weekly lesson plans on two separate days. I had unwittingly assigned, all in the same week, a math test, a spelling test, a social studies assignment, a book report, and their Gettysburg Address speeches. The kids sighed in relief when I rescheduled the math test and book report.

I said to them, "The Lord must love you. He intervened with a dream just to rescue you from too much homework." Probably Judee Kreg had interceded for them in prayer.

I enjoyed my students and believed that God gave me the necessary wisdom as we tackled learning problems and relational conflicts, and even grappled with spiritual crisis. Early one morning, I arrived in my classroom to see one of my students curled into a ball on the floor, sobbing.

"Sandy, are you okay?"

She shook her head. "I want to die." Part of me wanted to laugh at the drama in her tone, but I could see her pain and this was no joke. "I don't have any friends, and the girls hate me."

A flashback to my childhood combat with cruel notes and harsh words reminded me of the fifth-grade mean-girl syndrome. At least, that is how I began to think of it. Like picking apart a knot in a string of yarn, over the next weeks, I addressed the catty instigators. And that morning I prayed for Sandy.

Some twenty years later, I ran into her at the bookstore. She said, "Remember when you found me in the classroom that morning?" I looked mystified, so she provided another tidbit. "The girls had been teasing me."

"Oh yes. You had a tough time, but I remember how you overcame."

"You know, when you wheeled through the door, I thought you were an angel. I felt like the room lit up. I wanted to kill myself that morning, but you prayed for me."

In time, I came to see that being a teacher required me to play the role of mom, counselor, pastor, and a friend. I also appreciated that not every moment was serious.

One afternoon, I got out of my wheelchair and sat on a desk, reading aloud from *Hinds' Feet on High Places*. Then, *boom!* Only the explosion was not a .357 magnum but my wheelchair tire. We all laughed, and for the remainder of the day, I wobbled around in my chair, wheeling on one rim. The story became a favorite, which the kids and I revisited and laughed about more than once.

And so my first-year days encompassed the profound and the absurd.

Then, one evening as I drove home from work, an obscure Scripture came to mind. Before Jesus faced the cross, he said, "Unless a grain of wheat falls to the ground and dies, it remains alone. But if it dies, it bears much fruit" (John 12:24).

I sensed the Spirit of God asking me, "Lynn, do you give me permission?"

I wondered what grain of wheat he referred to—what loss was he talking about? But it didn't matter. "Yes, Lord, you have my life."

Within weeks of hearing, "Will you give me permission?" the news rocked our school. The church that had hosted us for eighteen years asked OCCS to leave. Evidently, over time, though they'd shared the property, the school and church had drifted apart. OCCS became merely renters or a disconnected appendage of sorts. Unable to find another facility, the school closed, and my dream of working as a missionary to San Clemente ended. I joined the ranks of the unemployed.

On the last day of school, after the ending ceremony and sad goodbyes, I headed off to a job interview at another local Christian school. Depression hung on me like a lead vest as I sat before the principal, attempting to answer her questions. I realized too late the foolishness of trying to prove myself a worthy candidate on the day the school died, when I waved off families, students, and coworkers, and I had cried off my mascara. I did not get the job.

Months into the 1990 school year, I still had not found employment. Then, one of the few remaining Christian schools in the region hired me as a long-term sub—the fifth in a long line of in-and-out staff filling in for a teacher on medical leave. By the time I came along on October 31, an unfortunate omen perhaps, many students seemed resentful of my presence. Moreover, the church that supported the school fought over issues of Christian doctrine, a tussle that eventually culminated in a church split. Though I had to climb a flight of stairs to get to my fifth-grade classroom—a slow, laborious process while an aide hauled up my wheelchair, I didn't mind so much. It was the school's conflicts that weighed heavily on my heart and seemed to create a tense atmosphere.

For two months, I worked to reinvigorate the kids' learning and earn their parents' trust. I wished I had more experience under my belt. Progress was slow.

Then on a January night while I drove home in a light drizzle, my car hydroplaned off the greasy, wet pavement. Since it was not yet a law or my regular routine, I had forgotten to buckle my seatbelt. As my car swerved and spun around, bumping over the center divider—lurching past the oncoming traffic, I flew out of my seat and bounced around like a beach ball. The auto stopped after slamming into the guardrail, dangling over an incline, with a golf course fairway twenty feet below. My hip screamed in pain.

Soon the ambulance arrived and took me to Mission Hospital.

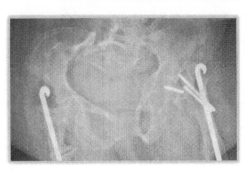 To my relief, tests showed I had not broken a bone. The rod in my left femur had only shifted and slightly loosened, giving me the sense of a fresh break to the bone that had never mended. Unable to walk, I could no longer negotiate the steps to my classroom. I lost that job, too. (Here is an x-ray of the injured area.)

Soon I moved from Susan's place on the furthermost edge of San Clemente and got my own apartment, closer to the schools where I substitute taught. For three years, I looked for a new, full-time assignment. I often qualified for a final level interview, but no matter how well the meeting went, I never got the job. Finally, one principal gave me a moment of clarity that I lacked.

141

When I first arrived for the job interview at a local elementary school, I wheeled up to the principal and reached out to shake his hand. When he saw me, his mouth visibly dropped open and his eyes widened. He exclaimed, "You are in a wheelchair!"

I smiled at him and didn't say anything, but he stood staring at me. For a good thirty seconds, I waited for him to snap out of it, close his mouth, and return my handshake. Inside, around the interview table, sat a panel of women educators, but only the principal asked questions: "How long have you been in a wheelchair? How do you write on the board? Why are you in a wheelchair?"

Completely lacking were inquiries I had received in other interviews like, "How do you teach reading?" Or, "What is your strategy for discipline?" He asked about none of these relevant issues, but he did add this one absurd comment to his interview dialogue, "You know, we have retarded people in our school." That one made me mad. A week or so later, the gentleman called to tell me I didn't have the job. "You just didn't have any experience like our other candidates."

I said, "I could tell by your questions that I would not be hired. You never got over my being in a wheelchair."

He denied it profusely. "No! That's not true! I gave you the same opportunity I gave others."

"No. You asked me why I used a wheelchair. You asked me how I could write on the board from my wheelchair and how do I manage to wheel around the classroom. You did not ask any questions about my teaching skills. Moreover, you forgot about my full-time teaching experience and three years of substituting. The truth is, you never gave me a chance."

"I am sorry." he capitulated. "You are right. I did not even consider you."

Shocked into silence by his flat-out confession, I missed the opportunity to say that which might have landed me a job: "I accept your apology, but what are you going to do about it?" But then, upon consideration, I did not want a job working for him anyway.

But now I understood. The resistance I faced, at least partly, had to do with discrimination. Though I prayed for favor and a miracle where God's power overrode man's prejudice, my hopelessness intensified. For years I had been overcoming obstacles in a wheelchair. Now I saw my biggest hindrance, not in limited access, but in the way people thought.

The issue intensified when it got even more personal.

"LYNN, I CARE ABOUT you, but I could never marry someone in a wheelchair."

I stared at Ned, shocked that he felt the need to explain and annoyed to be having this conversation in a yogurt shop. Also, it hurt. Ned and I had been friends for four years. I had met him at my previous church, and he now attended the Mission Viejo Christian Fellowship. We hung around the same crowd and went to the same church. When our dearest buds married, he took on the role of best man, and I, maid of honor. Together, with our cronies we laughed through many a game of Risk, each trying to conquer the world.

More than that, Ned enjoyed kids, and he favored me, so we often hung out together with my nieces and nephew in tow, like a little family, flying kites, shopping at Costco, enjoying a meal. I suppose we began to look like a couple. I liked his company. Given the time we spent together, I wondered if there might be more.

Ned was the third man that had joined *can't marry* and *wheelchair* in the same sentence—each word, like a nail in my coffin. I couldn't help wondering if they represented every man on the face of the earth. Although I considered them friends, I hadn't seriously entertained the idea of dating the other two men, but with Ned I did.

And what made it worse, Ned knew me. He saw up close how I played and worked—how I lived independently. How could he put *not marry* and *wheelchair* in the same sentence? I'd rather he had said, "I like you as a friend, but nothing more." Leaving out *wheelchair* would have been kinder. I needed no proof that, for men, my disability might be an obstacle. I thought back to when I was only twenty years old.

IN 1981 MY FRIEND'S boyfriend, Tommy and I were meeting up with my friends and family who already waited in line to see *ET*. I noticed, as we drove up, the queue to the popular film circled the perimeter of the theater. As I removed my wheelchair from the car, Tommy hopped out and hurriedly took off in search of his girlfriend. Quickly, I unfolded my chair, got in the seat, and took off after him, pumping the wheels to catch up. "Hey, Tommy, wait for me."

As I approached, Tommy hurried away at an even faster pace.

Amidst crowds of moviegoers standing idly, or sitting on the pavement, I maneuvered through bodies and caught up with him again. "Do you see them?" I asked, a bit out of breath.

"No," he answered shortly and surged ahead.

Each time Tommy raced forward, creating a distance between us. When he disappeared altogether, I got it: Tommy was embarrassed to be seen with me! Feelings of rejection knifed into my gut. Boys didn't beat down my door to date me, but ashamed to be seen with me? I never considered such a horror.

I KNEW OF LOVELY, healthy women seeking implants, Botox, tummy tucks, and all manner of discomfort to hold their own in a dating world that set the bar high. Already I had given up playing the game. I was four feet four inches, deformed, overweight, and in a wheelchair. The world would measure me by criteria impossible for me to surpass and the assessment of society determined the opportunities presented to me in friendships, dating, jobs, and the confidence others expressed in my abilities. These unspoken attitudes were the uphill mountains I climbed.

As I turned thirty, the issue boiled over.

Few things are as tormenting to the wanna-be-married than a girl in love. When I turned thirty, my two best friends got engaged and then married to two wonderful guys. Harder to withstand than their endless prattling about their men were the physical displays of affection between lovers when I hung out with them, or the evenings I spent alone because my buddies now had other lives.

With chums busily employed in their jobs, my days felt empty. I squeaked by financially, occasionally substitute teaching, but I worked at a different location every day and sat by myself at lunch—a stranger to them, invisible amidst a bustling crowd in the teacher's lounge.

After Ned broke the news, I grieved the death of a dream while the old resentment of being disabled jabbed at me.

CHAPTER 22

Cursed or Blessed

"DO YOU FEEL CURSED?" I could not believe my pastor, Ed Piorek, asked the question. He sure had a way of getting to the point. For the last hour, I had been telling him about my dive into depression and feelings of defeat, as though I had taken ten steps backward in my faith. My resentment burned. Life had played a cruel trick. A year had passed since the accident, I had lost my dream job, and my two best friends married. Health. Finances. Dear friends. Loneliness. The glass was not half-empty. From my angle, it turned upside down.

Eddie sat across from me in the brown overstuffed chair, listening intently, occasionally jotting notes on his yellow legal pad. He had a calmness about him. Whether he stood behind the pulpit or sat in a chair, he seemed controlled, lean, and purposeful—almost like an Olympic speed skater at the starting line. Indeed, he had been an athlete for many years, but his passion had nothing to do with the ice. His fondness leaned toward the chilly Pacific. Eddie surfed. He often told of when God called him to the ministry by saying, "You have been surfing waves, but now you are going to ride the waves of my Spirit."

His gaze pierced me. For many years, his quiet intensity had intimidated me. I always wanted to squirm. In my long association, and through meetings like I had that day, I overcame my uneasiness, seeing kindness in the man. His understanding of God's fatherly affection, coupled with his gift of counsel, made each rare appointment with Ed Piorek filled with powerful breakthrough potential. Today was the first of what turned out to be several office visits with my pastor, and in the nine years I attended his church, I was never disappointed.

Maybe I could have seen him more regularly, but I had a sense of reserve about talking to my pastor about my personal life, believing I needed to first find Jesus on my own. If I had a problem, which I could not resolve through God's Word or in prayer, I would go to my friends or my home-group leader. If all my attempts didn't work, I might even throw in a little fasting before I would pursue my final course of action, calling Eddie Piorek. Reaching such an impasse that day, I sat on the couch across from him, my chair beside me, feeling like a delinquent before the principal. "Where is God?" I complained. "Why doesn't he do something dramatic and save the day for me?"

"I know you are struggling to understand, but the Lord wants you to know, 'You are faithful.'"

What? Is that supposed to help? Annoyed, I continued venting. "Is there something wrong with me? I mean, why does God not answer my prayer for healing? Why am I single? Why can't I get a job?" I poured out my frustration, and Eddie patiently sat there—occasionally asking for clarification. With the precision of a surgeon, he uncovered my heartache.

When I paused for breath, Eddie said, "Despite all that has happened, the Lord keeps telling me, 'You are faithful.'"

I smiled and thought, That is sweet when you think about it. After God's done so much for me, harboring this anger has made me feel like a failure. It's nice to know he sees me differently. "Eddie," I said, "Why is God so near when I am hardly looking for him, but when I'm desperate he's a million miles away? He is the one who told me to go into teaching and now I can't even get a job."

Eddie did not talk as much as I. Mostly he listened—to me—and also to the Lord. "It must be confusing to you, but in the midst of your distress, God says, 'You are being faithful.'"

Am I faithful? Wow. How nice of God to see me that way given that lately, I've been miserable and whiney. I giggled and looked up at Eddie, now shy because God thought so highly of me. Then I continued, once again, asking questions, processing my frustration.

About an hour later, with all the broken pieces of my life scattered before him, he asked, "Lynn, do you feel cursed?"

You bet I do! I wanted to shout it. My story seemed tragic. Self-pity is a slippery little devil. As soon as you think you see it in yourself, it slips away—either through angry dismissal or because it seems the only logical conclusion for a disappointing life. Friends recognized my woe-is-me attitude before I did. LeAnn, my friend from the cruise, in her love and concern, and perhaps with a bit of irritation, said, "You need to stop feeling sorry for yourself."

Though accurate, her assessment didn't address the whole truth. If my confidante grew impatient at how long it took, it did not compare to my own eagerness to air out my inner world. I had hoped God would wave a magic wand over my life and I would instantly be self-assured and joyful. I found out that he did not lead me in the fastest route to my destiny but initiated a process of becoming—like the billions of years it takes for diamonds to crystalize.

In the environment of chronic pain, I fought in a war for survival. The aftermath of combat for a veteran might be PTS, but my repeated disasters resulted in PMS—poor-me syndrome. Perhaps another name for it is victim thinking, the opposite of faith, where I thought, *Why are others blessed and not me?*

People process grief in different ways. In the movie *Forrest Gump*, Forest loses the love of his life when she leaves him. He doesn't cry or pray or even try to talk about it. He puts on his sneakers and begins to run. He runs with such fervor, onlookers take notice and start to follow him. With his devotees trailing behind, he sees beautiful parts of the nation—mountain vistas and lakes so clear and still they reflect the sky above. Grieving has its beauty. Forest found that, and I discovered it when Jesus came to comfort me.

First, I had to accept that pain is painful. Before you laugh at such an insane statement, let me ask: Has anyone ever told you to just get over it? Have you ever pretended you were fine to make someone else feel better? Some people are honest to the core. Not me. I learned that "Ouch!" was not always acceptable—probably because at one time or another, the crowd following Forest Gump is *everyone*.

Some tried the shaming approach to squelch my grieving. After confiding to a friend a sad piece of my history, she wanted to console me. "Well, at least you are not blind," she said.

"Yes," I said. "It is good that I'm not blind." Obviously this "comforter" had not learned that pain is painful. Comparing my useless legs with darkened vision—the loss of Mom versus the loss of Dad—the loss of a reputation or the loss of a home—could never diminish despondency or bring relief. Losing my vision might be a worse fate, but the comparison did not cheer me up.

She could have validated my grief by saying, "I hear you. I can understand how painful that was for you." She could have empathized, "I feel sad that you went through that; I am here for you." She might have just listened attentively without saying much all. But inadvertently my friend condemned me for my distress, by pointing out what she considered an even more tragic predicament. These are the shame comforters. The idea is to make the person feel bad for articulating *ouch*.

Others tried withdrawal of affection. In teaching children, we call it "extinguishing the behavior." The idea is that if you ignore the one who is needy, then you are putting the lid on a burning skillet. Like removing oxygen from the flame, withdrawing attention will extinguish the offensive behavior. Medical personnel know all about this. When at my most needy, they often avoided my little room at the end of the hallway, and when the nurse did arrive, yesterday's kind and friendly caretaker might be curt and distant. I will never forget when the patient in the hospital bed next to mine asked me, "Why are they so mean to you? I don't get it."

Although I had noticed the situation, my roommate made me curious, so I asked for further explanation. "Why do you say that?" I asked.

She said, "After surgery, you have required much more assistance since you are unable to move. Now they seem more abrupt and unfriendly, almost as if they are punishing you."

Before this, I thought that maybe I only imagined these things. These tactics worked well on my young psyche because there is a kind of shame in being needy and plenty of reward for putting on a brave face. In contrast, the Lord valued my emotions, not allowing me to dismiss or stuff them; he joined me in sorting out my sorrows strewn around the room like dusty, discarded old garments. I wrestled with the debris, sometimes with grieving and sometimes with self-pity.

So what is the balance between grief and self-pity? I must say, it was a tender subject to my suffering soul. I read that when one of God's favorites, Elijah, seemed stuck in a poor-me attitude, God came to him gently in a whisper and not in a thundering condemnation (1 Kings 19:11–13). Of Jesus it was said, "A tender reed he does not break" (Isaiah 42:3) In my way, I had to finish jogging around the world with Forrest— till denial doors opened, till I could make peace with my losses.

Feeling sorry for myself was such an insidious trap that I tend to want to speak of it as a dangerous vice—and it is—and yet God did not go after it with a hatchet, and for that reason, I am slow to speak. He allowed me to grieve, showed me what unbelieving, self-pity looked like, and then embraced me with his presence regularly.

One summer night in 1991, I told my most recent tale of woe to my friend, Cathy, unaware of how negativity permeated my conversation. After the phone call, I felt more depressed than before our talk. I could not understand why my spirits had taken such a turn, but I did not have time to contemplate the shift. I rushed off to Marty's house.

Each Monday night, a group of us gathered together at Marty's house to make lunches for the day laborers who would be waiting at the local ballpark the next morning, hoping to get hired. We knew these men had a pretty tough time of it. Having come to the States to get work, they often crammed together into a small apartment and sent a good portion of their meager earnings back home to their families in other countries. It was a small service to them, but Rod and Jaimie, two men in my church, felt God's heart for them. They would bring the guys our lunches, pray for them, and sometime share with them about Jesus. I joined in on their efforts by making lunches. We had fine-tuned our operation down to an assembly-line approach that allowed us to prepare sixty lunches in a little over an hour. The next day Rod and Jaime delivered the goodies to the men. After we made the meal, the evening would end in a prayer time for the men needing work. That night just Rod and I stayed afterward to pray.

Rod's genuine interest in people always felt so loving. He often took time to visit with me, not seeming to be in a hurry to leave. That night he said to me, "Lynn, as we prayed I saw a picture of you. Every time you looked behind you, you had a tail that grew longer and longer."

His picture horrified me. I knew God sometimes spoke in the language of pictures to encourage and help us, but Rod's image didn't inspire courage at all. "What does that mean?"

Rod said, "I have no idea what it means."

I would not accept his answer, "Wait a second here. You can't tell me that God showed you I have a big, long lizard tail growing behind me and not explain what you think God is saying."

"Oh it wasn't like a lizard's, but a big, bushy squirrel tail. Every time you looked back, it grew."

His words hit home. For the first time, I recognized how self-pity got fed, how I helped it survive. I had earlier experienced the aftermath of having aired my gripes on the phone and the resulting heaviness that lingered. Like the squirrel tail that grew each time I looked at it, focusing on my woes created a cumbersome weight, which got harder to bear the more I chose to whine about it. Getting caught in this trap was easy, especially when pain became a constant companion, when it stabbed in the minutest of movements—lifting a glass, putting on my pants, or sitting up in a chair. With such anguish, my life got reduced, real losses occurred, and financial trials and other disappointments were harder to bear.

But this moment of clarity proved invaluable. Self-pity was a little less slippery now. It looked like complaining, a negative focus, and excuses for addictive behavior—because after all, poor me, I deserve that donut. The result was an inability to pursue dreams or sometimes just get up and out of the house. In my present season of loss, whether I justified it or faintly acknowledged the slimy sucker, my poor-me attitude threatened to steal my life away. Once again, although I had grown so much, I remained pinned down by self-pity's muscle men—

disappointment, anger, and depression.

IN EDDIE'S OFFICE, I looked at him, still waiting for the answer to his inquiry, "Do you feel cursed?"

I dried my tears. Blew my nose. I thought of all the ways God had taken care of me. Even through this season of unemployment, I had a roof over my head. One month, rent money showed up in my mailbox. When Mom and Dad sold their boat, I received their discards, an apartment full of new furniture and dishes. No one walking into my decorated home would guess that money was tight. And how many times had the Lord shown up making this wilderness journey rich with his presence?

I said, "You know, Eddie, how I feel and the truth are not always the same."

"No, Lynn. They are not."

"You know what my name means?"

He looked mystified. I paused, remembering how just the other day I had studied names in the Bible and asked God to show me what Lynn stood for. That night, my friend Sharon gave me the meaning of *Lynn*, written on a bookmark. I hadn't fully understood the significance of it till now. "Lynn means...abundantly blessed."

Eddie and I laughed at the irony.

Then Eddie said, "All the while you have talked, I keep hearing one thing, 'You are faithful.'"

If God's Word is a hammer, then Eddie hammered this point home (Jeremiah 23:29) When he said it for the fourth time, I received it. Believed it. I chuckled at it. Then, I belly laughed. *God, you are funny! I love you!*

I rolled out of Eddie's office, able to recognize that sneaky devil, self-pity. Though it now lay like a wounded animal in the middle of the road, it still had vicious claws, a few fangs, and a long, bushy tail. God saw me as full of faith. His vote of confidence inspired my next steps.

After my appointment with Eddie, I decided to look for the good in life. I came to think of my periodic substitute teaching as my vacation from work—a gift—a space of time carved out of my life where I could enjoy God and study his Word.

One issue kept robbing my joy, however, and I didn't know how to get past it. I begged and complained in prayer, reluctant to surrender to the Lord my desire for marriage, fearful that he would ignore my longing and I would forever remain single. So I poked at it continually in prayer. Like a scale with a brick weighing down one side, my obsessive focus made me unbalanced and heavy-hearted.

In this less than happy state of mind, I welcomed my favorite holiday, Christmas, at my folks. I had purchased ten presents—one for each parent, one for a sibling, Beth, since I drew her out of the hat at Thanksgiving, six others for nieces and nephews, and one for little J.J., the son of my brother Don's girlfriend. At Mom and Dad's house, the pile of gifts, already smothering the tree up to its shiny star and taking up half the living room, swallowed my measly few.

At 6:00 p.m., the dam broke. Dad played Santa, grabbing a package from the mass, he read the card, "To Laura from David." One by one, children to parents, parents to children, sibling to sibling, husband to wife, wife to husband, boyfriend to girlfriend, girlfriend to boyfriend— the combinations of the giver to receiver seemed endless.

Satin bows soared across heads of spectators to join the box for reuse next year. Colorful wrappings torn off by excited children big and small passed down the assembly line to the trash bag. One by one, the stack diminished, and our brightly lit, phony evergreen reemerged. It was now midnight.

I glanced around at my Miller clan, seated among gift debris stacked up in organized towers. The three gifts I received, two from my parents and one from a sibling, lay under the coffee table mocking me. I had no spouse. No lover. No kids. Mine had been a long night, my singleness no longer a heart-bruise, but a swelling goose egg.

Then Don drew everyone's attention. "What's this in the tree?" He reached into its bristling plastic needles and pulled out a small, red package. He read, "To Mom and Dad from Don and Dianne."

Mom and Dad stood like kids lost in a department store. They usually saved the last gift of the night for each other. In years past, Dad had given her a gas grill, fancy luggage, and a diamond ring. Mom, on Christmas Eves past, had startled Dad with a new set of golf clubs and a watch. Now Don had turned the tables.

Mom opened the box. Dad stood close beside her. She withdrew a note and a ring, and read aloud, "Dear Mom and Dad. Merry Christmas. Dianne and I got married in Las Vegas."

Don and Dianne laughed.

In unison, Mom and Dad seemed frozen, mouths open, eyes not blinking—the kind of scene when you put a movie on pause. Then, a long ten seconds passed, with the scene on pause, before they cried out, "Congratulations!" No one in our family had ever eloped before.

The news hit me like a knockout punch. I faked a smile and fled the scene as soon as possible for home, where an empty house greeted me. My tree held no remnants of Christmas cheer. I slid my opened packages under its branches, stripped off my festive attire, quickly donned my pj's, and sought refuge in sleep.

A cloudless, shining Christmas morning sneaked past my curtains to awaken me, but I could not escape my dark thoughts. For hours I wept, curled into a ball, hiccupping sobs. I lamented to God, "I am the last of my siblings to be unmarried. I don't know how to live with this, Jesus."

My family expected me to join them for lunch and afternoon fun, to play with the kids, and to compete in a game of Pinochle. I didn't call. And didn't answer the phone.

I never regretted leaving Chet, not even then. But that Christmas day, the ache for a spouse ravaged me. About 2:30 in the afternoon, eyes puffy and red, nose swollen and beyond the power of makeup to disguise, I begged God. "Please take my hopelessness. I don't know how to give it to you."

Then it happened—a shift in the atmosphere of the room. Peace walked in. I felt his presence, and in a way hard to describe, I saw his form.

Now I wept again because love poured into me. Shining rays of light deluged me. An awareness that my life was but a breath, a mere blink of an eye, could not compare to the eternity I would spend with him, lover of my soul.

In his presence, I found rest.

At about 4:00, I gathered my tissues, tossed them into the trash, and hopped in the shower, ready to join the family.

God had much more in store for me than this one moment of Christmas comfort. One would think it enough to feed me for a lifetime, but Jesus never once meant to imply, "Here, live off this for the rest of your life." Our deepening intimacy would always lead me to dependency on him, not self-reliance. Soon after the Lord began to teach me the difference between being lonely and alone. Childhood isolation in hospitals, unable to play at lunch and PE during my years at school, and time spent in a body cast left a core wound like an empty crater. I had looked for Chet to fill it. Now it consumed me. The Lord contested my perspective. It seemed sweet and silly, but from time to time, I would sense him asking me, "Lynn, are you lonely, or are you alone right now?"

After a few seconds of self-assessment, I concluded that although I was alone, I was enjoying myself. No longer would I think of aloneness and loneliness as equivalent. I found contentment in my own company and the Lord's. For the first time in my life, I sought solitary times with him, even preferred them. Hours spent on my own became "dates with Jesus" when opportunities to be romanced by him abounded in the simplest of activities. One of my favorites was a trip to the zoo. Excursions there usually meant going with my rather large family—my desire to observe animals frequently cut short by the more hurried pace of my companions. Early one morning, God awakened me with an invitation: "Let's go to the zoo today."

I UNLOADED THE SCOOTER from my van and rolled into the San Diego Zoo, unsure of what the day would hold. Did the sun shine brighter? I am not sure, but blessings seemed to abound. As I sat at the tiger exhibit, it was quite common not to see a feline anywhere in view or just to catch a glimpse of a hanging tail over the edge of the two-story platform where they slept. But today, as I gazed into the glass enclosure, the graceful spotted cat arose from his resting place in the furthermost corner of the jungle exhibit, leisurely descended the cliff and strolled over to me. He drank from the small pool of water, allowing me to marvel at his impressive size from only a few feet away. But for the glass separating us, I could reach out and scratch his ears.

Afterward I rolled over to the orangutan exhibit, where onlookers crowded the glass, making it impossible to see anything but the smaller monkeys in the treetops. Then, a thought interrupted my musings, "Go over there."

Not sure if I said it to the Lord or myself, I decided, *I am not going over there.* It seemed foolish to wheel over to the other end of the exhibit. No apes were there.

The words intruded on my thoughts again, "Go over there!" Now I recognized the Lord, and I felt a little bit like Peter when Jesus said, "Put your net on the other side of the boat." Peter reminded him what an enormous waste of time it would be since they had spent the whole night fishing without catching much. But then Peter lowered his net to please the Lord (Luke 5:4–5). Similarly, by the instruction of my "date," I wheeled my scooter to the other end of the glass.

Once I settled in my new spot far away from the throng, a woman entered the habitat carrying lunch. From my front row seat, I observed feeding time. Every critter in the enclosure gathered to the spot in front of me. Big Janae knuckle walked over to the ledge as the waitress threw the vegetarian chow over a ravine to her hungry clientele. Younger apes hurriedly grabbed what they could and began to munch. The old man of the group, Clive, gobbled fruits and veggies, yet not without a gracious hand-off to one of the babies.

Eating time soon developed into play as one ape started rolling across the grass, lazily munching on a celery leaf. One baby, so ugly it was cute, decided to annoy Clive by putting food on his head; the older male gently pushed the tot away. Not to be thwarted, the little monster then climbed on Clive's head. The show made me laugh.

After the orangutan entertainment, I circled a path just in time to catch the gorilla's chow time. What a difference, as the male gorilla guarded the food with a threatening stance and then ate his fill before letting the ladies have a turn.

My outing with the Lord hadn't ended, yet. When I got to the panda exhibit, the baby panda was celebrating his first-year birthday, so the zoo shipped in snow. I sat and watched as little Ping (or was it Ling?) played like a toddler in a wintery sandbox.

Disentangling from the fear of being single, enabled me to enjoy new experiences both rich and diverse. Not only a visit to the zoo became more fun, but also vacations with Jesus had unexpected twists that felt like arrows of love.

Most flights are decidedly dull, but that isn't the case with Jesus, for I have far too many stories to tell. Here is one of my favorites. On a long trip home from Kansas City, Missouri, I started reading the page-turner *Mountain Man*, full of action and danger, so I felt irritated when I had to stop to change airplanes in Colorado. The story told of a missionary to China who brought the gospel to remote mountainous villages where witchcraft and spiritism created fierce, life-threatening opposition. I couldn't wait to find out what happened next. After transferring flights—sitting in the aisle for the remainder of my trip home, I eagerly opened my book.

Out of the corner of my eye, I noticed the passenger next to me elbow her elderly mother seated at the window. She said, "Look what she is reading, Mom." Then she turned to me and asked, "Where are you in the book?"

"I just read about a guy named Howard coming to join the missionary in China," I answered.

Her eyes twinkled when she said with a grin, "Howard was my grandfather!" For the rest of the flight, I heard the sequel to the story after communism took over in China.

I had believed that marriage guaranteed I would never be alone. Many a widow would disagree. And what a lie—that if I never married, I would be a miserable, desolate old lady. God convicted me of leaving him out of the equation. In all our treks, Jesus taught me how to live more joyfully, whether single or not. And in his company, I experienced the delight of being loveable.

When the next Christmas loomed before me, I decided self-pity would not steal the show. The woman at the grocery store's flower department raised her brows. "You mean to tell me you want twenty-four long-stemmed roses, each individually wrapped?" When I explained my reason, she gave careful attention to each rose and even cut me a deal.

With my armload of fragrant gifts and not just a little nervousness, I rolled into the rehab center. *Will my plan be immediately thwarted?* I wheeled up to the front desk. "Excuse me, would you mind if I visited people and gave them a rose?"

"No, not at all. Just sign in here."

"Where do I go? Where do people need the most cheering up?" The three-story facility hosted active seniors on the premises and those quite ill.

"You are going to want our hospital care wing. Here is your badge. The elevators are over there." Before I could ask, she added, "Go to the third floor and turn left."

Is that all there is to it? I could be a kook. They must be desperate for visitors. I still felt apprehensive, wondering, *Will patients be irritated by my intruding on them? What will I say after I give them a rose?* I knocked on the door of the first room and called in. "Hello, anyone here? May I come in?" That is how I started my tour of the third floor.

By the twenty-fourth rose, I boldly strolled into the room and with a cheery smile said, "Hello, would you like a Christmas rose?" Always they said yes. Some were too ill to talk much; others easily chatted with the young gal in a wheelchair. Before leaving, I asked, "Would you like for me to pray for you?" Always they did.

Since I discovered an answer to my holiday doldrums, on the next Christmas, two years after Don's elopement, I bypassed the roses and brought to the center my brother David's Christmas gift to his new wife, Pam. David had asked me to keep it for him until his big reveal on Christmas Eve. With less trepidation than the previous year, I wheeled into the nursing home with a two-month-old Rottweiler named Daisy. I never made it up the elevator. For the next two hours still in the lobby of the facility, I sat and listened to Harry's stories. The whole while, he held Daisy, stroking her smooth, puppy body as she snuggled in his arms. Upon returning her to David, I feared he would find a bald spot from Harry's petting.

Early in my walk with Jesus, I relished, with utter amazement, how my invisible God drew near as I reached out to others. I not only found the God of love in secret places of service but also with those Christmas visits, I overcame the misery of self-focus. And more than that, my heart lit up like a holiday tree, radiating joy.

Being single at Christmas never bothered me again. Whether married or single, I could have joy.

CHAPTER 23

Treasures

WHY ARE JEWELS NOT found lying on the ground in plain view? Rather they are hidden in caves and fused into layers of rock, cloaked by a mountain. Similarly, in the dark days of my unemployment, underneath mounds of self-pity, I unearthed rare God treasures.

I did not welcome my heartache. Few of us do. But after my appointment with Eddie, I decided, in the midst of my troubles, I would look for God. Despair over unemployment, singleness, best friends marrying, a car crash, and financial struggles would no longer weigh me down. The grain of wheat had fallen to the ground. Now, amidst black soil, I hunted for a green sprout.

In the summer of 1993, I made plans to teach English in Phnom Penh. I figured if Orange County didn't want me, I had other options. It was an odd goal to pursue, given that Cambodia with its tropical climate and lack of sidewalks and curb cutouts would be about as accessible as North Dakota in winter.

My home-group leader and our church missions pastor, Mike Hudgins, partnered with Cambodia's native son, Sophal Ung, in planting

Christian churches throughout the country. Sophal had narrowly escaped Pol Pot's mass killings, only to be imprisoned and tortured by the Vietnamese regime that had ousted the Khmer Rouge—all because he continued to share his faith in Jesus Christ. Each Tuesday we would gather with Cambodians who drove down from Long Beach to pray for Sophal and for the gospel to reach this war-torn nation, devastated by genocide. Just one year earlier, Sophal had returned to his homeland, and almost immediately his church started to grow, then extend through church planting into more remote villages. Already, in just over a year, Sophal started twenty-one churches and an orphanage.

One learns a lot associating with a room full of believers who pray with the wild passion of those who have lost family and friends in the Killing Fields. They prayed loudly and all at the same time in a cacophony of desperation, fervency, and weeping. This was no tame prayer, checking off requests on a list. It was electric. And it jump-started my heart for a foreign people in a faraway land. Joining the team at the newly formed orphanage in Phnom Penh seemed like the best expression of what stirred in me.

I had my bags packed, had completed all my immunization shots and updated my passport. When I found Cambodian brothers to travel with, I quit my job substitute teaching and tutoring kids in writing. I swung by Mike Hudgins's house to tell him I had only to buy a plane ticket.

Noticeably standoffish, he said, "I think you should hold off on that. Let me talk with Sophal first."

In keeping the confidence of the leaders in Phnom Penh, Mike could not give me details for the delay, but as weeks passed, I did not understand, and my anger escalated. Having already purchased appropriate Cambodian attire, and having begun packing my bags, I now wondered, *Should I unpack? Should I look for a new job?*

I knew both the orphanage and church met in a three-story building, and getting around would be hard. In my estimation, my season of unemployment and isolation served as my boot camp and readied me for the obstacles I would face. But as time passed, I thought myself a fool for believing that a person in a wheelchair might find a place of ministry in Southeast Asia. *Why else would Mike not authorize my trip?*

Then, as summer approached, Mike called on the phone. "Lynn, would you be willing to tutor Makarah, Sophal's daughter this summer? Sophal is bringing her back to the States so she can begin fourth grade in the fall." He further explained that Makarah would stay in California with her older sister after Sophal's return to Cambodia. Teaching Makarah brought me solace. Not only did I get to tutor her in English, but I savored a small taste of Asian culture when visiting her home—having to remove my shoes before entering, eating spicy soup for lunch, trying to decipher meaning from Sophal's heavy accent. In a way, I did go to Cambodia to teach English. But I still felt confused, foolish, and even angry toward Mike.

Then, about mid-July, Susan's brother got married and celebrated the wedding reception around the corner from Mission San Juan Capistrano at a Spanish-style library. I had only just arrived when I ran into my old friend, Denise, who had recently returned from Cambodia. Late-afternoon light flooded the courtyard where we sat reminiscing. A two-tiered fountain gurgled nearby, and the sultry tones of a single saxophone played unobtrusively as background music. From time to time, we stopped to listen, appreciating the musician's artistry.

After catching up with Denise about her family after their move back to the States, Denise said, "We heard you planned on coming to teach English. Is that true?"

I felt embarrassed, so I laughed. "Yeah. I don't know what I was thinking. Pretty stupid idea, huh?"

"I think your moving to Phnom Penh would make a huge difference. You know, for about a year, Kirk and I prayed you would come."

"You must be kidding me?" I shook my head, perplexed. "Out of all the people you might ask to come, why would you want me? That doesn't make sense."

"So many young people have been maimed by war. They live as beggars, and many have no hope. I think you, just wheeling down the street, radiating joy as you do, would help them. Perhaps they might see what's possible for their lives." She paused and thought for a moment. "It is because you are in a wheelchair that I hoped you would come."

A dark cloud that had weighed me down lifted. As absurd as my desire had been, I now understood that perhaps it had been rooted in God. As the saxophone played, confusion slipped out the back door; peace came in with a flourish. I felt the release.

Soon after my talk with Denise, God showed through a dream that I still needed to clear the air with Mike. Within a few weeks, after making an appointment, I sat in his living room, the place of many prayer meetings and worship nights. Mike graciously listened. Discussing the events that hurt me, although uncomfortable, brought me closure and reconciliation. Though I never taught in Phnom Penh, I would, one day, team with him, in over twenty years of fruitful, full-time ministry, and I still partner with him today. I had no idea how essential these peace talks were to my future.

At the end of our meeting, Mike asked if he could pray for me. His kind prayer is long forgotten, but as he finished, Mike said, "Lynn, the Lord gave me a verse for you." He read, "'In a large house there are articles not only of gold and silver but also of wood and clay; some are for special purposes and some for common use. Those who cleanse themselves from the latter will be instruments for special purposes, made holy, useful to the Master and prepared to do any good work' (2 Timothy 2:20–21)."

Then he added, "As I prayed for you, I saw a vase like the one you might see in a kitchen. It was pretty. Then I saw another vase, an exquisite work of art, displayed in a place of honor in the home because of its value and rare beauty. God wants you to know that you could have been the nice vase in the kitchen, but the circumstances of your life have made you that masterpiece."

His words of comfort were honey. And that Mike gave me this encouragement added to its significance.

His illustration emphasized to me that I have lived in the timeless tension of the now and the not yet. I am holy and blameless, though I am being sanctified day by day. I am seated in heavenly places, as I walk by faith. I have won the prize, even as I run the race. The kingdom is within me, but I am to pray each day, "Thy kingdom come." By his stripes, I am healed, though I am still rolling around in a wheelchair. God, who stands outside of time, sees me as whole, my true self, and says that I lack nothing, even though I can't walk and I can't seem to say no to tortilla chips.

And remarkably, that which is at the top of my wish list of prayer was also, mysteriously, one of the things God most used. Not only does my disability not hinder God, but the glorious power of the kingdom is displayed most in the broken and weak places of my life. I am reminded that it was not the mighty miracles of Jesus that saved the world, but the bleeding man on a cross. As I follow my shepherd, the same holds true for me. Out of suffering, God brought forth treasures in the darkness. The act by a novice nurse that put me permanently in my chair also put me forever in God's kingdom. I had resisted responding to the gospel before then. She made me desperate enough to accept a God outside my box.

The worst became the greatest. The ugly became what most beautified. My view of God's kingdom turned upside down.

WITH CAMBODIA POSTPONED AND school districts unwilling to hire me, I decided the time had come to move on. A friend arranged an interview with a Fortune 500 software company.

Welcoming me with a smile, a young woman named Brianna introduced herself, then removed a chair at the conference table so I could roll up. I thought, *She doesn't appear shocked by my wheelchair. That's a good sign.*

She sat across from me, leaning back in her chair. Her striking appearance and general demeanor perfectly matched the office decor— upscale, beautifully put together, charming. Although she had my resume in front of her, she said, "Tell me about yourself, Lynn."

Feeling no pressure and no fear, in a pleasant exchange like one might have with a new friend over coffee, I told her of my education and teaching background. Brianna listened attentively, seemed sincerely interested, and when I made a joke, she grinned. Although I came to be evaluated by her, I decided she had my vote. Working for Brianna would be a pleasure. About fifteen minutes into the interview, I knew I had the job.

"You will be working closely with me to organize events. You will also collaborate with managers from several departments in a team effort..."

I stopped listening. Tears I could not hold back slid down my cheeks.

Brianna stopped.

I tried to explain. "I am sorry to have taken your time. You have been gracious to meet with me, but I cannot accept your offer. I know it sounds crazy, but as you described the job, I realized that I could not surrender the call on my life, which is to work with kids. God's given me an intense passion for them. I used to be terrified of children, but now..." I cried as I described what God had done, and tears trickled down Brianna's checks.

With the end of my story, the bizarre interview abruptly came to a close, but before I left, we hugged.

Afterward, Brianna told my friend she'd wanted to hire me, but I'd turned down the job. Then she'd confided, "I'm six weeks pregnant, and this morning I had decided to have an abortion. After talking to Lynn, I can't go through with it. I've decided to keep the baby. I know that's what God wants."

When my friend told me of Brianna's decision, embarrassment over wasting her time, and for being emotional, evaporated. Instead, in my failed attempt to forsake my calling, I had unearthed one of the most precious treasures of my life: Seven years later, while teaching Sunday school, a bright-eyed little boy ran into my classroom. Most first-time visitors are fearful when coming into an unfamiliar environment. Not this kid. He exuded an irresistible joy. I liked him immediately.

Then I noticed his mom following behind him—Brianna from my interview.

She said to her son, "Dylan, I want you to meet somebody who changed my life."

When he hugged me, perhaps I clung a little longer than usual. But to me, Dylan presented a picture, in miniature, of what my life's mission was all about.

Having settled the issue once and for all, I recommitted to finding a teaching job. Within just weeks of my odd interview with Brianna, I received a phone call from Dr. James Fleming, superintendent of the large Capistrano Unified School District. I felt like Joseph, getting a call to leave his prison and meet with Pharaoh.

At one of his board meetings, Dr. Fleming had been eulogizing the memory of a man who, despite his health concerns, had improved education for many children. As a result, Dr. Fleming hoped to open the door wider for people with disabilities. One of the board members had spoken up. "I know someone in your district who is in a wheelchair and can't get hired." Sheila Walsh visited the dentist office where my mother worked. For years, Mom had kept her abreast of my search for a teaching position.

Dr. Fleming took that to heart and looked up my employee file. When he called me, he said, "Lynn, I am not guaranteeing you a position, but I am setting up an interview with a panel of principals. All on your own, you have to convince them you are qualified." Then he added, "I want you to know, I would not be calling you unless your substitute file had been excellent."

I went to the meeting and enjoyed the ease with which I could answer questions—relevant ones like, "How do you develop computer literacy?"

In the fall, I began teaching fifth grade.

CHAPTER 24

Public School Teacher

I WOULD NOT DESCRIBE my return to full-time teaching as a cheery ride through Disney's It's a Small World (a ride that features dolls from all over the world singing about global peace). It felt more like Big Thunder Mountain Railroad (a Disneyland roller coaster) with bumpy twists and turns. For three years, as a substitute, I had not planned lessons or taught students for more than just a few days. When I finally opened up my fifth-grade classroom, the rusty door creaked.

Within the first few months, one parent accused me of hating her kid. My supposed abuse took the form of misspelling her daughter's name. In addition, in the mother's eyes, I maliciously withheld the reward of licorice when her child wore pink instead of red on Spirit Day. Another parent yelled at me for assigning too much homework— insisting her son be moved to another classroom; the principal obliged and transferred the boy. I felt ashamed. Then there was the mom who accused me of being satanic because I taught analytical thinking skills. I thought that last complaint slightly funny.

In time, I learned to better communicate with my students'

parents. In just a few years, another principal would assign to my class kids with problem parents, because I handled their demands with finesse. However, that first year working in a public school, I shed a few tears and worked late into the night, grading papers and preparing innovative lessons.

Ironically, I missed the long days of my more contemplative, unemployed life. Although I ached to work with kids, the administrative aspects of my profession took time to adjust to. And it hurt to have people not like me, to be told by a friend that moms complained about my deficiencies at their son's soccer game, as moms were apt to do, giving voice to their rejection and my failures.

While managing the ups and downs of work, my church life had become a trip out of this galaxy—an original Star Tours adventure (a Disney ride in a spaceship based on the Star Wars film). It began when our church leaders visited the Toronto Airport Vineyard in Canada. Christian pastors from all over the world traveled there because of an outpouring of the Holy Spirit that would in time reach every continent, bringing refreshment to believers, and a surge of church planting into unreached villages of third world nations. Weary pastors, and even burned out missionaries got reenergized in their work. There also were mighty healings, and many other manifestations of God's presence. The team came back full of excitement at the hand of God, which looked much like Acts 2 when on Pentecost the Spirit descended on one-hundred-and-twenty followers of Jesus. And I felt astonished when God willingly poured out Pentecost in our little neck of the woods just like he had up in Canada. Whereas I had become accustomed to experiencing God's presence, now he came in catalytic power to the whole congregation.

People were passed out on the floor for hours. Others would cry. It seemed to me like surges of power would blow through the room, hitting people like pins in the bowling alley. Although the presence of God brought a party atmosphere to our meetings, I didn't like it, nor did I trust it, and controversy from more conservative churches in Southern California validated my concern. Although I read the Bible, which described peculiar manifestations of God, the way my friends responded to the Holy Spirit offended me. In time, I would see the fruit in their lives—the passion for Jesus that caused them to pursue his purposes in the nations among the poor even at cost and danger to themselves. But at that time, because I did not understand, I felt scared. And because absolutely nothing happened to me, I felt despondent. Dear friends professed a life-changing God encounter, but I only spectated: the simultaneous rejections at my job and in my church only compounded the pain.

Then one Sunday night, after a Father Loves You conference that weekend, I asked Eddie Piorek to pray for me. When he did, the Holy Spirit swept through my body like a surge of electricity. I had had this happen twice before, but this time the Holy Spirit continued to wash through my body in waves for several hours. As before, I initially lost consciousness, and then I could hear laughing from what seemed like miles away. I didn't know where I was, but as awareness returned, I recognized the chuckling was my own. A phrase came to mind, "Laughter is medicine to the bones." I did not know the Scripture, but the next day I looked it up and found a similar verse in Proverbs 17:22, "A cheerful heart is good medicine, but a crushed spirit dries up the bones."

Soon after this moment, after one particularly grueling workweek with painful parent complaints, I dreaded returning to my job. In my state of despair, I agonized over being single again, never having children, and never walking. All of my life's disappointments surfaced. God had begun removing self-pity, but now I drowned in a flood of it, not sure if my faith would survive and doubly discouraged to have the struggle resurface. I turned to the support of friends attending a meeting in my home. As they prayed, I saw a vision of myself trudging through a valley of bitterness. There were skeletons strewn across the desert landscape—those who had gone before me to this bitter place and had never made it out alive. I feared *Will I die here, too?*

Desperately, I pleaded, "Oh, Father, help me. I don't know the way out of this valley of bitterness. I am so angry!"

Then the Father came. I felt his love flow from my head to my toes—warm and sweetly cleansing. I forgot where I was and who was praying for me. The arms of the Father held me. As my head nestled against his chest, I wept and poured out my heartache. Then, again, his glorious affection rippled over my body, and I laughed in his arms. That

167

night, God took away rejection and secured me in his love, giving me the ability to face onerous circumstances at work and transform them. Following this incident, with joy flowing so readily from my heart, I got the giggles while in the middle of social studies. I outright snorted, and my fifth graders erupted. In what would be one of my favorite moments of the year, for thirty minutes the entire room howled, and then laughed all the harder because no one knew what was so funny.

Struggles during my first-year teaching continued Monday through Friday, but Sundays were unfathomable. The Father healed my heart of old wounds and new ones in the most unusual touch of love I have ever known. I never fully understood how body casts affected my life, but sitting still in prayer would remind me of being in a body cast, as if crawling out of my skin or being mercilessly tickled. But during trials at work and outpourings at church, God invaded places inside no one else could ever reach. He did not take me back to traumatic moments in my past, but he deluged body memories trapped inside me. He filled up caverns of loneliness. I laughed and then I cried, not because of inner pain, but because his passion unraveled me—love pulsed through my veins.

In the past, God had often come to me gently. Now I lived with a new sense of awe because he forcefully descended in ways more profound than any other touch, and satisfied my physical, emotional, and spiritual needs. For two years, when we gathered as a church and even sometimes on my own, God's presence powerfully consoled and healed my heart. These moments with God have been his most stunning gifts in my life—heaven on earth. From such encounters, one knows it is not streets of gold or heavenly choirs or pearly gates, it is not even peace and having no more tears that are the riches of heaven—it is God himself who is the treasure of paradise. Everything else pales.

But two mysteries bewildered me. In light of such a mighty work from Almighty God, it astonished me that I did not become a big league saint like Mother Teresa. I could only conclude that God poured out his compassion on me, not for what I would give in return, but because his love is personal. I am not one in a billion; I am a daughter deeply loved. For this reason alone, he removed pain memories and the loneliness I felt in pockets of my soul and body. The other shocker is that I did not get physically healed. After electricity swept through my body, I opened my eyes and looked at my legs, still the same. How could such power have no immediate outward result? Only in time, did I see that though I did not rise and walk, what I received paved the way for other kinds of healing moments. These would come much later. Moreover, I also recognized a greater healing. After all, many a nondisabled person may have anguish because of an unhealed soul. I could be physically fit, even running marathons, and still not know the love of God or the grace of his embrace, which is a far worse state than being in a wheelchair.

That year the Lord also gave me the strength to overcome my Thunder Mountain teaching experience. I pondered, *Was my first-year teaching more challenging because of my wheelchair? Did parents find it hard to see me as competent?* I did not know. But in the spring, a coworker who had been part of the school community for many years, and my niece's teacher several years earlier, offered me an insight. We sat in the library on our break chatting. She asked, "So how do you like teaching at our school?"

I grimaced and said, "It has been far tougher than I could have imagined, but I am learning fast. I think next year will be better."

"When I heard you got hired here, I knew this community would have a hard time accepting you, Lynn. A few years ago, they signed a petition to get rid of an African American teacher who spoke out about racial issues. They considered her extreme and too brazen. I knew being in a wheelchair also made you quite different. I doubted you would have an easy time of it."

After working at the school for seven months, it had never occurred to me that I might not be the problem. I had assumed my roller-coaster ride was entirely my fault—my inexperience. I count it as the mercy of God that I did not find out until late in the year. It might have interfered with my willingness to grow and to improve. Still, my colleague gave me a broader perspective, which I appreciated. It helped my heart. And it allowed me to move on in my career—wiser and more equipped—able to make a difference in ways I had not imagined.

I SWERVED MY CAR between the two blue lines designated for disabled parking, and barely turned off the engine before hauling my wheelchair from the back and slinging my knapsack of graded papers and teacher books over the handles of my chair. A woman pulled in next to me. I didn't know her, but I knew the look—by the worn weariness on her face and the skilled way she pulled the wheelchair out of the van and lifted the child into the seat. A caregiver. More than that—a mom.

Like every mom, she had aspirations for her daughter, and while the pathway into that hopeful destiny is a mystery for all parents, this mom faced more than a maze. Having a child with special needs, she had ravines to cross and mountains to climb and no roadmap or GPS to show the way. Then she met me. Don't get me wrong. I wasn't her savior or her tour guide. My only contribution was that I had traveled a few miles ahead on a similar road.

"Excuse me," she said.

I stopped my hurried push to class.

"May I ask you a question? You are a teacher here, right?"

"Yes," I said.

"I have watched you and noticed how you get along so well. I have a daughter in a chair, and I wondered what advice you would give me in helping her live a full life like you do."

I had been teaching for four years, and although most of my world walked instead of rolled, conversations like this popped up from time to time. They didn't always happen at the school where I taught. They could just as readily happen at Wal-Mart, outside the bank, at the gas pump; well, just about anywhere. In 1996, I had begun the school year teaching second grade at Phillip Reilly Elementary School. In sharing their property with the Orange County Department of Special Education, my daily routine came under the scrutiny of this mom.

Overwhelmed by the task of condensing my life lessons into a few short phrases that would allow me to answer her question and still get to class on time, I thought quickly about my childhood and what helped me overcome. I answered, "Help your daughter be as independent as possible. Don't do everything for her. Allow her to do it for herself. You will serve her much better in the long run if she can get along without your assistance."

My hurried advice seemed woefully inadequate. I knew this

mom's concerns were too complicated for quick answers. But I thought back to my first-year teaching fifth grade and a third grader named Chris.

Chris had shaggy blond hair and a petite frame dwarfed by a wheelchair too big for him. A solemn little boy, he seemed representative of one of the many disabled students who could claim no one as a friend. He often sat alone during my recess duty, allowing us to hang out together.

One morning, I scuttled out the door of my fifth-grade portable, dodging pellets of rain and groaning because I would probably spend most of the day in damp pants. Sitting in a wheelchair made me an easy target for all types of weather. Although I didn't stand a chance, I made a dash for it, pushing along at NASCAR speed to the front office. Then I caught sight of a drenched Chris, stranded on the curb and shivering. I coasted up to him, my one hand propelling my chair forward, the other hand clutching the umbrella, and my stronger leg moving like an oar to keep my course straight. These maneuverings were second nature to me. "Chris, what are you doing sitting out here in the rain?"

"The bus driver dropped me off, but I couldn't open the door to the building. No one was around to help me."

"Okay. Well, let's get you inside." As I held the door for him, anger churned. How could an eight-year-old boy not be able to open a door? This didn't seem right at all. I said, "Hey Chris, how would you like to learn to open the door for yourself?"

Eyes widened excitedly. "Really?"

"I will meet you here on Wednesday and coach you. Deal?"

He nodded enthusiastically.

Two days later, Chris and I met after school. I taught him how to grab the door and hold it open while positioning his chair to glide through. In third grade, he studied reading comprehension and multiplication tables, but no one had taught him how to open a door. Independence was a missing ingredient for his success. Working on a school campus gave me a chance to help Chris become more capable of tackling his world, just like my father taught me to do.

To him, and to the other children I met at school also rolling through life, like the sixth grader who, impressed by my dignified teacher's status, rambled on excitedly, "How long have you been in a chair? Do you want to race? Are you married? Do you drive?" I was their glimpse into the future. She, Chris, and others, both parents and children, needed encouragement and hope. To them, my life seemed a happy ending. However, many more students not in wheelchairs entered my classroom. For them, I realized the benefit of being just a little different.

WHILE SUBSTITUTING, I GOT to know every high school, middle school, and elementary school in my area and the unique accessibility issues of each facility. Desks oddly clumped together. Kids like packing peanuts filling empty spaces cornering me in one spot for the day. And I visited modern schools built upon steep mountains and sprawling high school campuses. These disadvantages did not outweigh my conviction that being a substitute in a wheelchair probably benefited the students. I could tell by their initial responses that my leadership role and disability seemed incongruent. Weren't disabled people weak and helpless? And the fact that I am not a buff guy in a wheelchair, playing wheelchair basketball and marathoning across the country also mattered. I am, well, I am an ordinary little gal. They didn't quite know what to think about me. I am sure I confronted a few stereotypes along the way, but often by the end of the day, kids had already adjusted to my being just a little different. And I considered that a breakthrough in their lives—perhaps, as important as the day's reading and math.

Once I got hired full-time, however, I knew that having a disability now had a more profound influence. During my first-year teaching fifth grade, my principal called me into his office. He said, "Lynn, have you talked to the kids about why you are in a wheelchair."

"No. I haven't." It had not even occurred to me.

"Evidently they are all wondering about it, but don't feel they can ask. Would you mind sharing your story? It might help the class feel more comfortable."

Hmmm? Are they feeling uneasy? Fearful? "No, sir. I don't mind explaining my disability to them. Thanks for bringing it to my attention. I tend to not think of my being in a wheelchair."

So, I told my class about my bone disease. Quietly they listened, all ears as if I read numbers to a million-dollar lottery. Then they interviewed me Oprah-style, "What's it like in a body cast? How did you go to the bathroom? Is being in a wheelchair fun?" And I let them ask away.

Children are inclined to draw pictures and write love notes to

their teachers. I noticed many of my students showed an unusual interest in doodling my wheelchair. One talented third grader, to honor me with a gift, assembled a wheelchair out of construction paper. A second grader, Bita, wrote a note to me in her childlike scrawl, "I love you, Miss Miller!" With impressive skill, she colored a picture of my little body in a wheelchair. When I opened the card she had written, "You are the best teacher in the world. I have waited my whole life for a teacher like you." The humor was adorable, given she had only waited all of two years—kindergarten and first grade. I knew from their cards and notes, more than those to whom I merely subbed, these kids gained a deeper level of acceptance and respect, getting to know me beyond my most obvious accessory.

I also found that for children, a wheelchair has an irresistible allure. Kids ache to touch it, push it, and put their foot out in front of it, just to see what will happen. I think the contraption even ranks higher than a bike. Occasionally I gave in to the plea, "Miss Miller, can I push your chair?" But I soon discovered just how fleeting the attention of a second grader could be when I strolled into a bush or dove off a curb. This happened more than once. Each time I joked, "Now you can tell your friends that you push your teacher around."

They always laughed at that.

Almost every year I taught, I took one day out of the year to sit down on a bench and let kids wheel around in my chair. I got such a kick out of their joy. Boys would always try performing wheelies. Girls would take turns pushing each other.

During my first-year teaching in CUSD, on the last day of school, one significant insight came from a fifth grader, Jonathan. We both laughed as we walked out together, in our final moments of fifth grade. He said, "Miss Miller, you know what I learned by having a teacher in a wheelchair?"

"No. What, Jonathan?"

"I found out that a teacher in a wheelchair is fun!"

What a compliment, indeed. But Jonathan's praise came unexpectedly. Up to that point, I had not realized that I might be imparting to another generation a different way of seeing disabled people. His words gave me hope that one day Jonathan would hire a person in a wheelchair or choose to befriend someone a little different. Perhaps he would open his heart because I got to be a part of his life when he was only ten years old.

CHAPTER 25

My Calling

ELEVEN YEARS AFTER EARNING my teaching credential, working in private schools and public schools and teaching all ages, God did an unexpected thing in my life. I thought I would die an old-lady-schoolteacher. Not so. I am still alive and kicking, but I am no longer a schoolteacher. Unfortunately, I couldn't negotiate the old part.

As is the case with me, a new season often comes with a significant dream. Once again, God gave me a glimpse of his plan. While deep-sea fishing on a motorboat, I caught a porpoise and reeled it in. Then I awoke. The meaning seemed clear—playing on the word *porpoise*. I believed God promised me a new purpose in life. With no other plans or career aspirations, I had no idea what he meant.

Then our assistant pastor and missions pastor, Mike Hudgins, who had spoken such a powerful word to me about God making me into an exquisite work of art, felt called by God to start a new church in the region. My best friends, Stuart and Cathy Greer, decided to join Mike and Janiece. But was God calling me? I could not imagine leaving Ed Piorek's church. But I also felt the magnetic pull of Mike's zeal for reaching the region with God's love. While fasting and praying, deciding to wave off my friends if that were God's will, I sought him for wisdom—a kind that was personal, like a father counseling his daughter. Several weeks passed, other friends joined the church planting team, but I still had not heard from the Lord.

One day I sought for answers at a park overlooking Dana Point Harbor. I said, "God I need to know what you want me to do. I feel as if I have so much to give and if it doesn't get used, like fruit on a tree, it's going to wither. Please show me where I belong." While I waited, a young couple sat down on a bench beside me. Their toddler, drawn by my chair, came over to explore my odd vehicle, sticking his chubby fingers between my spokes.

"Jeremy, leave that nice lady alone. Come on over here to Mommy and Daddy." Jeremy's mom shook her head, "I am sorry for disturbing you."

But I found Jeremy adorable and dutifully watched him entertain his mom, dad, and I as he investigated my chair. Then I heard God's voice intruding like a whispered thought, "Lynn, all children are a blessing."

"Yes, Lord. I know they are," I said silently.

"A new church, like a baby, is also a blessing." Without words, I knew God called me to take care of his "new baby." Then I sensed him saying, "You will help many young couples like this one."

No one knew God changed my life while little Jeremy, bolder now, came around to play with keys dangling from my brake. I swiped them away quickly and laughed. Then, I asked his parents, "Are you from around here?"

"We're from Oklahoma." They spoke in unison. *What a cute couple!*

She explained, "My husband transferred to the marine base at Camp Pendleton. We just moved here."

I chatted with them for a bit longer, a young couple alone in California with no relatives around. I thought them lonely and yet somehow brave. So this was God's purpose, to help Mike and Janiece with the new church, to help families like this one, and to love on little Jeremy kids.

I rolled further down the path and gave my attention to the panorama of harbor boats, Baby Beach, San Clemente on the left, and a limitless ocean before me. I silently praised God. "Thank you, Lord. Thank you for showing me which way to go."

AT FIRST, I TRIED helping with the new church while teaching full-time. But within just a few years, and working eighty hours a week, I got burned out. Though my passion for sharing Jesus with children intensified, my interest in educating kids in the three R's waned.

As the world rolled into a new millennium, I entered a new era in my life. Mike hired me on as children's pastor at Vineyard Community Church, the third full-time employee to join the staff. First, he hired MaryAnn, the accountant, receptionist, and office manager. Next, he brought on Aaron, the youth pastor and maintenance man. When I first came on staff, I took on the duties of children's pastor, took over the receptionist job, and became pastor on-call for all those dropping by the church in crisis. I also copied the bulletin, sent out church-wide mailers, and designed flyers and signage. I even cleaned the classrooms, because Aaron's duties did not include cleaning tabletops and disinfecting toys. My desire to serve in the ministry made cleaning toys for a living a wish come true.

When I looked back on my journey, I could see that I had been heading in the direction of full-time church ministry for many years. Though I had long since acknowledged my call to kids, I never once foresaw God's fuller purpose, to disciple others in their faith, children of all ages, particularly his little ones.

I had come a long way since that parking lot where I sobbed in terror over face-painting kids. Because God had been my joy and strength through the ups and downs of life, I felt like Joseph, "What the enemy had meant for evil, God meant for good." (Genesis 50:20)

THE SAME YEAR I joined VCC's staff, meaningful events transpired in my family. Eleven years had passed since I'd moved out of my folk's home, my siblings much sooner than that. Even though Don lived far away in San Francisco, and the rest of us spread out all over Southern California, we continued to gather for holidays, playing cards, watching football on TV, talking all at once—just like our family times in my childhood. Nieces and nephews had grown into young adults and teens, our clan adopted new dogs, and my oldest nephew, Michael had a newborn baby. Mom and Dad had long since sold the boat and purchased a cottage up in Lake Barriessa. We all gathered together for family vacations—fishing off the pontoon boat, and zipping around the twenty-seven-mile-long lake on Sea-Doos, with water so calm you could hydroplane at sixty miles an hour, where only deer and hawks could see us explore remote inlets. I worked hard, preoccupied with our growing ministry, but I made sure to join on most of our family gatherings.

Then in 2000, I had a dream about my dad, which left me feeling deeply concerned: As we stood together outside our family home, a tornado came up the road and took a direct path toward Dad, aiming to kill him. When I rebuked it, the tornado instantly stopped, but drew so close he could reach out and touch it. Then I awoke. For several months after my dream, I felt quite burdened to pray for my dad's health, his job, and his relationship with Jesus. I even called him up and asked, "Dad, is everything okay? What's going on with you?" With uncommon forthrightness, he told me of pressures at work and changes in his company that affected him, even threatening his job security. I continued to pray for him, and often I experienced an unusual presence of the Lord while I interceded.

Then one night, the Lord visited me in another dream. I awoke with the feeling that death was imminent. But more than that, God imparted to me a sense of what it felt like to be dying—the fear—the sense of regret, and the feeling of loss. I wondered, *Am I about to die? Is someone dying tonight?* I prayed, "Jesus, I sense you are talking to me, but I don't know what you mean. Please show me." No clarity came.

Soon after this second dream, on December 19, my nephew, Daniel, celebrated his sixteenth birthday at his favorite restaurant, Joe's Crab Shack, and the whole gang gathered. Our huge family sat at two long wooden tables, in a room loud with conversation, and the occasional interruption by waiters singing to their patrons "Happy Birthday." I thought, *I guess this is Daniel's idea of a party.*

While conversation buzzed, Mom leaned in close to me and said, "Lynn, I want you to pray for your dad. He has gone to the doctor's twice because of severe heartburn. I am worried about him."

Somewhere along the way, I am not sure when, Mom began asking my sister and me to pray with her for all manner of personal concerns. Beth also worked in full-time ministry at Inland Vineyard of Corona, and over the years, Mom witnessed our sincere faith and came to have respect for our church communities. She attended Women's Teas, Christmas pageants, and my niece Michelle's baptism. She even joined in on several of our services and came just to hear me preach. Often, she bragged to her friends, "My girls are not Catholic anymore, but they are the most Christian women I know. I am so proud of them." Then she added, "If you ever need prayer, let me know. I will call them." And because Beth lived so close, she and Bobby visited Mom's friends to pray for them.

Her request to have me pray was not unusual, but because of my dreams, I felt especially concerned. "He has struggled with heartburn for years, Mom. What is different about this?"

"It's so severe and sudden," she worried aloud. "Twice while golfing he felt pain in his chest." She held her fist to her chest as if she could feel it herself, "The pain hurt so badly he had to stop playing; he thought he was having a heart attack. I rushed him to the doctor, but the doctor said it was just acid reflux and gave him a prescription for some medicine."

Dad overheard our chat, so he piped in, "Betty—I'm fine," and then he shook his head and rolled his eyes insinuating Mom had to be slightly daffy for bringing the subject up.

Later that night, my parents followed me out to my car because Dad offered to latch down my backseat. He leaned between the car seats and bent down low at an awkward angle to snap the mechanism in place. When he got up, his face looked ashen, and he breathed heavily. This was no ordinary acid reflux. In my most bossy voice, which I had fined tuned in my teaching career—the one that could silence a room of thirty-five kids, I said, "This isn't right, Mom; something is wrong. Promise me you will take him to the doctor's first thing tomorrow."

"I'm fine," Dad interjected.

Mom ignored him. "He already has an appointment for a physical at one o'clock."

"Good. Make sure he keeps it!"

The next day, while Dad took a cardiac stress test at Anaheim Medical Center, he had a heart attack.

At that very moment, when Dad lingered between life and death, a surgical resident (Dr. Kumar) happened to be walking by the door and heard the commotion. Upon seeing Dad passed out on the floor, he quickly applied a defibrillator to restart his heart.

Dad first felt the pain of electric volts hitting his heart like a sledgehammer when he came back to us. After that, he drifted in and out of consciousness.

I got a call from Mom. "Lynn, Dad has had a heart attack," Her voice got husky, "I am scared. They want to do a quadruple bypass."

"What hospital are you at? I'll come down right away."

"No, he is in ICU and needs to rest," she said. "Besides, there is nothing you can do except pray." Then she added, "Lynn, if Dr. Kumar hadn't been walking by that room at just the right time, Dad would be dead. It's like he was an angel."

Immediately, I called my friends and asked them to pray. Then, because of the dream I had about dying, I knew I needed to see Dad.

All my life, Dad kept his relationship with God private, but that morning, as I leaned over his bed, he shared more than I ever knew about him—about his secret prayers—and about his fear of dying. I wished to share with him more about Jesus; I longed to help him find greater peace. But I also felt it would be hard for him to receive from me, his youngest daughter. Besides, just as the moment came to pray with him, a nurse interrupted us and said, "I need you to leave. We have tests to run."

As I drove home, I called my friend, Jim Nelson, a pastor at our church. I figured Dad would relate well to him, so I asked, "Jim, would you come down and pray for my dad?" He arrived at the hospital within the hour, shared with my dad, led him in a prayer, and helped Dad find greater peace in his relationship with God.

Even though I felt like God had gone before me and knew of this moment in Dad's life, Mom, Beth, and I felt as if we still had to battle in prayer. Dr. Kumar had told Mom privately, "Don't let your husband get heart surgery at this hospital. They only do it several times a year. Get him to the hospital in Los Angeles where they do heart surgeries four times a day. He will have a better chance there." Mom requested a transfer, but the ICU at Los Angeles Medical Center had no available beds.

Mom, Beth, and I gathered in a holy huddle outside on a bench; fervent prayers—fierce prayers—poured from our lips. That's when I discovered the warrior in my Mom; she didn't offer weak, faithless petitions. For Mom, intercession was familiar turf. When we returned to Dad's room, we discovered a shift had occurred. A bed had opened up at the Los Angeles Medical Center.

Though relieved at this shift, we continued to call on the Lord. Then another threat arose soon after our breakthrough. When ambulance drivers came to transport Dad, one of the paramedics spoke loudly, even harshly as they began to move Dad. Immediately I started to pray, "Jesus, please shut that medic up. Dad is looking terrified." I wanted to intervene, kick the guy out, or kick him in the shin, but my years in hospitals, in this moment, only served to muzzle my voice. With no sense of how to behave—as if he wanted to agitate his patient (my dad) instead of keeping him calm, the ambulance driver continued his loud blustering. As a result, Dad became anxious, and the machines hooked to Dad's chest beeped an alarm. We watched in terror as nurses swarmed around Dad—checking vitals and shoving a pill under his tongue. I assumed they gave him nitroglycerin.

Outside Dad's room, fury pumped adrenaline through my veins. Pulling aside the head medic, I said, "I don't want your assistant anywhere near my Dad. What is wrong with him? Is the guy trying to kill him?"

"I'm sorry, ma'am. He is standing in for my partner. It's his first night. I'll talk to him right away."

"He better cut it out, or I am reporting this to your boss," I said. But after Dad's heart episode, the drivers refused to transport him, saying he wouldn't survive the trip.

Mom, Beth, and I prayed again for divine intervention, and soon afterward, Dr. Kumar came by to see how Dad was doing. We did not hear his conversation with the ambulance drivers, but they seemed to come to an agreement. Dr. Kumar came over to Mom. "They are willing to take Bob to the hospital in Los Angeles as long I go along with them."

Our angel intervened once again.

The paramedics took off with Dad and Dr. Kumar. Mom, Beth, and I immediately followed, though we sat in rush hour traffic. Dad arrived there safely.

Everything happened so quickly my brothers couldn't join us. Yet it seemed appropriate that only us girls kept vigil; we spent the night at a local motel. The next day we waited and prayed together, while Dad—at only sixty years old—had quadruple bypass surgery.

He survived it beautifully.

THOUGH THE MOVE INTO a new millennium started out rough, it also came with a renewed sense of the importance of family, of my church, of prayer, and especially, with death coming so near, the relevance of my calling to help children receive salvation. All the things I felt most passionate about came together when I joined the ministry, but I had much to learn about setting a manageable pace, and how to merge church, work, and fellowship all in one place. Without boundaries, I had a sure recipe for burnout. We started out with forty people the first week and doubled to eighty the following week. In the blessing of fast church growth increasing to over 1,200 members after only a few years, I needed a way to get refreshed.

And so I bought a little red motorized scooter that became an answer to the stress of overwork. I needed time to play. After purchasing the scooter, I adopted a miniature schnoodle from the pound. Traversing nature trails with my dog, Misty, became my favorite pastime.

In time, new leaders joined the staff. A receptionist took on phone calls and the bulletins. A maintenance crew took charge of the building. I continued as children's pastor and began teaching adult classes and leading a women's group. Since our church had grown quickly, I stayed busy organizing kid's ministry for weekend conferences, creating programs and retreats, organizing themed harvest festivals, teaching kids on Saturday nights and Sundays, and leading a volunteer team of a hundred church members in our children's ministry. I also made sure to get out in nature on my scooter.

My parent's 60th wedding anniversary, eighteen years after Dad's bypass.

Top: Mikailynn, Joel, Kyle, Nicole, Michael, Mom, Dad, Brittany, David, Don, Thomas, Kathrin. Lower: Beth, Bobby, Lynn, Daniel, Heidi. Middle: Michelle with baby, Hayden.

Chapter 26

Sneak Attacks
and Balancing Acts

MOST DAYS BEFORE BEGINNING our workday at VCC, the staff met for fifteen minutes in the sanctuary to connect up with each other and pray. One Monday morning, leftover decor remained on the stage—a Moroccan tent, plush with rich burgundy and gold velvet pillows, ornate rugs, and silk curtains. An out-of-town guest speaker had come that weekend, a missionary from Istanbul. Like kids having a campout in the backyard, our church staff lounged inside their luxurious hideout, having a brief prayer huddle, amusing and offbeat, I wanted to join in. I could not.

In order to access the stage, I had to circle around our sanctuary and wheel up a ramp, an endeavor fraught with unknown obstacles in the dark. After hunting down the light switch, inconveniently placed on a wall opposite the door, I would have to ascend the incline past a twenty-foot ladder, discarded paint buckets, and thick fabric that grabbed my front wheels and wrapped around them like an octopus on its prey. By the time I got through to the tent, our little fifteen-minute meet up would be disbanding. Having thought through my one option and dismissing it, I rolled up to the edge of the stage, deciding to contribute from my more distant location.

I sat among four hundred empty chairs, looking up at the cozy gathering, straining my ears to hear, unable to make out a word. I felt an outsider, the kind who stands in the snow, gazing through the window at friends having a Christmas party. Emotion welled up inside. Soon it would spill out on my cheeks.

As I plotted my escape, Chris, the guy who, during the kids' Easter production, resurrected out of the tomb amidst smoke from a fog machine, unfolded his lanky frame and climbed down from the stage to join me. My disintegrating ceased. *How did he know? I can't believe he left everybody to join me down here.* Smiling at him, I said, "Thanks, Chris."

He gave a one-shoulder shrug, "Of course," dismissing his gesture as nothing.

The following Sunday I shared with the kids about friends who looked like Jesus. Because, days later, Chris's kindness still comforted me.

After years of being disabled and the myriad of experiences related to that, I am stunned that I am not too old to hurt. I see myself as mature, and too professional at doing life in a wheelchair to be bothered by my restrictions. I call these seemingly inconsequential moments that slip past my defenses, sneak attacks.

After all, I am used to not feeling part of things. Most conversations are three feet above my head, and often I only catch bits and pieces. There is a disconnection when life happens at belt-buckle level. I am not offended by it, nor do I notice it most of the time. But now and then, I get a lump in my throat when a person gets down on one knee to chat with me or looks for another chair so that we can be more face-to-face.

Most of my friends tend to forget I am in a wheelchair. They park the vehicle and are walking into the store before it dawns on them, "Where's Lynn? Why is she still in the car? Oh yes, I need to get her wheelchair out of the trunk."

Forgetting I am in a chair is the best kind of compliment, and most of the time I don't have it on my radar, either. But when my friends Cathy and Stuart moved, though they are both as tall as Christmas trees and might appreciate vaulted ceilings, they preferred a downstairs place where I could come and visit. And since Cathy knows me so well, she has even scouted out foreign lands, saying, "I would not suggest traveling to Mozambique, Lynn. I think you would be frustrated. Now you could go with us to India, especially to the city where we are going. I checked it out last time we visited." Then, with a smile she might add, "But I would suggest staying at a five-star hotel."

We both laugh, because who wouldn't want to stay at a five-star hotel?

Friends and family have adjusted their plans to accommodate me, and sometimes pushed me past my limits. Carol, to the water's edge in a adaptive beach chair, so that I could stick my toes in the Pacific. Jessica, up a slope so steep I thought I would tip backward. Beth, at a hotel in Kansas City—luggage piled on the back of my chair, so heavy we did tip backward—falling in a heap together, giggling. Susan helping me across ancient cobblestones outside the Palace at Versailles where I broke down and cried because the antithesis to a stroll in a California shopping mall is rolling over a half-mile, fourteenth-century stone path in the rain. And the threesome, Susan, Elissa, and Cristina taking turns getting me over a rugged trail around a lake in Colorado so high we walked through clouds.

I learned accessibility must be a loosely held term, for it all depended on who I traveled with, how much money I had to pay for modifications, and a measure of faith. More than once, I have flown into an airport and taken a bus to pick up a rental, only to find the task took hours as attendants brought one automobile after another. Do they have a two-door? Can I get the wheelchair in by myself? Will my chair fit without destroying the leather seat? Can I reach the pedals? Can I see over the steering wheel? Can I afford it?

With one rental, for a week, I kept my eyes on the road from *under* the steering wheel. Scary. On another trip, after trying every car on the lot, while the midnight hour passed, after a long day I just wanted to end, I drove off the lot with my wheelchair packed in the trunk. For eight days, I traveled around Missouri asking strangers at each destination to take the chair out and put the chair back in. So much for being independent.

However, it did make even going to Wal-Mart an adventure. After all, how do you pick a person to say, "Excuse me. I am disabled. Would you mind getting my wheelchair out of the trunk for me?" They have to have some muscles. And they have to appear safe enough to not steal my purse or kidnap me. They also have to be nice—willing to lend a hand, not in too much of a hurry, not with a sore back, not pregnant, not a mom carrying a small child, or a guy returning a TV.

I am glad to say, all week long, no one robbed me blind, and I never had to spend the night in my car.

BUT IN LOOKING BACK over the years, despite using a manual "ultra-light-weight" chair, it is true that I burdened, and even tortured, family and friends when they offered to lend a hand in traversing my world. I will never forget the first time I visited the San Diego Zoo. Dad trucked me around the exhibits, and even though the incline must have been a 45-degree angle, he schlepped me up to the monkey habitat. He got me up there, but in a way reminiscent of a sprinter at the finish line—holding his side, sweating profusely, and sucking in air. He wanted me to enjoy the day, but I had little pleasure when he could have a heart attack. In the years since then, the zoo offered a scooter for its disabled visitors, but the cost of the convenience, forty dollars, hardly made it a gracious solution.

Then there were times when my nieces and nephews were still little and I took them to winter retreats, long after admitting each trip won tops for the most challenging weekend of my year. I had yet to attend a wheelchair-friendly site and driving kids at night on icy roads in thick fog, sleeping in a cabin of boisterous youngsters hankering for an all-nighter with their buddies, and the trappings of snow, with stairs and slippery slopes, made it hard, and sometimes scary. I would not have inconvenienced myself, except the reward always outweighed the grief.

When Michelle was only ten, I thought I would have a reprieve from the drudgery of snow when I brought her to summer camp with a handful of youth from my Sunday school. Our Vineyard had joined together with other local churches for a group event. When two burly young men said, "Don't worry, Lynn. Come with us. We'll get you around kids' camp," I expected our weeklong summer outing to be much smoother than our snow retreats. But I did not know about the dirt hill upon which the camp sat: bunkhouses at the top, meeting hall at the bottom, and archery and fire circle through wooded, bumpy paths on its outside edges. Unable to navigate the quicksand, my well-intentioned hulks took turns grunting their curses as they heaved me over to the fire pit, lunch line, and meeting room—the first day. By the second day, I had pushed them past their endurance.

So the kids took over. All week long, youth teamed up and muscled me through soft dirt, insistent that I join them for every activity.

At nighttime, I had no help when hurriedly rushing downhill to the john—push, sink in dirt, wheelie, push, sink in dirt, wheelie—all in weak moonlight, while haunted by howling coyotes and shadowy critters scurrying into the bushes. Of course, rushing is an exaggeration since one did not hurry over such obstacles even in daylight. So on night two, I settled on the cloaking abilities of a pine tree and regretted having hitched a ride to the retreat with a friend, instead of driving my own vehicle in which I could escape.

Since I had no alternatives, I prayed, "God, please rescue me. Help! This is a nightmare." Then I turned my focus toward the children. I had only brought about twenty kids from my Sunday school, but one of my little flock, Kristin, had yet to express interest in God, for whenever teaching began, Kristin tuned out. In addition, we hosted nine-year-old, Sammy from one of the other churches, overweight, with thrift-store clothes and a taunting smirk. If I were to guess, she suffered from an oppositional disorder. Her disruptions at every meeting screamed for negative attention. Already, Sammy fell in line with her role, almost as if she wore a sign around her neck that said, "Bad Girl." Then there was my Michelle, who had a rough beginning when the girl cliques proved impenetrable. And we took care of all the others: the children missing home, sick in the tummy, afraid of spiders, bored, and grouchy from late nights.

I set my mind and prayers to reaching them.

During the afternoon workshop outside at the picnic tables, kids enjoyed my interactive approach. Then I instructed them on the art of making key chains with plastic lanyard, creating a handle as thick as a man's thumb. This gave me many enjoyable one-on-one moments with youth, including Sammy, and prepared the way for me to speak into their lives at the session on our final big night.

Though I lost my independence, I observed the pleasure kids took in being my legs. I decided to forgo catching a Greyhound home. "Don't worry Miss Lynn," they said. "We will get you to archery." And although they pushed a long way through soft-dirt hills and booby trap brush they shoved and dragged and lifted me there—my heroes.

Finally, the last night arrived, and with it the monumental feat of keeping the attention of a roomful of kids. The Lord had inspired my teaching while in prayer, and so I created a humungous four-by-four-foot heart with a middle pocket. Its size captivated. I told the story of a boy named, Joel. After being bullied by older kids, he became angry and unable to forgive. Then, in kind, he cruelly teased his young brother and rebelled against his parents, lying and sneaking out. I added black tissue to the heart's opening, making it bulge. Then, I tilted it toward my audience for a view of its dark interior.

Eyes widened in respectful horror.

Then I continued Joel's story—how he came to camp and heard about Jesus, and how he asked for forgiveness and gave his life to Christ. I flung the black sin tissue around the room and replaced it with white tissue, explaining how God comes when we invite him in. After tipping the prop again, my audience saw how God had filled Joel with love— fatter than a stuffed turkey. Tears welled up in Kristin's eyes.

Then I described how goodness spilled out from Joel when he returned home: he helped his mom clean the kitchen, he played catch with his little brother, and he even did his homework without his mom first yelling at him. As I described Joel's transformation, I distributed from the heart's innards bundles of white tissue with sweetheart candy hidden inside. Sammy got the most enormous stash of all.

I laughed out loud at her shock and delight. She received the candy as I had meant it, as an arrow of love. During our ministry time, little Kristin cried and poured out her secret pain to Jesus. Sammy also wept and received prayer. Afterward, her face shone with joy like she had swallowed a moonbeam. Children throughout the room found meaning in Joel's story and asked Jesus into their hearts. I would not have traded my joy—kids touched by love, their eternal destiny shifted by a decision to say yes to Jesus, for a smoother rolling week on my home turf.

After my nieces and nephews grew up, and for the twenty years I have pastored children, I continued taking kids to winter camp. My nephew, Daniel, became a camp counselor for several years, and Michelle now helps me lead our retreats.

I have been tempted to keep my jaunts predictable because of the burden I have been to others. But as I experienced with the kids at camp, some of my favorite moments have been when I could push past limitations, because God, who slows his pace to walk with me, also provides for me along the way. This is where faith has added a whole new dimension to life in a chair.

For instance, a huge box sat in my living room for three months because I could not figure out a way to get it out to the high storage cabinet in my carport. I became so accustomed to the large, unsightly, brown box, that when people came to visit, I forgot to enlist their help. Finally, one day, I had had enough.

I prayed. Then, by faith, I shoved that box toward the front door using my wheelchair like a kind of bulldozer. I pushed it out the threshold, down the curb, across the street, and then stopped with it before the shed. As I sat there wondering what to do next, a man appeared and said, "Hey, let me help you with that." In a matter of minutes, he tucked the box away in the cabinet overhead. I am not sure if the Lord sent an angel, or the guy lived in my complex, but I thanked him for the divine intervention.

At Christmas time in 1992, I didn't have my friend Kathrin to help me set up my tree like she usually did. Since Kathrin had returned home to Switzerland, I asked God for his help. Off, I went to buy a fresh-cut evergreen.

The man at the tree farm tied my prize to the roof of my car. "You got someone to help you unload this at home?" he asked.

"No, not really."

He looked confused. "Do you need us to deliver it, then?"

I had long since discovered that money could level most of my obstacles, but I was not blessed with millions. "No, that's okay. Thanks anyway." I counted on the Lord to provide.

After pulling up to the curb outside my apartment, I clipped the ropes off the tree. The answer had not arrived. I half expected the Lord to show me some innovative way I could haul it inside. Pulling the tree down from the roof, I leaned it up against the van. "Well, Lord," I said, "You know this is it. What's next?"

Right then, my upstairs neighbor arrived. "Let me help you with that," he said. Within minutes, he lifted the Christmas tree, put it in the holder, and without losing a breath, placed it in front my sliding glass door, positioned for decorating.

I hadn't expected a neighbor to come to my rescue. But afterward, those neighbors and I became friends. I found out that his wife hailed from New Orleans and made the most delicious Cajun catfish I ever tasted. Once again, as I found in childhood taking strolls around the block with my dog, my handicap served as a bridge to get to know people.

Though I have unearthed many unexpected treasures rolling through life—benefits like friends and Cajun catfish, there is also another side to having a disability that is harder to work out. The balance between needing others and being independent is not always so precise.

I never wanted people to say I could not reach for my goals. Could not live alone. Could not teach. Could not travel. Could not lead a normal life. As a result, I became fiercely independent. Only with more self-acceptance and having less to prove, has receiving help become okay. My identity is no longer up for grabs when somebody opens the door for me. Nor does it rob my sense of strength.

Though people are willing to lend a hand, even the good ones reach their limits in situations where I leaned on them frequently. One time, while someone hung out at my house, I asked if she could change a light bulb in my ceiling.

She said, "Lynn, I am tired of you asking me to do something for you every time I come over." Her comment shocked me. I had no idea I had been so needy.

Later she called to apologize, but for a long while, I decided not to ask for assistance from anyone. But what could I do? Going for a year without light in my bathroom was ridiculous. I settled on hiring handymen and asking family for most things. Along the way, I have had

191

friends who have allowed me to lean on them when changing light bulbs or coming to get me when my wheelchair breaks down. But it is always hard on me. Always, it is a balancing act.

Every year, while I taught in public school, my sister, Beth, joined me in setting up my classroom before my new students arrived. We arranged student desks and bookshelves, hung bulletin boards, and set up learning centers. It took days, but Beth didn't mind. She is a rare breed. My brother David, the most gifted handyman I know, has come at the drop of hat—too many times to count—to rescue me from some mishap or other, installing easy-to-reach shelves in my garage and an accessible sliding shelf in my kitchen. They have allowed me to lean on them, and this is no small benefit.

Occasionally I need to ask a passerby to come to my aid, like when my minivan rolled back on my chair and trapped me under the bumper. Or when I'm at the grocery store and need canned artichokes from the top shelf, or I can't get in my car because someone parked too close to the side for me to get my wheelchair in—and, yes, I have given my keys to a stranger to back up my car for me.

People are so gracious. Many times, without my asking, they have offered to carry in, lift up, get down, put away, or take out. And though this is the case, quite often when they offer help, I thank them but refuse. Then Jesus changed my mind about this when he said, "Why won't you let me help you? Wouldn't you let a husband carry that?"

So now, if I think about it, I am more willing to say, "Sure. Thanks!" And of course, then I am more likely to hear their story and pray with them, too. Don't get me wrong, though. I love the conveniences of my modern, curb-cut-out world. I appreciate wheelchair parking and the wider lanes up to the cashier at the grocery store. Accessibility empowers my independence and allows me to be more productive and less of a burden to others.

I wish every culture had a value for creating independence. I took a trip to Europe in 2000, and while in France, I went to the Paris train station. We were told that the only wheelchair-accessible entrance was around the back of the building. I thought there would be a ramp or an extra wide doorway. Instead, I found a doorbell. When I rang the buzzer, an attendant came and pushed me around the terminal. When I needed to board the train, they didn't have a ramp like the buses in California. Instead, the attendant enrolled the help of two other stewards in carrying me, and my metal chair, onto the train. During our stay in Paris, Susan had made a reservation at a wheelchair-accessible hotel. Only when we arrived did we realize it had been defined that way because it had an elevator—one that started on the second floor. Their view of "accessible" seemed ridiculous—hauling my luggage and dragging my butt up a flight of stairs. I loved the centuries-old architecture in France and their fabulous food. I cherished touring the Louvre and Musée d'Orsay. But in France, accessibility had little to do with establishing independence.

In England, the wheelchair-accessible hotel room was also oddly named. Though my chair is smaller than most, I could not even roll through the narrow doorway to the bathroom. However, kudos to them, the elevator did start on the first floor.

So I discovered, when traveling in Europe, I must consider my intention to be independent as a loosely held concept.

ALTHOUGH I HAVE HAD to weigh, "Am I being too demanding?" with genuine need, I am aware that I must at times boldly assert my independence. Because, for some people, I am merely an obstacle, or a fire-code hazard, or someone "less than."

When I first adjusted to life in a chair, I noticed how waitresses would always seat me next to the kitchen—conveniently tucked out of the way. I got sick of clanging pots and pans, so I quickly learned to speak up and request another table. I would only enjoy a quiet meal if I boldly stated my preferences.

The situation didn't improve as the years passed, which I believe derived from either increased insensitivity or stricter fire-code laws. I am not sure which. In 2007, I bought a plane ticket and spent quite a bit of money to join my friends at a conference. When we arrived at the auditorium, I removed a chair at the end of the row and settled in next to my companions. Moments later, the usher informed me I must move to the place reserved for my wheelchair. This was not a pleasant seat in front. I had to leave my buddies and park in a vacant spot in the last row. The usher told me it would be my home for the week of the conference and that one friend could join me. This put in me quite a pickle. Given the terrible view, asking a companion to sit beside me would hardly be kind.

A year later, when I went to a popular event at a venue in Los Angeles, attendees waited in line for hours that day. Since I used a wheelchair, I waited in a line that would allow me to go in first. I long since accepted this necessity since most seats are in aisles. When the doors opened, instead of giving me a wheelchair-designated place, the staff took me, and all the other people in wheelchairs, to the uppermost level of the arena, *behind* the speaker and the band. Despite the designated wheelchair spaces throughout the auditorium, ushers forced me to sit *behind* the stage up in the rafters, better known as the nosebleed section. Many of my fellow wheelchair comrades, quietly accepted their fate without complaint. I understood their resignation, it's easier to give in, but I could not keep silent. Deeply offended, I choked back angry tears and asked the usher to relocate me. He refused. I again requested a transfer. He sent me to the head usher who said, "Listen, lady, you need to be grateful you even got a seat."

My pleas hit deaf ears. I continued to reason with them, encountering a stubbornness and pure meanness hard to recover from. Reluctantly they conceded. I moved over to a wheelchair spot near my companions. All the other disabled spectators remained behind the stage in the clouds.

Restrictions that unnecessarily isolate are a part of my life—when I go to movies, concerts, sporting events—especially if I go with my large family or more than one friend. Although these have become commonplace, I have never become accustomed to discrimination or being treated as a nonperson. I see it in the waitress who asks my friends for my food order, assuming I can't talk. I think it funny that my friends find it irritating. With an annoyed tone, they will say, "Why don't you ask her?"

Independence is a high value in my life, but sometimes I've benefited from accepting help. Other times, I have had to be fierce about being treated like everyone else, and quick to forgive.

Usually I order my life in such a way as to avoid being stuck. If the church is having a church picnic at the beach, I either do not attend or arrange for someone to help me get out to the gang. I understand the barriers and plan accordingly. But when facing unexpected roadblocks, I am grateful for the One walking with me, and the One who sometimes pushes my chair from behind. Because of him, I reach beyond my limits.

CHAPTER 27

More Power

SINCE THE CEO OF any church is actually God, our weekly staff meetings often begin with prayer and worship before diving into the work of reviewing the calendar and discussing the affairs of church life. One day, Mike—my pastor and boss, decided to ask the impossible. He said, "Let's take a few minutes this morning and thank God for the worst things in our lives."

I thought, *What is he talking about? Thank God? Are you kidding? God isn't behind my sorrows, more like the work of the devil.* I sat there wrestling with his request before deciding to lift the ten-ton prayer of gratitude. It began like a mumble, as I picked up and gathered every jewel I could find in the most grievous adversities of my life. I said, "Thank you, God, that this bone disease created in me desperation to know you. Thank you that my suffering as a child produced a ferocity about kids experiencing the love of God. Thank you for how body casts developed in me perseverance and fight. Thank you for the accident that landed me in a wheelchair, because it caused me to seek your salvation." The list went on, and while I barely eked out my praise in the beginning,

I ended it shouting victoriously. Once I started, I didn't want to stop as wave after wave of shining revelation located the buried treasure—the ways God worked all things for good in my life with *osteogenesis imperfecta.*

For many years, I had been moving from depression to joy, self-pity to hope, fear to faith, and disappointment to gratitude. Staff meeting that day brought an upgrade, though I did not conquer a land and then sit back to rest under an apple tree in idyllic bliss. No. Not a land conquered. What I am talking about is strapping a bazooka on my back and marching through life with a more effective weapon than I once had. And for that I am glad, indeed.

Gratitude is my bazooka.

God is found everywhere for those with thankful hearts. He reveals himself in fistfuls. He resides in the moments where we appreciate. Self-pity fuels offense and keeps alive the constant drama of unmet expectations. When I began looking for what God was doing instead of what he wasn't doing—I could celebrate small incremental shifts as a movement toward an eventual breakthrough—as standing in the middle of a miracle. And so, after coming into full-time ministry, I took up counting my blessings and discovered a God whose glory not only fills the whole earth but my life and every circumstance.

Although I did not believe God authored every tragedy, thanking him for the treasures mined out of my worst hardships proved powerful medicine. I found the principle also seeped into the crevices of my most difficult relationships. Searching out the good in those who have caused me heartache transformed the way I looked at my offenders, removed judgment from my heart, and delivered me from many an enemy landmine. A new lens for looking at people crystalized a life-altering antidote, much like Dorothy said when landing in Oz, "Toto, we're not in Kansas anymore."

The landscape of my life took on new colors. Ordinary, everyday prayers, always an important part of my life in God, also reflected the fruit of my newly acquired bazooka. With each remembrance in my gratitude prayers, I could still breathe in the perfume of past blessings. I found that twelve red roses may romance some, but as for me, I will take a dozen answered prayers. Its fragrance tells me I am not alone—my little life matters—I am deeply loved.

Often, I would gather with others to pray for our region, for our government, for kids in schools, for elections, and all manner of things. Mostly, I just chatted with God throughout the day. Though pressing issues prompted many of my requests, talking to God extended to every arena of life whether big or small. People think of prayer as a crapshoot; answered prayer merely a coincidence. Oh, what humor is lost when little blessings are dismissed. A God who cares about such inconsequential requests conquers my heart. Some people think of it as an organized set of petitions carefully crafted, possibly by some saint long dead. For me, prayer became like chatting with a friend over coffee, and occasionally sweetly intimate, like pillow talk with a lover. At other times, it's been slightly violent and in danger of waking up the neighbors. But it is in places of praise and thanksgiving he most inhabits. This joy gets me through storms.

One February, in 2007, I took kids up to Big Bear for a winter retreat. That first night, I desperately sought the Lord for any crumb he would throw my way. I was bone weary and sleepless. I had made it up the mountain with seventy others, most of them, kids, for our annual weekend camp. Volunteers were a little slim that year, so I scheduled myself to speak on the final night of the retreat. I also filled the job of administrator, the one who assigned cabins, the carpool organizer, a driver, and the MC. For the last week, I worked intensely and gave late nights to the event. I had been praying, asking the Lord what to teach, but being distracted by the details, I never heard from him.

The first night of camp ended, and now I lay in bed, earplugs stuffed in my ears, curled around my comfy pillow from home, but sleep eluded me. I said, "God, I need you! I feel like we have hardly connected the last few days. I don't have a clue what to talk about at our big session tomorrow night. Please, show me!"

Nothing but silence filled the cabin.

I got into my most ardent prayer position on my knees. I love intimate times with God on my knees, but my prayer can last only a few minutes because my legs hurt. Still, I got on my knees and poured out my request once again. "Jesus! Where are you? Please guide me. I feel worn out and don't have time tomorrow to work on this. I can't sleep.

Help!"

Nothing.

Getting back in my chair, I took another approach and spoke in tongues—a gift of the Holy Spirit given for moments like this one. By faith, I voiced my unknown language, but my heart remained dull, my mind uninspired, and my body bone weary. "Lord, I don't know what to do. I need you!"

The truth is, it was more than a Scripture passage I needed that night. It was a new heart and a renewed spirit. I needed *life*. But I could only focus on the fabulous, engaging sermon I had to muster.

By 3:00 a.m. I had not yet fallen asleep or found my answer. I decided that it was hopeless. I am just going to thank God and focus on the positive. "Thank you, God, that we made it up the mountain." That seemed to hit the ceiling and drizzle down the walls, as if my praise was a waste of time. "Thank you, God, that I have eyes to see. Thank you that I am not in pain today. Thank you that so many kids got to camp this year and the congregation provided scholarships." That prayer was a kite on liftoff—breezier—easier. Then I said, "Lord, I thank you for the Holy Spirit and how he lives in me."

Given my struggles, I felt new appreciation at being inhabited by a Holy God—this joining together of weakness and strength, imperfect with the perfect, earthly with the heavenly. What a wonder. I said, "Thank you that One so great hangs out with me." How many times has the Holy Spirit washed my feet, meeting me in my tears, removing my doubt and sin? "Holy Spirit how kind you are to never give up on me." Earplugs still crammed in my ears cocooned me in silence, the world shut out, but gratitude and worship flowed out of my mouth and tears streamed down my face. Into the night and the empty room, I gave my thank offering, and rejoicing overflowed like Niagara as I celebrated the gift of my beloved, indwelling Holy Spirit.

Afterward I crawled into bed and slept soundly.

When I awoke the next morning, I heard whispered mumbles from guests in the room next door. As the retreat leader, event staff had given me private sleeping quarters downstairs nearby attendees from a youth camp. *Oh my! I can eavesdrop on everything they are saying. Did they hear my ranting last night?*

Crowds of teens and leaders, packed the hall where my young campers lined up for breakfast. Wide eyes and crooked smiles greeted me. I now realized my neighbors had heard my 3:00 a.m. rejoicing. *Oh no! Shall I apologize?* Though mortified I also wanted to laugh. Instead, I pretended to be oblivious.

Though I had begun the night vigil seeking a passage of Scripture to teach, what I got was far more. I do not recall my message that next night, but I remember an eight-year-old child curled up in my lap. In a holy afterglow hovering thickly, she unloaded the pain of divorce and her dad's drug addiction and how her stepdad had an accident that paralyzed him. As kids quietly played and giggled in corners of the meeting room, she shared her heartache, and I helped her give it to Jesus. Then she whispered a prayer with me, "Jesus, come into my heart; be my Savior and fill me with your Holy Spirit."

Bouquets of answered prayer are sweet, and mountain-moving miracles are no little thing, but the promise of meeting God allures me most. It is in these places of private fellowship, when I have focused on meeting him with a grateful heart, that I receive more than a sermon; I become the message—a carrier of him. Though these moments have been bountiful, most I have forgotten. But then again, these are just ordinary, everyday prayers.

An old friend, Judy Morton, who I knew from Blaine Cook's church years earlier, began attending VCC with her husband Scott. We began working out in the gym together and taking hikes on various trails in our region. One day, Judy and I went for a walk. My little red scooter had broken, so I pushed my chair along Arroyo Vista Trail in Rancho Santa Margarita— my progress slowed while I hauled myself uphill. Judy offered to help, and I willingly accepted. Now that I had my hands free, I took a swig from my water bottle. From behind me, she chatted away while pushing me, "Why don't you get a power chair? Seems to me it would make things a lot easier."

Good question. Many others have asked it. The answer is simple really: for much of my life, walkways and bathroom stalls, homes, the dentist office, and a myriad of other locations have not been broad enough, offered wheelchair ramps, or provided a level entrance. They still don't. My lightweight, manual chair provided more mobility getting up steps and into tight spaces. It meant more access, because the bulkier power chair had less maneuverability in stores, in friends' homes, and among crowds of people.

But arms were not designed for propelling from a thick-carpeted classroom to my thick-carpeted office, over the curb at my apartment or up the step into my parents' house, or into the Laundromat, carrying a basket with my rose-print comforter and queen-sized blanket. When I lugged tubs of Harvest Festival decor across the church parking lot, set up the buffet tables, and dragged a compressor out of storage to blow up some zillion balloons, a minor injury in my arm deteriorated into a rotator cuff tear. Already swollen nerves from continually grabbing and releasing my wheels had developed into carpal tunnel syndrome in both hands, which kept me awake at night as I took on and off wrist splints, unable to decide between sweaty palms or numb fingers. Enjoying more access using my manual chair came with a cost to my body.

Using a motorized chair came with another kind of price. The twice-as-expensive, heavier power chair also required a conversion van for transporting. This took lots of cash--about $66,000 worth. In time, after rotator cuff surgery and operations on my wrists, to protect my shoulders and hands from the strain, I would purchase such a car and a power chair. And though Mike eased my burden with a gracious raise, and friends gathered funds to pay for my new power chair, I eventually had to forgo dental work, skip vacations, and acquire a second job.

Just as I adjusted to my funeral home-discard at age nine, and enjoyed the freedom it brought me, the same is true when I incorporated a power chair into my life. I still preferred my familiar manual chair at home and when ministering to kids at church, but hiking trails, the grocery store, and decorating for our Harvest Festival became a breeze when using my speedier power chair.

I have noticed people are curious when they observe my mobility in the power chair. Mostly they are confused by my independence. They sometimes wonder where my caregiver is, and will bluntly ask, "Who takes care of you." I discovered afresh that people have a limited view of disability, as the "dis" in *disabled* implies. I prefer to think of myself as "differently" abled. So I use a long-pronged grabber to get down canned tomatoes from up in the cupboard, and I store my glasses on an easy-to-reach shelf down low. So I cook without being able to see inside the frying pan on the stove and chop my veggies at eye level on the cutting board. You see—differently abled.

Having this viewpoint means, if one of those curious strangers talks to me about their disability, or that of their loved one, I will validate their grief, but I will also pray, and believe there is a way to move on. It's because I see myself not as disabled, but as differently abled. And I find that people need to hear this. People who feel loss and grief, who are stuck waiting and waiting to get their old lives back—even their old health back.

I had one such discussion with the guy who bagged my groceries. A muscular physique gave Jason the appearance of fitness and health, but he donned black wrist braces and noticeably limped when he pushed my groceries to the van. I had used similar apparatus to alleviate my carpal tunnel when I slept. Before my surgery, my hands swelled, causing a prickly sensation much like low-voltage electricity resonating in my fingers.

Jason wore his wrist splints while he worked—clearly not a minor affliction, and I felt compassion. I put my oar in the water to see where the conversation steered. "I see your braces, Jason. What's wrong with your hands?" Having my own set of unmistakable maladies gave me more leeway in asking Jason a personal, direct question about his disability. There is no written code to follow, but our mutual physical hardship gave us common ground, like when two strangers are walking their dogs, and stop to chat about their canines as if they are old friends.

"I have bad joints in my hands and knees," he replied.

"I asked because I used to wear braces like that, caused by years of propelling my wheelchair."

He bent down to peruse my power chair like one might study an alien spaceship. "You push this thing?"

I had named my little vehicle "The Tank." With it, I gouged chunks out of doorways, crushed cans, mangled shoes, and inadvertently pulled down on top of me the six-foot shelves and storage tubs in my garage. Afterward, I sat trapped, but in one piece, until a landscape guy heard my smothered cry for help. While shopping at

Kohl's, I accidentally snagged low-hanging lingerie on the toggle switch, ramming a whole rack of bras into the wall. And so at 350 pounds, I could not strong-arm my impressive "tank" anywhere. The thing was savage! "No, this thing runs with a motor," I explained, "but for years I exclusively used a manual chair."

"Oh, an old-fashioned kind." Now he understood.

I thought it cute that he believed my self-propelled chair was an archaic transport, as if a horse and buggy. He could not know that I preferred the easy maneuverability of my manual chair and the way it felt less intrusive—less chair and more me.

I had been eager to chat with Jason; little did I know he also wanted to gab with me. He said, "You know, my aunt hurt herself and can't walk very well. It's been about fifteen years now, and she hasn't been the same. She is depressed all the time." He shook his head, as if trying to dismiss a painful memory. "She used to be a mountain of a woman and so radiant. It hurts to see her sad."

Like shelved books at the library, my groceries lined the trunk. I thought, *Time to go.* Instead, I stopped to listen—and to sympathize, remembering how pain can wear away at one's soul. "Does it hurt for her to stand?" I asked.

"Yes, she has a walker, but it doesn't help. All she says is that she just wants to die. I love her so much, but..." He said no more; just gave a resigned shrug.

I knew what he had not put into words. His support couldn't bring his aunt back to the woman she once was. I touched his arm. "I'm sorry, Jason."

From time to time, I get into conversations like this—one benefit of rolling through life with a visible handicap. One woman asked if she could have my cell number so I could encourage a beloved sister in Florida who had become despondent and reclusive since having a severe accident. The woman saw something in my mobility that she wanted for her sister. She wished for more than getting her sister outside the house; she longed for her injured sibling to embrace life again. Then I met Doris. As a retired schoolteacher, she never anticipated she could be so tired, until her husband's health declined and she took on his care. She noticed me rolling into my conversion van after leaving the bank. She came over to share her story and express a longing to see her spouse more active again. We ended up praying together. She also asked for my phone number.

Jason's aunt wanted to die. Cooped up at home and clinging to the hope of walking, yet she refused to exert herself to avoid the pain. She missed out on everyday activities that made up a full life—shopping, walks under a blue sky, or coffee with a friend. What a vast world would await if she would only take a stroll on a scooter or get a power chair.

I saw the transformation in my sister-in-law's life. Pam (David's wife) had lain in bed for several years, but when I gave her an old, unused power chair someone had donated to me, she could go out to the store, and get up and make herself a sandwich. At Thanksgiving she could sit at the table, play Cranium, and slaughter us all because she is a trivia genius.

"Jason, I know Jesus can help your aunt. Would you be willing to pray with me?"

His face brightened. "Yes."

We bowed our heads in the parking lot.

HAVING A BAZOOKA AND a tank gave me more power to navigate life, but Jesus also had more in store for me. Mike believed that God wanted him to ordain his leadership team: me—the children's pastor; Robin and Ryan, who led our young adult's ministry; Brent and Erin—our youth pastors; and Paula, who led in our women's ministry. Family and friends were invited to join us for the ceremony and also for the luncheon that followed at a beautiful home overlooking the ocean in Laguna Beach. Mike and Janiece asked Ed and Janet Piorek to help officiate the ordination. It seemed appropriate that apart from my parents, all the leaders who had the most influence in my life would give me their blessing. I considered it a quadruple honor.

There in the front row sat Mom and Dad, in their seventies now. Beth and Bobby, and their son, Joel, attended. Also, my brother David came; he had just that year began attending a church in Costa Mesa. Many friends, even those that had moved on to other churches, returned to witness to God's work in my life, his calling, and to celebrate.

On the morning of January 6, 2013, the worship seemed as electric as it had the very first time I entered a Vineyard church. I thought my heart would explode at the sense of God's presence; and I could feel his smile shining on me as I worshipped with my Miller clan and my church family, too. Mike preached from the Bible about the ordination of leaders, and afterward each pastor prayed for me. Mike and Janiece had known me for twenty-three years, and their prayer reflected our long friendship. Mike called me a fighter with a heart of a marshmallow and a victorious champion. Janiece called me an amazing friend and an inspiration. They took the time to recognize and applaud my family, and the honor given them meant so much to me. Then Mike and Janiece prophesied what they saw God doing in my future, and Ed and Janet imparted to me the anointing they received from John Wimber.

Having never had a wedding or a baby shower, there have been few events like this in my life. While it felt honoring and joyful, I believe it also made a spiritual deposit that is reflected even in this account called *Dry Bones Dance Again*, and their blessing still rests on me as I continue to serve the Lord.

Chapter 28

Wired for Love

IN THE SPRING OF 2013, I took a ride in my power chair out to the hills near home and decided to stray from the cement trail, loving the sense of adventure this bumpy dirt road brought on other occasions. Before the path changed to rockier turf, I pulled over to soak in the sunshine. Up ahead, I would enter a shadowy forest and cross a shallow brook that would soon disappear when summer dried the winter runoff. Most of the wildflowers had already died, but yellow mustard plants sprinkled the green fields creating a vibrant aliveness to the landscape.

Lost in silent appreciation, I barely noticed the man who jogged past. It was not unusual to have a runner pass by. What was odd is that he turned around and doubled back. "Excuse me. I am David Whiting, a writer for the *Orange County Register*. I write outdoor articles." He handed me his business card, then added, "I would like to do a story on you. You can check up on me, and if you're interested give me call."

"Okay," I replied. On another day, a reporter had stopped me to ask my opinion about the lifelike statues of children at play inhabiting our town center. I figured David Whiting probably wanted to know about accessibility in Rancho Santa Margarita and not so much about *me*. I was glad to oblige.

A few weeks later, David came to my house to interview me. Although a wiry, athletic man, he didn't seem impatient or in a hurry. He relaxed, sitting back in my living room recliner, able to live in the moment and ready to enjoy a look at my simple life. Having achieved success as a paid writer on a prestigious paper, he came to hear from me. I felt honored, and also a bit curious. I asked him, "What kinds of things do you write?"

"Each week I write three front-page articles and one outdoor article. Recently I wrote about the Boston Marathon and interviewed victims of the bombing. I have written about gun control and genetic testing, and a few weeks ago I wrote about Medal of Honor winners who motorcycled with Veterans Across America." After this amazing list of topics, I asked the most obvious question, "So what are you doing here in my living room, David?"

"Well," he hesitated a moment, then confided, "I figured a lone woman in a wheelchair, out on the trail in the middle of nowhere, had to have a story. At first, I thought I would write about accessibility. Then I read about you on your church website, and I thought you had more to your story than that."

For the next two hours, I told David Whiting about my life with osteogenesis imperfecta and my passion for teaching children about God. So he decided that any article about me must also have pictures of the kids. Several weeks later, the photographer from the *Orange County Register* came to my Sunday school class. He didn't blend in or strive to be inconspicuous. He shot photos from across the room and then, with the camera clicking, mere inches from my face. I pretended not to notice the man with the camera. The kids, taking their cues from me, hardly seemed to notice. I learned long ago how they followed my lead about what I gave attention to, but never having been a model, I could only fool them, not the camera, and not myself. My smile felt stilted, so I would not smile. Then, my expressionless face seemed fake, so I'd smile again. I couldn't win.

That day, I invited a member from our congregation to be our guest speaker. Noel and Kelly Salas had become good friends, and I often marveled at the way God used Noel to touch people with healing or a message of encouragement. Noel made the day fun. Kids raised their hand and shared their snippets of stories about prayer and healing. Noel had the rare gift of engaging a room full of kids whose attention was always up for grabs at the slightest provocation. Noel had been a professional surfer and out of respect for his cool hobby, or because he had exciting tales of God healing people he met in Starbucks, at a soccer match, at the beach—or wherever he went, the kids eagerly listened.

After inspiring God-stories, we took the time to pray for each other. Today's guest speaker added a certain joyful nuance to the ministry time. I should have been at ease, off the hook from having to teach since I could sit back and enjoy a stirring message and kids eager to pray for kids. Instead, I tried hard not to be self-conscious as the photographer took pictures of Pastor Lynn Miller for the article.

In the midst of my preoccupation, six-year-old Josiah got my attention. Small for his age, he always sat in the front. Playful brown freckles sprinkled his nose and reminded me of his dad at that age, only his dad had been a towhead and much more trouble, if I remember correctly. "I would like prayer," he told Noel and me.

"What would you like prayer for?" I asked. He showed a barely perceivable old owie on his finger.

Noel said, "Hey buddy, it looks like God already healed it."

Josiah looked for another injury and pointed to his knee. Now Noel had already moved on after realizing this little guy didn't need healing at all. Josiah searched his brain quickly and tried another tack, "Well, my mom…" He didn't complete the thought. Noel was gone.

Sad eyes turned to me. He didn't have words to describe why he needed prayer. But I knew. I knew it well. Josiah longed for love. The camera zeroed in as I prayed my best prayer for this little one who could not yet articulate the most basic desire of his heart. Love!

Of all the pictures taken, guess which child ended up on the front page of the Sunday *Register,* June 9, 2013. Little Josiah as we prayed together. I thought it a fitting exclamation mark to my story, for how often I have been like Josiah. With all my visible and less than visible owies I have brought to the Lord, my most desperate need—always love.

All along the way, God showed up in my disappointments and pains, redeeming it all: not married, yet able to testify of being deeply loved and satisfied; no children of my own, but nurturing the faith of hundreds; no great beauty to commend me, but radiant with joy; no great wealth to secure me, but always provided for. And although I roll through life in a wheelchair, my walk is supernatural. The Lord puts some wonders in plain view, but as the star of Bethlehem, which just a few shepherds and wise men searched out, only the curious will discover the miracle hidden in an ordinary child of God.

With unchanging affection and his abiding presence, the Father, the Son, and the Holy Spirit have transformed my life. His love has brought forth treasures from darkness and filled me with joy. This is my great miracle.

I pray it might be a signpost on your road.

CHAPTER 29

Worthy of it All

As I OVERCOME BARRIERS to intimacy with God, I receive the joy of dry bones dancing again. Trauma created a spirit of accusation in my heart. As a child, no church-going or lip service worship could deny the secret judgment of my heart. When I broke a bone, I cried, "Why God?" I would never say out loud, "God is a jerk!" for that would be blasphemous. Instead, I lived in distrust of him. God let me down somewhere—way back there. Whether before time or in the womb or after my first breath, God decided something so entirely unkind that I had this bent in my heart. My body represented evidence that God, who was supposed to be kind, was also frightfully scary and had a different definition of good than me. God couldn't be trusted.

Then I met Jesus. I mean, I did not just choose to believe a theology, although I think this happened. No, I met a mysterious person, as real as the air I breathe. I met a lover. This messed with my mean-God religion and broke my accusing finger.

I have thought a long time about the cross. I have gazed on a man in agony hanging on a tree, crying out with a loud voice, "My God,

My God, why have you forsaken me?"

Jesus also asked, "Why?"

In his humanity, and in that most vulnerable place of obedience on the cross, he was separated from the Father as he enfleshed my sin. I am awed by his embracing not only my human wilderness and the agony of the crucifixion, but also this great tormenting *why* in his time on this earth.

I have imagined a conversation, which I find comforting. What if God, who stands outside of time, in some distant eternity said, "Lynn, you have lived in a world of pervasive evil in your time on the earth. It touched you deeply. My enemy delighted in every blow, but my child, I wept with you, and because you allowed me, I turned everything the evil one had done into glory. I knew this tragedy would occur, but I loved you before you were born, and I would not imagine an eternity without you. You have allowed me to incarnate in you. You have reached out in faith for the impossible, and unearthed miracle after miracle. You resisted the lie that I don't care. My desire for you to experience heaven on earth was the most critical battle in your generation, and you fought well. You praised my name whether healed or not."

And I say like Mary did, "Behold, the handmaiden of the Lord."

Perhaps my greatest hour is in the middle of my darkest moment, when I say, "I worship you! I love you! I am yours."

War, suffering, and sickness exist in the world because evil prevails. I am convinced that a child born with a deformity is an image bearer of the glorious One and an innocent victim of a cosmos that is resisting God and his children. We are all beloved of God and hated by the evil one who desires our destruction and suffering. Though this is true, through Christ we overcome every circumstance.

I have known Jesus Christ in my suffering and my joy, I will receive unspeakable glory for my yes, and that is why I am on this side of paradise dropping my accusing finger. Perhaps there will be a day in eternity future when I wish I could have done far more for his name.

One afternoon, I sat at Dana Point Harbor and talked to the Lord while I looked out over the sailboats passing by on their way out to sea. As I drank in the scene, I had a vision of God's glory filling the entire harbor and city. Suddenly, in a revelation of his grandeur, I saw myself

211

and *all* who ever called on the Lord's name before his throne. A thought got anchored in my heart. If I gave him everything, if I died for him, and if all humanity were to give him everything and also our very lives, he would still merit far more.

Though I am the treasure of Jesus, and we are all his prize, he is far superior to our offerings. What a mystery that I can prevail over his heart in such a way that he divested himself of glory and purchased me with his life's blood. Then, after this extravagant price, he became even more personal—went after me to conquer my resistance and spent a lifetime with me, even slowed down his pace to walk beside me like a Daddy with his toddler and called me forth to carry a destiny I never imagined. Even though I have this place before him, his majesty is beyond comprehending.

We will one day say, "I wish I could have done more for you my God." We will revel in our God so infinitely stunning, and with hearts speechless with wonder, drop to our knees and discard our hard-earned crowns, even throwing them down. We will see how deserving he is to receive all the glory and honor and praise angelic beings sing about night and day (Revelation 4:11). We will be glad—I will be glad—that I laid aside my complaints, put away my accusations, and received the God who is worthy of it all.

For I reckon that the sufferings of this present time
are not worthy to be compared with the glory
which shall be revealed in us.
—Romans 8:18

Epilogue
Physical Healing

HOW DO WE LIVE in the tension of a promise not yet fulfilled? What does it mean to live by faith when God's rule is not fully manifested on earth as it is in heaven? How do we receive a miracle? The answers as to how to wait joyfully, to press on expectantly, and to obtain in this life, at least partially, the benefits of Jesus Christ's redemption at the cross came to this sojourner in bits and pieces.

In the years following my shift to full-time church ministry, I discovered new territory in my faith. Up to that point, my healing culture and the prayer of believers often left me feeling stripped of my dignity as they sought for reasons why I was not healed and were sometimes accusing. I once heard it said, "You can tell a mature healing ministry by how many unhealthy people can endure hanging around." I wonder if the person who made that observation used a wheelchair?

For me to experience God as healer, I needed not only the comfort of God to invade my hidden scars, but I also required a more accurate theology. I look at it this way. When a little girl skins her knee and runs to Mama, she is not looking for a diagnosis, or to understand

213

the science of coagulation. The only real consolation is arms that hold. Arms that say, "I am here. I understand. It is going to be okay." The law of coagulation is at work, and how very important that it operates automatically to mend wounds. But it is not comfort. In our humanity, as beings with a body, soul, and spirit, removing sickness and injury often requires a more holistic approach. For this reason, God offers himself, as both Comforter and Truth.

Before I share my healing account, let me tell you about three friends. Their stories shed light on essential biblical truths that those with pain and chronic disability find hardest to believe and most up for grabs.

The Elderly Lady

She hobbled along in slow, deliberate steps while leaning heavily on her walker. I observed her labored movements as I sat at a patio table outside a taco bar. Pain seemed to sear through her leg with each footfall. She had not set out on a leisurely stroll through the neighborhood. This was therapy.

Our eyes met, and although we were strangers, there was also a connection. We shared common ground, she on her walker and me in my wheelchair. Stopping in front of me, she said, "Why? Why? Why?" Like a record replaying the same note, stuck in a groove, she repeated the question over, shaking her head, openly mystified.

"Why?" she said again, apparently looking to me for an answer.

I remembered how, as a child, I asked the same question. Why me? I studied the woman waiting for my answer; I wondered if she felt as I had. Did she think God deserted her?

Her old eyes looked confused and sad, like a child whose feelings have been hurt. "Why would God do this?" she said again.

"God did not do this." I responded gently.

"But why, why, why?"

Searching for a key to share a meaningful answer, I repeated what I knew, "God does not have wheelchairs in heaven, and he does not pass them out. He loves you!"

Her eyes widened in surprise, and I thought, *Epiphanies strike like that.*

The whys ceased. "Thank you!" she said. "God bless you!" She continued her plodding steps down the sidewalk.

My words were plain, our exchange only a brief moment. I could have given much more—could have even offered a miracle-producing prayer. I just didn't have the faith, sitting outside the taco joint, that day. I didn't even think to meander down the signs-and-wonders trail.

But I shared what I believed in my gut—most days.

God is love.

Underneath her why-me, the thorn cut, lacerating deeper and deeper. God is behind this. God doesn't care. She and I both had to reject this lie; walk, or in my case, push our way out of the dungeon of God rejection. Jesus Christ, the perfect representative of our heavenly Father, in his earthly ministry, never gave out disease, but always extended his hand in compassion (Luke 6:19). He has not changed.

Waiting with joy is itself a miracle, possible because I stopped pointing an accusing finger at God.

Kara

Kara sat in my living room recliner, meeting with me for a pastoral appointment. She had attended my Prophecy II class the previous fall, and as the weeks passed, she got to know me and trusted that I would be a safe confidant. I poured us coffee. Misty settled down, curled into a ball on the rug in the corner.

As if opening a long-locked door, Kara presented her life, a narrative of sickness, abuse, and emotional torment. I listened without interrupting and let her dictate the direction of our conversation. Then a question came to mind. "Kara, is there a lie you have been fighting since your recent car accident?"

She thought for a moment and replied, "All I can think of is, 'Why me? Why do bad things always happen to me?' I just don't understand."

Why me! Only God could arrange this. "Okay, well, let's think about that. Tell me: why is this happening to you?"

At first, she laughed at the audacity of the question turned around on her, and then she quietly contemplated her answer. "Well, I guess God knows I can handle everything I have gone through."

"Okay. Any other reason?"

"So that I can help other people..." She trailed off. I supposed, hearing her belief spoken aloud echoed like a belly flop, didn't even sound convincing to herself.

I reflected back what I heard, "So you believe God sent this because you can bear it. Also, he did so because he cares about other people?"

"Oh, I don't think he sent it, but he allowed it."

"Yes, he did allow it." I waited before continuing. I knew we navigated tricky terrain as we skirted around the theology of God's sovereignty. "Do you think everything God allows to happen is his perfect will? God permits us to sin, and grants us the freedom to murder and commit adultery."

Tears welled up, soaking her cheeks. I passed the Kleenex. I continued. "Do you think, rather than God condoning these hardships, he may have grieved for you?"

In some dark place inside her, light broke through.

After waiting a few minutes, I asked, "So, Kara, can you deal with everything you have suffered? Could you endure it as a little girl?"

The answer gushed out of her mouth in a sob, "No! I never could handle it!"

Indeed! Who could put up with such horror? And what does it look like to "handle it?" Who would say to a child abused and soul-battered, "Hey, you need to just get over it." Healing balm can flood the soul when you stop holding it all together; stop pretending, and you recognize some pains are God-sized. "You are right, Kara. You can't handle it," I agreed. "God never condoned the abuse, but he can help you overcome it now."

She wept. But not tears of self-pity making her more depressed. The difference, I understood well. I waited while years of pain and confusion about God poured out. Then, she looked up at me sheepishly through tears, a new light in her eyes and a crooked, serene smile. As I observed the transformation, I said, "Kara, you *will* know the joy of all this working for good. It will be a great consolation."

Kara laughed. She believed it, too.

Some people believe that God, who is all-powerful, orchestrates all events. They reason, If I am sick, God must have ordained it—the car accident—the cancer—the divorce. Since I prayed and he didn't deliver me, God wants me to stay in this state and suffer. Although God works all things for good, it is a distortion of the gospel to accept sickness as a friend or ally when Jesus openly opposed it throughout his ministry.

Kara and I can throw logs on faith fire, and enter a new audacity in prayer, when we accept that God works through prayer, anoints believers with gifts of the Holy Spirit, and uses people with skills, talents, faith, and love to do the works of God. These are ways he has chosen to release his will on the earth, as it is in heaven.

We don't have to accept evil as if God's sovereignty has determined it. That is why we can ask God to heal us.

Abdul

After parking my car, I wheeled up to the mall entrance where four friends waited. From the outdoor seating area of California Pizza Kitchen, came quiet murmurs and the clang of dinnerware. Heidi stood with her back to me. On a bench in front of her sat Carol, Jessica, and Karen. I nosed into the discussion quietly, already regretting that I had left my coat in the car. Although the sun shined, I shivered under the shade of a large palm tree.

We had just come from Vineyard Community Church for outreach to the mall. As Heidi filled us in on her plans, Abdul strolled by and suddenly crashed in on our huddle. "Are you talking about God?" he asked.

"Yes," Heidi said. Heidi had a kind, friendly manner and a charming German accent that put people at ease. Whenever I spent time with her, I would most likely find myself talking to a stranger about Jesus or praying for someone who had a painful limp. I considered her a gentle evangelist. The gentle part made her a rare breed.

"Good," Abdul said. "I will make you an offer. If you let me tell you a story, I will let you say to me whatever you want about your Jesus."

I think he wanted to pick a fight. He boldly hurdled over that

217

invisible wall of protocol meant to keep our chat safe. The one that said, "Don't talk politics. Don't mention religion. I have my view. You have yours. Let's leave it at that." Perhaps it is an adult form of peer pressure that seems to whisper in my ear, "Don't make waves. Just keep quiet." I felt that squeeze on my conversation the day I met Abdul. He had broken the protocol, and it looked like he itched for a fight.

But Heidi laughed and said, "Sure, why not? Tell us your story."

He spoke with a strong Middle Eastern accent, and although a small man, he projected a forceful manner. Now about seventy, his tale occurred at only seven years old. Abdul described his vibrant family life and how his innocence had been wrenched away when war broke out in his country. Evil men ravaged his nation; even the land became marred by violence. He spoke of terrible atrocities and his terror. For days he, his family, and other refugees slogged through villages and deserted roads as they fled their homeland, exhausted and hungry. Voice husky with emotion and indignation, he told of swelling numbers of discarded, dead bodies abandoned on the roadside.

How does one respond to injustice and a man's rage against it? How does one reply to a man's heart scar more than sixty-three years old? Did Abdul spend those years spewing his anger on other strangers? Did it poison his family? Or did it just erupt today, a buried landmine from the past, the surfacing of a long-suppressed memory? I do not know. But he had been bleeding a long time.

Abdul ended his narration saying sarcastically, "Okay, now you can go ahead and tell me about your God of love." Clearly, in his view, we could have nothing to say.

I often carry on conversations with God in my head. No one around would suspect I am in prayer. I ask his advice. I ask for patience with a particularly rambunctious child in my class. Heck, I will even pray for a parking space. That day, Abdul had me in a desperate private chat with the Lord. "Oh, Jesus, I should be a puddle of tears, but this guy irritates me. I know I should feel concerned about his suffering and the horror he went through, but I am freezing. Please, just end this debate and get me out of here."

Unlike me, Heidi had compassion on Abdul. "May we pray for you?" she said.

Willing to endure our prayer now that he had monopolized us for the last twenty minutes, he shrugged and said, "All right."

Good, I thought. Maybe I won't have to say anything. Heidi will pray, and then we can go.

Heidi began, "Jesus, help Abdul know your great love..."

Then, to my chagrin, Jessica poured out a long, tender prayer. Also chiming in were Carol and Karen. Everyone waited for me to speak.

Silently I pleaded, "Jesus, I don't want to pray. I don't even know what to say. Help me!" At times when praying aloud, counseling, or preaching a sermon, I have known an unusual power beyond my ability. In my Christian circle, we call it "anointing." My response came from such an anointing. I considered it God, not me.

I spoke in the volume of a shout. I shocked Abdul and even myself. Chatter from the restaurant quieted. Passionately and immodestly, I bellowed, "Jesus, you *hated* what happened to Abdul! You *hated* what happened to that nation and the people who suffered! You are a righteous God, and you will judge evil!"

Abdul reached into his pocket and pulled out a hanky to dry his eyes. Then he slipped it away.

"You came to bring justice, Jesus. You deplore the violence of brother against brother!" Way past my comfort zone, I roared. As God's truth poured through my mouth, love for Abdul flooded my heart. No longer was I disengaged.

When my prayer ended, we waited in a holy silence. Then Abdul again reached into his pocket and pulled out the hanky, blew his nose, and dried his eyes. "Thank you." His voice trembled. "I feel loved." Bitterness had kept Abdul pinned down, unable to see the face of a good God.

That day, in my interaction with Abdul, I received a gift. My extreme response by a divine unction reminded me that God's hatred is as righteous as his love. That he never stands at a distance, dispassionate as we suffer. Jesus came and got mixed up in the fray, a radical response to our cry for justice and our ache for healing.

Once I settled that God is love, I conceded he must also hate that which is contrary to love. God's fiery emotions of love and hate, motivating him to endure the cross, make possible my surrender to him of bitterness, offense, and unforgiveness. It creates for me yet another pathway for physical health.

My Healing Journey

When I first gave my life to Jesus, for a period of a few months every time I read my new Bible, it opened to Psalm 34:17–20. "The Lord hears the cry of his righteous ones...He saves all their bones, and not one of them is broken." I figured my Bible must have developed a crease so that it always fell open on that page. Still, I wondered, *Is Jesus telling me that I am not going to break any more bones?* I did not know how to hear a promise from God. I had no idea if I could trust this incredibly relevant Scripture.

As my Bible opened to the passage, I dared to hope that maybe, just maybe, this coincidence was the finger of God. Then one Sunday I went to church, and a young man, Lonnie Frisbee—highly regarded for his prophetic gift, quoted the same verse. I surrendered my doubt and, from then on, received it as God's oath. Thirty-five years later, the promise proved valid. Despite corrective surgeries, car accidents, and falls, I have never broken another bone.

Though I am a living miracle, not everyone sees that. Most people see only my wheelchair. And because not everyone who attends a church is compassionate or doctrinally sound, having a disability made me a target for every kind of weird prayer. With faith in God and expectation, I allowed people to pray for me. But my leg would not grow out. My back would not straighten. Without immediate success, believers searched for reasons why their prayer didn't work. I felt like Job, whose counselors would rather believe the worst about him than accept the tension of his dilemma and suffering.

Those who ministered said, "You need to forgive your mother." Though unaware of anything to forgive, I dutifully exonerated Mom of any wrong. Whoops. Still no luck. Next, they tried casting out a spirit. Nothing ever happened, but in their minds, because I had a bone disease, I had to be demonized. For years this undermined my confidence as a Christian. Sometimes, I would wheel away crying, because it hurt to have church family think I had demons. I felt shamed.

Desperate for healing, I endured their tactics.

Like in the Dark Ages when a penitent crawled up the steps of the Vatican on his knees to earn the favor of God, such prayer put conditions on my faith, my cooperation, my trying to walk or perform. And I did it all, over and over, and felt like a fool for the healing that never came, even condemned for my insufficient faith.

One time when visiting the Toronto Vineyard in Canada, while in the middle of worship, quite joyously engaged in the adoration of my king, a lady interrupted my song and asked to pray for me. Though shocked at the intrusion, I politely refused. She pursed her lips and shook her head; her accusing eyes splashed cold water on my face, "No wonder you are not healed!" At a church conference in Florida, a lady came up and grabbed my hands and swayed back and forth as she prayed as if her gesture would empower me to rise and walk. Behind her swaying body, I could see my friend. Jessica's eyes widened, and her jaw dropped at the audacity of the woman. I wanted to laugh, but I saw the sincerity of this kooky lady. I gently ended her antics.

I could not understand why people would assume their untimely, inappropriate approaches would be welcome. But to them, I was an invalid—not Lynn. Sincere believers moving in compassion may desire my wholeness, but just as often as not, when I didn't rise and walk, the prayer disintegrated into control and presumption.

Desperation and faith led me to seek a supernatural breakthrough, but make no mistake about it, I took a risk. Will the prayer be manipulative? Condemning? Shaming? Will it be answered? Can my emotions handle the tension of what might *not* happen if I reach out by faith once again? Even now, though I am a pastor, my niece who is an adult has had numerous friends ask her, "Since your aunt can't get healed, what sin has she not repented of?" These notions make it hard to ask others for prayer.

How do you process *not* being healed? Whose fault is it? Is it yours? Is it God's? Is it the lack of faith in the people who pray? God's promise of healing in the Word and the witness of it in the church always pressed on my bruise. Though I pray for the sick, I've had to fight the unbelief, the lack of a breakthrough, even condemnation for not having enough gumption to seek God in fasting until I looked like Gandhi.

My buckets of tears didn't move the matter. And my healing culture zeroed in on the most significant issue of my life, with very little success. How uncomplicated, and less painful, it would have been to say God does not heal today. How much simpler it would have been to ignore the testimony of healed friends. How much easier to believe there was no battle involved, no enemy to fight, and just surrender.

But I could not. Affectionate words and touches from my Savior continued to testify—God is real. He is alive. He has not changed.

In the summer of 1990, I joined the ministry team at Ed Piorek's Father Loves You conference in downtown San Francisco. I had become good at praying for matters of the heart. We had had an incredible time of ministry with about eight hundred people in attendance, but the last session he devoted to physical healing. I had interceded for this ministry time days before the conference. While in prayer, I saw many people getting touched, especially one young woman in a wheelchair getting filled with the love of the Father. Many attendees, emboldened by their experience of love that weekend, came forward to receive healing from the Father. There in the crowd the young woman in a wheelchair rolled forward.

Despite my vision of her weeks earlier in my prayer closet, I suddenly felt ill-equipped to pray for her—or anyone. *What am I thinking? How can I pray for someone to be healed? I can't even get myself better.* Paralyzed by my defeated reasoning, I watched the sick and the lame partner up with someone to pray for them, even my young friend in the wheelchair. Relieved to be let off the hook, I proceeded to sink into a mire of inadequacy.

That is when an older lady across the room, waved me over to her. I searched the crowd, hoping to find a more capable miracle worker, but everyone was busy. *What is this woman thinking? Can't she see I am in a wheelchair? This poor woman needs someone who can really pray.* But she persisted in waving me over.

I rolled to her side. "What would you like prayer for?" I asked.

"I am having back pain, and I have one leg shorter than the other," she replied. Since I had a two-inch difference between my two legs and had seen this kind of prayer modeled many times, I knew not to pull on her leg or pull off her shoe to get the desired results as believers had tried with me.

So I held her feet in my hands and ordered, "I command this leg to grow out in Jesus's name." Nothing. I repeated, "I command this leg to grow out in Jesus's name!" Again, nothing. I prayed a more flowery prayer, "Jesus, you love her, and you died so we might experience your life. Release your love upon her. Come." But still nothing. *I knew it. I don't have any authority. I need to find someone else.* I combed the auditorium. Everyone was occupied. Now I decided to have a private conversation with the Lord. "Lord, what is going on here?"

I sensed Jesus saying, "She needs to forgive her mother."

"Oh no, don't tell me to say that! Jesus, I hate saying that. Blame is what people do to me. They focus on something wrong with me, and I never get healed. Please, just fix this."

But I could not escape this thought, "The enemy has access to her life through unforgiveness."

Looking past her outstretched legs resting in my hands, to her expectant face I said, "Is everything okay with your mom?"

She burst into tears. "I've been angry at her for years!"

While holding onto her feet, I led her in a forgiveness prayer. The woman wept, releasing her mother of all offenses. Almost as an afterthought, I glanced down at her feet. They were perfectly even. My shocked eyes determined there must be a mistake. I pushed on the lady's shoe in case it slightly slipped off. Her shoe didn't budge, already fitting snuggly on her foot. Her leg grew out!

Our excitement and praise met in a hug as we rejoiced in the power of God.

Even as far back as my psychology class at UCI, I learned of the link between forgiveness and healing, awed that secular research agreed with scriptural truth. For this very reason, with people I trust, I have discussed and prayed through my relational conflicts. From the cross, Jesus declared, "Father forgive them, they know not what they do." This same understanding helped me in my troubled relationships. God gave me an inside look at the destitute condition of my offenders culminating not only in compassion but also in recognition of their inability to grasp the horror of their actions, as when humanity crucified God.

Despite my efforts to live at peace within myself and with

223

others, never did my forgiveness conclude with tossing aside my wheelchair. Then again, few of Jesus's physical healings required repentance. Most were unconditional acts of compassion.

After the lady's leg grew out, my timid faith went from zero to ten. Scanning the crowd for someone else needing a miracle, I noticed my young friend in a wheelchair. She looked miserable. Two men and a gal stood around her, hands on her shoulders and head, praying earnestly but getting nowhere. I recognized well the torment of God rejection. I rolled over.

Believers saw her need for physical healing as the priority. I knew something her prayer team might have forgotten. Love is healing. As I prayed for God to embrace her, tears of joy flowed down her cheeks; her face shined like a bride on her wedding day. And her whole body trembled as her affectionate Father invaded her being in a mighty demonstration of love, supplying her most essential need.

In the same way, whether physically fit or not, God's love changes the quality of my interior life with the decor of joy and hope and perseverance. There are times when I sense Jesus near. There are times when a new injury and new pain makes my cry desperate again. I am glad I never surrendered my theology on healing to my limited personal experience.

In 2006 the pain in my left hip became chronic. Though unable to sleep on my left side for decades, stabbing twinges of pain made even minimal movements in my wheelchair an agony. I ended up at the doctor's office. He told me I needed surgery to remove a pin, pull the hip down out of the pelvis, and add new pins to stabilize the twenty-four-year-old injury. The procedure, familiar to me, had been performed after the nurses turned me over against my will, breaking my hip. At twenty, my recovery took the form of four months in a body cast. Horrified by the prognosis and suggested treatment, I pursued a miracle with fresh fervor.

Now anyone would notice my need for healing, but it is the rare person who could see beyond the exterior to behold the real woman — one with faith, life in the Word, intercession, gifting, and callings. This is when I found being in a smaller local church of infinite value. My church family became the safest, most anointed place for miracles. They didn't search for skeletons in my closet. They knew me beyond the skin. They offered prayers of faith, trusting in God's grace to heal. I turned to them.

I had booked my surgery. Continuing with my routine, I attended an intercessory meeting for our community. I sat at the door of our little prayer room, the first seat for those entering. Everyone knew of my plight, and they felt concern. As each member walked in, they laid hands on me and prayed. Suddenly, the power of God coursed through my body. I didn't know what happened and I forgot where I was. Hysterical laugher grabbed my attention. Again, just like before, as I gained awareness, I realized the laughter came from me. Another wave swept through my body. I giggled as if I just heard the best joke.

Another friend walked in the door, and laid their hands on me, saying, "Bless her, Lord. Heal her hip. Come Holy Spirit." Love crashed down in another hilarious wave. For two hours, God affectionately, mysteriously, tickled me. While I cracked up, I also marveled that this invisible God I'd once thought so distant could touch me deeper than any other love I had known. He took my fears, loved away my doubts, and brought me that inner calm that comes from knowing pure affection. Exhausted by my divine encounter, I drove home and took a nap.

Light filtered through the blinds awakening me from a deep sleep. It had been years since I had known such rest, free of discomfort. Then, it dawned on me—for the first time—in a very long time: I felt no pain. As I lay in bed, I rolled back and forth, but no piercing spasm hindered me. Bolder now, I rolled more vigorously. Still nothing. Then I did the unthinkable; I turned over to my left side. No sharp stabs or even an ache. I could barely grasp the implications. *Have I been healed?* Now I did a workout, trying to get the pain to return. Shock gave way to praise.

Two weeks later, the pain returned, at about sixty percent of its previous intensity. Having the biblical understanding that heaven invades earth, but not without resistance and a fight, I turned to my friends Rick and Maria Adams. That night, their home group laid hands on me and prayed. The pain ceased.

Three days later, it came back. Only now I felt about thirty percent of the previous pain. I knew not to give up. I was in the middle of a miracle. I knew it, yet I struggled with a history of disappointment. I said, "Jesus, thank you for taking seventy percent of my pain. I ask you to keep coming."

That weekend at church, my pastor, Mike asked me how I felt. After I described my battle, he prayed for me. "Jesus, come and heal Lynn. Pain, go." He rested his hand on my shoulder and waited for a bit. Then added, "Heal her Lord."

The pain never returned.

At my presurgery appointment, I notified the doctor of my improvement. Baffled, he immediately took an X-ray. The metal pin had migrated out of the hip and lodged in the fleshy, fatty part of my thigh. With a small incision and one stitch, he removed the ancient screw.

Instead of looking at the ministry of Jesus to guide my thinking, too often it has been my disappointments that determined my theology. To help me sustain a biblical view of healing, I keep the pin in a bottle, a souvenir of what great things God has done for me.

A few years later, in the healing rooms at the International House of Prayer in Kansas City, Missouri, God instantly cured me of restless leg syndrome and swelling feet. Then while friends prayed for me during one of our Sunday services, he suddenly removed debilitating pain in my body following rotator cuff surgery. On another occasion, he took away my acid reflux.

In many ways, healing is still a great mystery to me, but I am grateful for the way he has rescued me. I am also looking to him for more—for others and for myself.

Though I may have my unanswered questions, what diverse, rich pleasure to delight in him and search him out. Suffering is one context by which I discovered some part of that vast ocean—God! I encourage you not to miss out. May you also experience healing—in body, soul, and spirit. Don't let your suffering be wasted. Get from it every drop of truth and comfort, abundantly available to the brokenhearted.

What an adventure it has been to know the God of joy—whose voice and embrace have made these dry bones dance again!

Acknowledgements

IN WRITING THIS MEMOIR, I have on many occasions recalled with gratitude those who have been vital to my survival, integral to my accomplishments, always present to comfort, and the hub and creator of so many joyful memories. First in this are my parents, Bob and Betty Miller. I am truly blessed that you put each other and your family first. This story is also about you—my heroes.

Beth and Bobby, you nurtured my faith so often in the early years, and your journey with Jesus paved the way for me to follow. Beth, you have always been my greatest fan. After all these years, you are still captain of the cheerleading team.

I am indebted to the leaders who made possible so many of my victories and are also mentioned in my story. To Mike and Janiece Hudgins, you continue to inspire me by your example and unceasing passion for God. Thank you for inviting me to serve with you in our noble adventure. Janiece, you have championed me in this endeavor and many others—always able to cherish a diamond in the rough. Ed and Janet Piorek, your faithfulness, counsel, and the community of faith you led provided some of the most healing moments of my life. Also, with appreciation, I remember John Wimber, who passed away, and Bob

Fulton. Both these men created a pathway for me to come to know Jesus through the Vineyard movement.

Jessica Healy and Christine Hittenberger, it is because of you I got started. Jessica, you helped me trust myself and believe in my story. Christine, I still remember the day we sat in my living room and you said, "Before you write anything, you have got to tell your story." It is because of you, I settled on writing this memoir. Your wisdom continues to be a compass in my life.

Tricia Martin, Dan McCollam, Kris Valloton, Jay Grant, and Ravi Kendal, your words spurred me on past my doubts and strengthened my resolve. P. J. Cifulleli, you and your mom, Judy, celebrated my first chapters and your excitement invigorated me. Cathy Greer, how I appreciate your friendship and support. Thanks for being there Paula Davis; you breathed life into my dream. And I must mention Maralys Willis and her students, who seemed to enjoy my efforts and took the time to give me feedback. Bea Rios, you have been my greatest inspiration in these last two years. I am honored to be your friend. Jeff and Christine Hittenberger, thank you for valuing my message and contributing to my story so graciously.

I wish also to thank those who have helped in the final stages, lending me their support as I have navigated the often-confusing task of getting this book into the hands of readers. Joel, my nephew, thank you for coming alongside me to take me further than I could imagine. Pat Novak, I am thrilled that you took on the first editing task. You fueled my efforts in crossing the finish line with your genuine praise and commitment to my story. Jean Ardell, Ginny and Joanna at Book Helpline, Lindsay Linegar, and Susan Smith, thank you for your skill and kindness in taking care of my baby. Donna McCone, your willingness to lend a hand is such a beautiful testament to the kind of friend you are. Janet Guerin, how dear of you to dive in and create a fabulous photo. Dean DelSesto and Wendy Baisley Roache, thank you for sharing your publishing journey with me, and offering insights.

Thank you to my family—and also to my friends, some as far back as elementary school and high school, who make up my Facebook community. Your reception of my book encouraged me greatly, and your willingness to answer polls inspired my subtitle and book cover.

There are others who have prayed for me, for this book, and for all of you my readers. The ones who stand out are those already mentioned and include Thomas and Kathrin Meano, Vickie and John Staph, Candy Edman, and Kit DelSesto. I would also like to thank those who asked how the book progressed and supported me—the staff of VCC—particularly Heidi McMahan who encouraged me and offered great advice, Brent McIntosh—the best kind of pastoral editor, Lynn Schrader, and Kent Larson. I am honored to serve with you.

Michelle, you are a niece more like a daughter to me. Thank you for whisking me away from the computer so we could play and go to Disneyland. You bring me such delight.

Most of all, I thank my God for all he has done for me. Writing this book is my gift to him.

References

Dawkins, J. L. "Bullying, physical disability and the pediatric patient." *Developmental Medicine and Child Neurology,* 38 (1996): 603–612.

Erickson, W., C. Lee & S. von Schrader. *2016 Disability Status Report: United States.* Ithaca, NY: Cornell University Yang-Tan Institute on Employment and Disability (YTI), 2018.

Picard, Andre. "Don't Shut Disabled Kids Out of Society." *The Globe and Mail.* January 30, 2012, updated May 8, 2018. https://www.theglobeandmail.com/life/health-and-fitness/dont-shut-disabled-kids-out-of-society/article4420381/.

Note from the Author

SHINING A LIGHT SO that you and others might have strength in the battles you face, and come to know the love of Jesus, has motivated this memoir. You have heard my story, but I would love to hear yours. Has *Dry Bones Dance Again* been an encouragement to you? Tell me about it. I count it a privilege when I can pass on the healing message that has transformed my life or be an advocate for the disabled.

Did you know seventy million people are in need of a wheelchair but cannot afford one? If you would like to give hope, freedom and renewed dignity through the gift of wheelchair, you can donate to Free Wheelchair Mission. Learn more at: https://www.freewheelchairmission.org

You can contact me @ LynnMillerauthor.com

Made in the USA
San Bernardino, CA
18 November 2018